WHO INVITED THE BAND?

The Diary of an England Fan

DAVID SMITH

Any similarity to real persons, living or dead, is coincidental and not intended by the author.

Published by David Smith
Publishing partner: Paragon Publishing, Rothersthorpe
First published 2015
© David Smth 2015

ISBN 978-1-78222-391-7

Book design, layout and production management by Into Print
www.intoprint.net

Printed and bound in UK and USA by Lightning Source

For William

Contents

6

FOREWORD

I stumbled into watching England abroad in 1981 as a very naive teenager.

As time progressed I went from being a wet behind the ears novice, to becoming one of England's top fans.

This book covers the early years I was following England – the eighties. It is not a book in defence of hooligans, but more a journal of how it was.

The contents will probably shock some people, but this is an honest account of the brutality, violence and racism of the real world.

Norway

September, 1981

I had a heavy drinking session the night before I left for Norway, as my local for some reason had a lock-in until about 1 a.m.

I was on an early train to Newcastle with Pat, a lad from the pub, then we were on a 2 o'clock sailing to Bergen. We had cheap seats at the bottom, and near the front of the boat, and once on board we left our bags by our seats and headed for the bar.

There were a number of England fans on the boat, including a Manchester group, some Leicester lads and a few Wolves fans from Wombwell, plus an older bloke and his young son from St Helens.

At the bar it was £1 a pint, which was quite expensive, in those days.

The Manchester lads were travelling in a battered Hillman Avenger. The Wolves lads had already broken down on the way to Newcastle, and had hired a mini metro to replace the broken down car. They had not told Kennings, the hire company, that they were taking it abroad.

After a couple of pints, we went to the cafeteria. I ate some left over food from a plate, as the prices in the café were high. On seeing this I was given a steak by a Norwegian passenger, who said that it wasn't cooked enough for him.

After chatting to the various lads, once we were back in the bar, it was decided a football match on deck was a good idea. The deck was really slippery. It was strange as we sailed past oilrigs, that appeared from nowhere in the darkness of the night.

A Yank, who was also travelling to Norway, had a tennis ball so we used that, but after the game had gone on for while, in the dark and the spray, plus with the odd broken bottle to contend with, as they were accidentally dropped on deck as we were getting more pissed, the Yank kicked the ball overboard.

Back in the bar one of the Manchester lads then decided to have a go about me coming from Matlock. I let it pass as he was after trouble, and had his mates to back him up.

At about 2 a.m. we went back to our seats, got our sleeping bags out, and slept on the floor in the aisle between the seats.

Saturday

The next morning we woke and we were approaching Bergen. We went to the bar and had a beer for breakfast and I took some photos of the boys we had met, and the fjord we were sailing in.

When we docked it was pouring with rain. We agreed to meet up with Wolves lads in Oslo; they said they were staying in the youth hostel there. Before we got off the boat we had bought some duty free vodka Pat also bought a bottle of port.

We headed towards the bus station. And we saw the Avenger squeak past us with the Manchester lads in it. They were all fat and the car was struggling to get up the road it really looked on its last legs.

Next the Mini Metro, with the Wolves lads in it, passed they were on the way to Klevik, where they had heard the nightlife was good.

The St Helens bloke and his son then came by. We were getting soaked by now and when he offered us a lift we jumped at the chance. We got in the back of the car and headed towards Oslo.

It was a long journey that included three ferries, tunnels that were up to a mile long, and mountain roads. On one ferry we had some food, the young lad moaned about it too his dad, saying the food was crap, but the waitress understood what he said and said that he was very rude.

His dad told him off, after that, he kept his moaning to himself.

We stopped for petrol. As it had stopped raining Pat and I went for a beer in a bar across the road. There were some village teenagers hanging around, but although they looked to be no trouble their girlfriends kept looking over at us and a couple of the lads didn't appear to be happy about it.

We had a beer and then went into the street. It was early evening and a woman on horseback was peacefully walking down the pavement. The St. Helens lad crept up behind her, and shouted as loud as he could. The horse bolted and the fat middle-aged woman was hanging on to the horse as best as she could. The lad smiled to himself as he walked back to the car, another foreigner upset.

We got back into the car and eventually got dropped off in Oslo at about 9 p.m. We thanked the St Helens bloke and he said he didn't want any petrol money when we asked him.

We decide to dump our bags at the left luggage lockers, in the train station. The station was full of dossers and druggies so, after depositing our bags, we walked to a nicer area and went for a drink. In Norway the fashion seemed to be to cruise around in custom cars, we spent the evening looking at lots of nice cars and lots of nice blonde girls.

As we had our England shirts on, a lad in a bar spotted us and started singing 'Switzerland'. England had recently lost there, and England fans had been involved in a major riot. We decided to play it safe and went to a quieter bar for one more drink, then started looking for a hotel.

The hotels were really expensive and most were full anyway, so we headed back to a square we had seen earlier. Here, there were some benches that we thought we might be able to sleep on, as it was quite warm. It was near midnight, we picked a bench each and waited for the town to quieten down.

A lad in his twenties walked through the square and asked if we were English. As I had my St Georges flag with me to use as a pillow and we had our England shirts on this was fairly obvious. He was a bit over the top about the flag. He said he had been working in Norway for a year and kept saying it was wonderful to see it, like it was rare, or a long lost friend!

After a bit of a chat, where we explained we had nowhere to stay. He told us he was staying at his girlfriends, but said we could stay at his place and, as luck would have it, he had left a window open. He gave us his address and we said thanks a lot and went for a taxi.

We got to the flat and let ourselves in, where we dossed down on the lad's sofa and chairs. It was really good of him and saved us an uncomfortable night.

Sunday

The next day we got up late. We let ourselves out of the flat by climbing out of the same window, as we couldn't undo the door from the inside.

We had a walk round Oslo and I bought Deb, my girlfriend, a postcard, which I wrote and sent. Unfortunately the next one I bought I wrote it, but it stayed in my pocket and it was all creased by the time it reached her.

She was not impressed when I got home.

We did a bit of sight seeing and had a look at the Royal Palace, but again, it seemed to be surrounded by druggies and drunks especially in the gardens. We decided to get our bags from the station and go by tram to the youth hostel, which was situated by the Winter Olympic Ski Jump Arena.

At the hostel we met up with the Wolves lads. They had got international youth hostel association cards, but said that Pat and me could sleep in their Metro, if we wanted to.

The car was parked in the car park. We decide that for tonight that would do. I would have the front seats with my feet hanging out of window, while Pat would have the back.

It turned out you didn't actually need a card to get in the hostel, but they did impose a curfew, which meant you couldn't get back in after midnight.

We went back into the centre of Oslo for a drink and one of the Wolves lads was telling us about a fight he had had at a match. He said he was just about to hit a Leeds fan, who had been knocked to the ground, over the head with a bottle, when his mate moved the Leeds lad's head and he smashed the bottle on the pavement instead. He said it saved him from possible murder rap.

We got chatting to a lot of girls as they passed the pub we were in. The pub was called 'Bills Bar'. During the night I went and sold my duty free Smirnoff vodka at the 'Bottle shop' and made £20 on the deal. I needed the money, as the bars were really expensive.

To help with finances we bought some beers from a supermarket, but we had to be careful drinking them, as if you got caught by the police, it was illegal to drink in the street and they just poured it away down the drain.

A load of Millwall fans arrived that night and the atmosphere was rowdy, but all right in 'Bills Bar'. At the end of the night Fred, one of the Wolves boys, and me ended up in club next door. It was really expensive to drink in there. We decided to knock it on the head and get the last tram back to the hostel, Fred went into the hostel and I slept in the Mini Metro.

Monday

When I woke up I had a major nosebleed, it took ages to stop, so I went for a walk and then tried to clean myself up. It probably bled because my feet were out of the window above my head all night!

In the afternoon we went for a drink. In the bar there was a lad who could bend a coin by hitting it with the bottom of a pint glass. He was really hitting the coin with the glass and the barman didn't look too impressed.

During the day Pat bought a badge from a market stall, which said 'fuck off I'm English'. Fred said 'that could cause some problems', and a few days later it did.

The police were really friendly towards us, and we had a few photos taken with them. Some of the policewomen were really pretty.

I met a girl called, Toni, a typical slim blonde Norwegian. I took her for a pizza and a beer in the 'Scotsman Pub'.

She was really pretty, and I was getting on well with her, when a Norwegian started talking to her as well. I eventually lost out as he kept trying to talk to her. I went back to 'Bills Bar', and then to a nightclub but it was full of punks and weirdo's, so I had one drink, and then went back to the car.

Tuesday

Today we booked into hotel. It was expensive but I needed a bed. By now there was lots of English in town, one lad I met was Gary from Wimbledon. He was drunk when I first met him and after another beer or two, he was out of it. After a while he collapsed on a street corner. I helped him up, and left him to sleep it off on a bench.

A lot of Scousers had now arrived in Oslo; most of them seemed to be stealing crates of beer from the local supermarket. They were just putting their coats over the whole crate and walking out.

While they were at it they were stealing whole chickens, and other food. No one was able to stop them. The supermarket lost loads of stock before some police arrived. The police ended up guarding the door.

The Manchester lads, from the ferry, finally turned up in their Avenger. They sill had some cans of English beer in the boot, so we bought some off them and drunk them in the car. Afterwards we took them into the pub, while they told us what they had been up to. This appeared to have been, just getting spaced out of their heads.

A Local radio interviewer then asked me if I would do an interview. It was live and he asked for my thoughts about the game and any potential trouble. I didn't say anything bad and it went all right, the interviewer then bought me a pint for my troubles.

Peter Shilton and Ray Clemence, the English goalkeepers at that time, were having a beer across the road in a bar. They seemed to be doing ok, as they had lots of women swarming around them.

The first arrest happened in the afternoon. It was an old England fan, in his 50 – 60's who was pissed up and had hit a policeman for no apparent reason. After this the atmosphere turned a bit nasty, especially when the police were pouring England fans beer away.

We then heard that a bouncer had been glassed at the 'Scotsman Pub'. I decided to phone up Debbie to let her know I was all right and see that she was ok.

Later that night we met up with two girls. They were really nice and after a couple of drinks, they went back to our hotel with us.

Pat poured some drinks from his bottle of port, bought on the ferry. He was trying to get the girl he was with, pissed. The reason for this was trying to get his end away; meanwhile the bloke in the next room kept banging on the wall, shouting at us to keep the noise down. I decide to walk the girl I was with, Christina; back to where she lived, which was a boat, that was moored up in harbour.

We started kissing as we walked to the harbour and she asked me to stay. I decided I couldn't do it to Deb, so I saw her home and then went back to hotel. By now the manager has been to our room and bollocked Pat for all the disturbance he was creating. The girl he was with, had used this opportunity to escape and had got a taxi home. Finally I managed to get some sleep, but my mattress was soaked in port.

Wednesday

We met up with the other lads at dinner and sat in the park. We had booked out of hotel and paid cash before they managed to see the damage caused to the room.

I decided to put up my flag in the park as it was on a stick. One of the Manchester lads said it would attract the coppers and told me to put it down.

As we are drinking from cans in the park he was right and it might have been a problem, but that day, there were loads of England fans drinking all over town, so I left it up.

The Wolves' lads turned up and one was wearing a full England kit apart from football boots. While we were sat on the grass I met a lad I had seen at Wembley.

His mate was on about his bank manager telling him that he had got to stop following England. I was impressed, and it sounded like they did most of the England games.

As the day progressed a big fight erupted near the underground station and then spread out to where we were on the grass. All the local Norwegians were complaining to us because their police were getting beat up, and it did appear to be the case.

I lost Pat in the too-ing and fro-ing but stayed with Fred. He had got a Bank's Mild flag with him, which is a beer sold in Wolverhampton. Another lad had a 'do it all flag' from a local builders yard, and he reckoned he should get paid for advertising.

Around the tube station there was a lot of fighting. It seemed that some of it was between Manchester United and Brighton fans and the locals were not really involved. There were some British coppers on the actual tube train, but they didn't do much to stop the trouble.

Once we had got to the ground, there was a pub directly outside, but it was absolutely packed full of English fans. The local Norwegians all seemed happy but the average English fan was not, whether this was because of the price of the beer or just how it was, I wasn't sure, however quite a few Norwegian lads got a slap just for smiling.

There was more trouble with the Manchester United fans. They seemed to want to fight any other group of fans whether they were English or Norwegian. Just before kick -off quite a few fans were being arrested and put into police vans. A lot of the England fans were singing 'to Norway' and also 'to Paris' to the tune of a Television show, 'Top of the Form'.

Once we had got into the ground there were loads of flags up on the perimeter fence.

In the stadium there was a big surge down the terrace because of the lads pushing to get in, from the back. The fans at the front were squashed, so much so, that part of the containing fence came down.

A load of lads spilled onto the running track that went around the perimeter of the pitch, and I saw Big Paul (someone I would get to know, at a later game) getting arrested. It took four policemen to carry him out of stadium.

By this stage there had been lots of arrests. The police, and police dog handlers with their dogs, were trying to restore some type of order. Some lads started feeding the dogs sausages they had bought from a fast food stall. The dogs didn't know whether to bite them, or roll over and have their bellies tickled.

Eventually everyone was put back on the terrace behind the fence. Some of the Norwegians started complaining because they couldn't see the game so the police decided to pull down the England flags, that were blocking their view, from the fence.

This caused another surge as the English lads didn't want their flags touching, and the fence came down again, and the whole process was repeated.

Eventually some groundsmen drove some stakes into the ground to keep the fence up.

England ended up losing the game 2-1. After the match the Wolves lads were straight off home in their Mini Metro. I couldn't find Pat, so I went into town and booked into a hostel. It had ten beds to a room. I had to be careful that my money and camera weren't stolen but at least I got some sleep.

Thursday

I met up with Pat back at 'Bills Bar', which seemed to be the meeting place and our local while we were in Oslo. Pat was with Rob Jones and the Belper lads. The lad who could bend a coin with the pint glass was also there and he said 'do you know this song'. He sung it, and it was about three verses long.

Rob gave him a strange look as though he was a weirdo and said 'I don't think so' and walked off leaving him deflated and on his own.

As Rob did so, he didn't realise he left his camera, but when he went back for it, it was gone. He wasn't too bothered about the camera, as he had taken out the film and had still got it, in his pocket.

Pat was pissed and kept singing. I just watched and noted that he still had that badge on.

We decided to go back to the Belper lad's hotel, which meant catching the underground. While we were waiting for the train some Norwegians, looking for revenge, possibly from having a beating the day before, saw Pat's badge and attacked us.

There was a stand off, but one bloke kicked Pat in the jaw, from behind and you could here the bone snap as it broke. As the train came in Rob held the doors open, a Chelsea fan was also taking a few punches, and another Norwegian was hitting me. I managed to punch the lad who was attacking me, and jumped onto the train just as the doors closed.

Pat had to go to a local hospital. An 'X'-ray showed that his jaw was broken in two places. At the same time the Chelsea fan had his ear stitched up. It cost Pat a lot of money for the 'X'-ray and for some pain killing tablets.

That night we got the overnight train to Stavanger. Pat had a few beers to numb the pain. I finally posted the post-card to Deb, before boarding the train but by now it was really tatty, and didn't impress her one bit when she received it. I managed to get a bit of sleep on the train.

Friday

We arrived at Stavanger and two girls we met on the train took us for a cheaper beer in a bar they knew. As we had got to catch the boat, nothing happened, though Pat was still trying his best to get off with them.

On the boat, I got talking to couple of Leicester lads, they were a good laugh and, at least on the boat the beer was cheaper than it had been in Oslo. A Force 9 gale started to blow and we were told one of the stabilizers had stopped working so; it was a really rough crossing.

When we were later on the dance floor, it was really easy to dance because the boat made everyone move across the floor in unison.

Pat started chatting to a girl he met, he ended up shagging her under the tarpaulin of a lifeboat. I met a Saints fan in the bar; he told me that he had got a spare bunk in his cabin, so once the bar had shut I had a decent night's sleep.

Saturday

We arrived in Newcastle and got the train home. We had a couple of cans of beer on the train. When we got to Matlock, Debbie was waiting at the station. We got a taxi to the 'Black Swan' and, when they saw him, everyone in the bar was laughing at Pat. He had to go and get his jaw wired at the hospital, and spent the next six weeks drinking his liquidized dinners through a straw!

Scotland

May, 1982

I travelled with a mate from work, called Joe Smith. We went for a drink around Matlock and got talking to two girls in the Castle pub. We ended up having to run for the train and dropped two cans of beer as we got on the platform and had to leave them as the train was pulling out. Another Lad from work was on the train and he drank another of our cans. At Stoke a load of lads got on. They were all banging the windows and playing up.

We got to Crewe and went into a pub near the station. After a couple of beers we then went for a hot dog at a fast food van in the car park. Four or five locals decided to have a go at us, but we stood our ground and some coppers came over and split us up.

We bought some more cans from the buffet, and got onto the Glasgow overnight train. There was quite a lot of Scots on the train, including some top Rangers boys; they were on the piss and they started tearing the train ceiling down.

A load of live wires were hanging from where lights used to be. Ordinary passengers in the compartments were jamming their doors shut, to keep themselves safe from a load of pissed up Jocks and England boys.

The next day there were a couple of fag burns on my arms from night before, and I never even felt them as it happened! At Carlisle a load of coppers got on and arrested a few of the lads for the damage that had been caused to the train.

We pulled into Glasgow at about 5 in the morning and decided it was a good idea to get some sleep on the concourse at Central Station. Unfortunately the police, who thought it wasn't a good idea, moved us on. We decided to go for a coffee and read the morning papers to kill a bit of time in a fast food place.

At about 9 o'clock we jumped onto a train that was going to Mount Florida, the station for Hampden Park. We got some cans from a shop and bumped into two English lads, John and Timber from Rotherham.

When we arrived we went into a bar, it only had about us four

English in it plus a load of Scots. As it happened the Scots were ok with us, they were content just singing at us, and even offered us drinks of whiskey, which we accepted.

When we got to the match, it was really hot and sunny. We had to try to get in; Timber and John bribed a gate man, so we did the same, it cost us a fiver each which was quite good value and we stepped over the turnstile.

We got in, in time for the pipe band and then I heard the flick of a knife. A Scot behind me said 'if England score, I'm going to stab you'. I took my silk England scarf off to make me feel safer.

Some Rangers fans came across and beat the Scottish lad up. They were saying he was a 'fucking Celtic bastard' the police moved in and took the battered Celtic git away. The Rangers boys said that I would be all right now.

At end of the game all the Scots were singing 'what a load of rubbish', as they had lost 1 – 0.

We decide to walk to Central Station, as the trains were packed with disgruntled Scots. It was a long walk back to the station, when we arrived we jumped on the first train going south, even though its final destination was Manchester.

I got talking to a girl on the train and she was travelling to Sheffield. We changed trains in Manchester, got on the Sheffield train and after it arrived went for a drink in Sheffield in some good pubs. She ended up giving me a lift to her house and I stayed the night.

WORLD CUP 1982
Spain

The night before I set off I met my girlfriend, Julie, who I had only just started going out, with and agreed to give her a phone call when I got back.

I had already sorted out, and serviced my car, a triumph 2.5 TC, and set off on a Friday night. I Picked up Bill, my cousin, from Burton, and we drove to Dover. We went through London and past Buckingham Palace. When we got to the port, we found out that we had missed our crossing as we had read the time on the ticket incorrectly.

The sailing was at 8 p.m. (20.00) not 10 p.m. but the bloke in charge of boarding let us get on the next ferry, as we had read it wrong and were obviously a bit thick!

It was a nice smooth crossing, there was about twenty England fans on the ferry and we had a few beers with them in the bar.

Once we had docked and disembarked we drove to Abbeville. On the way there was a massive thunderstorm, so we decided to park up and slept, by now it was about 2 a.m. Bill had fallen asleep as soon as we had started driving in France, I was struggling to stay awake as I drove.

Saturday

We had breakfast at a local café then drove south. I had to keep remembering which side of the road to drive on and also to watch the speed. Bill started opening and closing the glove box, something he would do about one hundred times or more on the trip!

We were driving through Le Mans, past the racing circuit when a posh bloke in a Bentley pulled up alongside my car. He said 'I say, are you in the green car park.' I replied 'no mate, were going to Spain to watch the World Cup'. He replied 'oh jolly good, hope you win!'

It was nice and sunny and we stopped for lunch at a roadside café, we had our England scarf's hanging out of the back windows. A Lad on a motorbike chased after us and as we pulled up at the café he stopped and asked if this is what we did when we were going to football in England. He seemed to be very impressed.

Later, some traffic police stopped us. They told us to put the scarf's inside, they weren't very impressed! After a while of driving in the sun I noticed a funny wiring noise coming from the wheels, but I decided it might just be the crickets that were in the grass verge.

Meanwhile a friend of mine called Rich was on a ferry sailing to Santander and was watching England's first game of the World cup. As Bryan Robson scored all the English boys in the bar went mad, but when the French equalised someone threw a bottle through the TV screen.

Apparently there were loads of England fans with fingers in the television trying to get it to work again even though it had no screen.

We arrived in Biarritz at about seven that night, and parked up in a car park near the front. There was an England camper van, also parked up, that was full of Stockport lads. They were all on the piss but were good lads and we had a few beers with them. We returned to the car and tried to cook up some dinner, but realised we didn't have a tin opener so we gave that up as a bad job.

As we were making this discovery, one of Stockport lads came back with blood dripping from a number of cuts on his face and arms. He said that he had just been mugged. He had lost all his money and his passport and was not in a good mood.

We went into some of the bars of Biarritz and I met a really fit French girl. I ended up with her for the rest of the night. At one point in a darker part of a bar I was kissing her and ended up with my fingers up her, but I didn't manage to sleep with her as I was sleeping in the car, and she was with her mates and she said that she didn't want to leave them.

In the end I just went back to the car and met up with Bill. We decided to get our sleeping bags out and slept outside the car on the grass by the beach.

Sunday

After breakfast we drove to Bilbao. We passed through customs with no problems. As we arrived in Bilbao we noticed its dirty yellow polluted river. We parked up in a side street and went to the 'Winston Churchill' pub, which happened to be on the way to the ground. Bill had put his Derby shirt on and some lads in the pub started saying 'give us a Derby song'.

He sang 'by the light of the silvery moon' back to them, a song popular with Derby fans at the time and one that he said they were singing at the Oldham v Derby game near end of the season.

A massive West Ham lad was leading the singing in the pub. He was a skinhead and also had a massive Viking boat tattoo, on his chest. Apparently he'd just gone AWOL from the army so he could watch England in Spain. He later appeared in the book 'Hooligans Abroad', a book written about this World Cup.

For this game it turned out that hardly anyone paid for their beer. This was because the Spanish expected you to pay at the end of your time in the bar. By kick-off time large tabs had been built up and nearly everyone just did a runner.

At one point the local police decided to steam into the bar and drag the West Ham lad out. There was a bit of a standoff in the road, but the police had massive sticks with them. When they waved them in the air, it created electric charges in them. If the police then hit you with these not only did you get a whack, but also the electrical discharge and this threw you backwards. After a tame effort from us, at trying to get him released, the police took West Ham AWOL away for some questioning.

This involved a few questions and a lot of beating.

We were stood outside the pub when a little Austin 7 1930's car rolled up; it was bedecked in England colours. A Union jack was painted on roof and it had red, white and blue tassels around it. Just after this some Derby lads spotted Bill's shirt and came over to him.

They had the Derby flag, taken from the roof of the Ley Stand at the Baseball Ground with them, Bill was made up, and had some photographs taken while holding it aloft.

About ten Sportswide coaches, a firm who were running escorted tours for fans to the world cup at high prices, came down the avenue and we all sang 'what's it like to get ripped off'.

Next loads off cop vans parked up across the road. The police got out; they were scared of our boisterousness and singing. They started to wave their batons in the air to build up the static charge, then ran across avenue and hit us with them.

As I was hit the force of the static charge and the impact, sent me flying backwards and I grabbed Bill and ran down the street.

At this point we still didn't have tickets for the match, so we decided to try a local travel agent, which we had been told was selling them.

We managed to buy two tickets for near enough face value and as it was approaching kick-off we went to a shop and bought a bottle of wine each and made our way to the San Marmes stadium.

We watched England win 2-0. The tickets we had bought were in the seats and I had a bit of a sleep in second half as I was pissed and the sun was so hot.

After the game we stayed behind and watched as, behind both goals, all the English lads were doing the conga across the terrace. They were going up to the coppers, who were standing at the sides in a mass conga, then turning at the last moment. You could see that the police were shitting themselves.

It was still really warm, one of the things I remember is how the stadium had loads of English and Union Flags all round it. England had won and we thought things were pretty good.

We walked back to the car, and came across a Scouser called Rob; he had missed his bus back to San Sebastian. As that was where we were heading, I offered him a lift.

He was a good laugh, but he kept complaining that I was driving too slowly and the bus, that he has already missed, would have been quicker.

We parked up near the beach and cooked up some soup with the little gas stove we had bought with us. After that we went into town with Rob and had loads more beer, he nicked some food from a shop and shared it with us. As he ate he kept singing 'Gibraltar is ours' to the locals.

We pissed it up in the old bars; they were old type Spanish bars with hams hanging from the ceilings and sawdust on the floors. After a while Rob went back to the campsite with his mates, Bill and I walked back to car along the beach. I slept in the front, Bill had the back seat.

Monday

We spent the day on the beach and had a football match with a load of England lads. Later we decided to book into hotel for a couple of nights. The hotel was a bit old fashioned but it was all right. I parked the car nearby and then went to a local supermarket and got some bread, cheese and beer.

We had a wander around San Sebastian and bumped into Bobby Moore, the ex-England captain, with his wife and daughter. For a laugh Bill said 'have you stolen any necklaces?' to him, but he didn't think that was funny. It turned out; a lad we met later called John Paul, had been into his hotel and had had a shit in the foyer toilet, leaving a massive turd in the hand basin, so perhaps he wasn't having a particularly good day.

As we walked round the headland, a group of Chelsea fans were catching fish using bent nails, some bread and string. When they caught a big fish, a bloke from the press told them to hold it up so he could take a photo, but the leader of the Chelsea boys told him to 'fuck off'.

At night we went out for drinks and in one bar I got talking to a really fit Spanish girl. She was keen on me, but two Spurs lads who were in the bar, told me a story about their mate taking a local girl home at an earlier Spurs game in Spain. Her father came home and caught them at it. The father took umbrage and reported the Spurs fan to the police and he was now in a cell awaiting trial for rape.

I decided not to risk it!

There was a mad Basque bloke in the bar and he had no teeth. He was wearing a beret, when we got talking to him; he showed us that he had a gun in his belt, hidden under his long shirt.

We then met up with a lad from Bristol and decided go to The Hollywood Night Club with him, which was down the street. We managed to chat up some local girls, and I let one of them get my dick out and play with it in a darker corner of the club. The Bristol lad couldn't believe it, and kept saying 'she flopped his dick out.'

He ended up sleeping on our bedroom floor as he couldn't get back to the campsite, and, the last thing he said before going to sleep was 'she flopped his dick out'. Apparently he had slept on street for the last few nights, as the campsite locked the gates early, and he couldn't get in if he stayed out on the piss. Bill did a dead good impersonation of him saying 'she flopped his dick out' in a West Country accent.

Tuesday

The day was spent down on the beach again. We had another game of football and a swim. A group of us decided to swim out to the island in the bay, but one of the lads started to get into difficulties with cramp.

We had to commandeer this young German lad's rubber dingy, which he was rowing nearby. Between us we helped get the cramped lad back to the shallows by hijacking the dingy and holding on to it. The German lad's dad was not impressed at all when we got out of the sea and he had a right go at us.

While we were swimming back, a dead rat floated past, and we remembered the colour of the river in Bilbao and presumed the sewage was just pumped straight into the sea.

Some of the lads later made a naked man 'sand castle'. They used a litre bottle of coke for his dick. The locals didn't like this as they walked past, and the police were called. That afternoon two more England fans were handcuffed and marched off, to the cells.

In the afternoon we went to a bar to watch one of the other games and bumped into John and Timber from Rotherham.

John kept saying 'el braga' to the local girls, which apparently meant get your pants off! When we clapped at one of the goals, one of the local girls came up to me and said 'why are you clapping when you could be fucking'. They ended up buying us some food and we bought them some beer in return.

During the day the police made a number of arrests up at the campsite. Apparently they were going in with snatch squads. Quite a few of the lads were now residing in the local nick. Some of them were there for hi-jacking a donkey and getting it drunk on the local wine.

At night there was a big fight outside the Hollywood Night Club and someone ended up shooting a gun. We wondered if it was our mad Basque friend with the beret.

We liked it in San Sebastian, and all the boys were singing 'we are Basque', in the bars. Later on that night Bill had too much to drink and was sick all over the pavement.

Wednesday

We went on the beach again, the weather was sunny and hot, and we had an easy day, just looking at the topless girls and sunbathing. I moved the car nearer to the beach, and during the day we went to brew a cup of tea. Unfortunately the local police didn't like us doing this, and told us to switch the cooker off. Perhaps it was a fire risk but we were by the side of the road and I think they were just being awkward.

We decided to go for a proper meal, in a restaurant. While we were in there, some other English Lads told us that an English fan has been shot last night. We had a few more drinks after the meal and decided to go to a different nightclub that night.

I was wearing my 'the empire strikes back' t-shirt which had printed on its front, a bulldog standing with one foot on each island of the Falklands while waving a Union Flag.

A Spanish bloke in the club kept pulling my shirt. I told him to piss off, but he produced a police badge and told me to leave the club with him.

He told me to go across the street and down an alleyway that was across the road. Then he pulled out a gun. I was not happy about this, but like a fool went down the alley. He aimed the gun at me and was shouting in Spanish about my T-shirt. I could see his hand shaking, as he was about to pull the trigger.

Just at that moment a car turned round in the street opposite the alleyway and its lights shone up, illuminating the alley. We were in the cars headlights, and it was obvious what was happening, so the copper ran off. I ran in the opposite direction, and then back to the hotel making sure I wasn't being followed.

Thursday

We had arranged to give Timber and John a lift to the match. We met up after breakfast, at the car. After getting in the car, we drove off, which meant I left my trainers, which were under the car, behind.

As we pulled into Bilbao, we were all shouting 'el braga' to all the girls that we saw on the pavement. As we drove past a cemetery for some surreal reason there was a full-scale gun battle going off.

I parked the car in the same place as the last time, and again we went to the 'Churchill pub'. We ordered beer and a burger, but this time you had to pay for it before you were served.

Baz Smith, a lad from Stoke came into the bar and reckoned that, as it was a bank holiday, in Spain, he couldn't get a film for his camera. More likely he was too tight to buy one. Like a fool, I gave him one of my spare rolls. He said he would repay me by getting another one for me, but of course he never did. I should have just asked for the money.

West Ham AWOL was there again, standing on a shelf at the back of the pub. He was singing 'God save the Queen'. Silk and Rob Jones came in and we had a chat, they had been staying on the French side of the Spanish border at a place called St Juan de Luz and had had a good time.

As we were talking the police baton charged the pub. We legged it down the street, but the cops grabbed hold of West Ham AWOL, so we grabbed him as well, and pulled him along with us. The next thing the police started spraying us with a water cannon.

We ran down the road and bumped into Fred who I had met in Norway. He suggested going to a quieter bar, which seemed like a good idea so we did.

At the match, this time we had tickets behind the goal. We beat Kuwait 1 – 0 and afterwards most of the English lads started doing a mass conga the width of the terrace. As we approached the police by the fence, they had their fingers on the triggers of their guns, or batons drawn, but at the last minute the conga changed direction and you could sense there was a mass sigh of relief from the cops.

All the English fans were in high spirits and we gave rousing versions of 'This Time', 'We'll fly the flag' as well as the usual 'Rule Britannia' and 'God save the Queen'.

The local Basques in the stand above had stayed behind to watch and applauded the English. Basque flags were tossed down to us, for us to keep, and I caught a Real Sociedad hat, thrown into the crowd from the Spaniards above.

After leaving the ground we found the local police had also stayed behind and they baton charged us down the street.

We arrived at the car to find John and Timber waiting with a few bottles of cheap wine purchased or stolen from a local supermarket. This was to be payment for the lift! We got in the car, and headed in the general direction of Madrid. Unfortunately at the first island, I managed to cut up a motorbike cop; luckily he only asked to see my license and did not breathalyse me.

After an hour or so's driving we stopped off at a small town for a drink and some food. I had found a way of overtaking the bigger Lorries, by shooting through the petrol stations that were every so often alongside the main road, then back up the slip roads. Bill was still messing about with the glove compartment.

We parked up and the town seemed deserted. It was like a Wild West town surrounded by craggy topped mountains, the local dogs were howling at us and this added to the atmosphere. We looked for a bar but couldn't find one so ended up using the only hotel in the town. We were surprised to find the Kuwait national team in there. Their manager was really fat, but friendly enough and we talked to him and some of the players before they left.

In the hotel bar the television was showing that night's game. It was Spain v Northern Ireland and we wanted Northern Ireland to win. At half time the England game's highlights were shown and the local Spanish spat on the floor, and stamped on it, when England scored. John enjoyed this, and it made him cheer even more than he would normally have done.

The atmosphere was really ugly in the bar, and the Spanish turned on us. We walked out of the bar backwards, and smashed our bottles on the tables outside, as the Spanish came at us. We decided to throw the bottles, and a few chairs for good measure, at the Spaniards who were after us, and then we ran towards the car.

We realised we wouldn't make it to the car, so we split up, and hid in alleyways. Eventually the Spaniards gave up looking for us, and we sneaked back to the car, keeping to the shadows.

I was pissed and just wanted to sleep in the car. The lads said it was too dangerous, so we drove to the next service station.

I parked up, and using a towel for a pillow, I slept on the grass next to the car. The other lads were fast asleep in the car.

Friday

I woke up and I was covered in dew and was freezing cold. It was about 5 a.m. so I got in the car and drove with the heater on, but just kept nearly nodding off. After an hour or so, I pulled over and went for a coffee. I was still sleepy, and the sun was low, and I knew I kept nearly nodding off, but eventually the other boys woke up and it was easier to keep awake. We arrived in Madrid at about mid-day.

I asked various pedestrians where the Bernabeau Stadium was, but they either couldn't understand me or didn't know, so I had no luck. After we had driven round Madrid for about half an hour, I decided to park the car in a multi-storey car park and to try our luck on foot.

We jumped on a bus that had a sign saying that it was going to the stadium. We wanted to buy tickets for the next two games, which were against West Germany and Spain.

The Bernabeau Stadium had none for sale, but we were told to try at the nearby bullring. Again no tickets were available and the travel agents, we tried on the way, also had none. The local Spaniards didn't seem to like us and kept shouting things at us as they passed-by.

We thought about getting a hotel in the Del Sol area but in end decided to try the campsite that we had heard about. Eventually we found the car park, and the car, and drove out to the campsite.

The owner required us to give him a passport, so Bill gave him his and we booked in for a few days. The ground was so hard that we couldn't get the tent pegs into it and ended up using a mixture of pegs and rocks to hold the tent up.

The campsite had a swimming pool, so we went and lazed around it for the afternoon. There was lots of different nationalities are on the campsite, some were Germans, they had all the mod cons, some Israelis in the pitch next to us had stacks of food.

All we had was a two-man tent, and a camping stove between the four of us. Bill cooked us up some soup for dinner, and then we went to the campsite bar for the night.

One lad we met was a right laugh. He was from Hemel and was called 'Fat Freddy Fuckfinder'. As his name suggested, he was up for anything. Another lad was from Portsmouth, so we called him Pompey, as you do, he had managed to get a dose of the clap and spent some time explaining about the state of his dick.

Two Basingstoke lads were also there. I would become great friends with them later. Sprake was six foot four tall and his mate, John Paul, was religiously keeping a diary of every day of the World Cup. The trouble with this was that his misses would find it on his return and finish with him because of what he had done and what he had written.

One of their mates was Alf, he was trying to organise a coach so they could all go and watch Northern Ireland play the next day.

Two of the English lads ended up naked, and after dancing on a table in the bar area, went off hand in hand, skipping round the campsite. The owner saw them and chased after them waiving a big stick. Due to his massive nose we named the owner 'El Conko'.

John and Timber were still with us and on the way back to the tent we stole some of the Germans plastic chairs, and some wine that had been stored behind a building. At the tent John stole some of the Israelis food. As we were eating and drinking the police toured round the campsite in a car. Bill panicked and ended up hiding under a caravan.

We got rid of the chairs then I slept in the tent along with Bill while John and Timber slept in the car.

Saturday

The Israelis accused us of stealing their food, which we denied. They packed up their tent and cleared off. John and Timber decided to go in search of a cheap hotel in Madrid. Bill and I had a lazy day round the campsite.

At one point Bill went to get his passport back but 'El Conko' wouldn't give it to him, when Bill asked again he pulled a gun out. Bill came back to the bar and he was shitting himself.

We went to the pool but they had tightened security and you were supposed to pay for a ticket. I got in but Bill had to pay. We were running short of money and it was a bank holiday weekend so we were going to have to be careful.

In the pool we met Steve a Chelsea fan from Jersey who was a cracking good lad. We had a right laugh for the rest of the afternoon, and then we went back to the tent and finished off the food, wine and beer that was left. We noticed that the Germans had reclaimed their plastic chairs.

On the campsite there was also an Australian bloke, and his young lad. He had been to every world cup since Mexico 1970.

That night we went back to the bar, Freddy was eating octopus and offering tentacles to all, the Basingstoke lads were also there. We had a good laugh even though our money had nearly gone. Bill ended up falling asleep in the bar to the amusement of the rest of the boys.

Sunday

We had arranged to all go into Madrid, in search of tickets today. I drove to near the Bernabeau Stadium and parked up. We met up with the campsite lads in a bar and then went to get tickets from the stadium, as a ticket office window there was open and selling them.

It was red hot standing or sitting in the queue that had formed outside the stadium and we took it in turns to go and get cold beers from the supermarket. In the queue was West Ham AWOL. He told us about there being a load of trouble at Dieppe, in France, when he was on his way out.

Apparently there was a big fight with the locals and a Citroen dealership ended up getting trashed. As he told the story he was pulling large swigs from a bottle of cheap Spanish Brandy.

A load of Spanish lads then turned up waving a Spanish flag. They approached us and were gesturing that they wanted to fight; we ended up chasing them to the corner of the road and managed to get their flag off them, which was ceremoniously torn up.

A German lad from Hamburg was with us. Every bit of his denim jacket was covered in HSV 'sew on' badges; he seemed to be a good lad, especially when he went to the supermarket and stole a load of beer and offered some of the bottles to us.

We were then told there were no tickets left, so we went across the square to the Sportsman Pub where Fat Freddy, John, Sprake and Pompey managed to buy tickets from a tout. We ended up drinking all afternoon and as night fell we carried on drinking down in Madrid's red light district, which is called 'Del Sol'.

We caught the metro there, and decided to all stick close together for safety. After more beer and a MacDonald's it was decided it would be a good idea to try out a whorehouse.

One of the girls in the brothel was really fit and Steve from Jersey was straight in there. I spoke to another nice one, but by the time I got upstairs with her, the price had doubled so I decide against it.

Bill and I went into a bar and three girls started rubbing us up, at this point Bill informed me that he was still a virgin, so I offered him some money to go with one of them, but he decided not to.

As we all walked down the street the girls were getting cheaper, but you had to go to a flat nearby with them and then wait, while people took turns in the two available bedrooms. I was waiting with a girl that I had picked up, for a room to become free, when her friend arrived.

She was not very nice looking and had thick glasses, but she had her own flat. I decided I didn't want to wait, and definitely didn't want to be left on my own, so I paid for the ugly girl.

I told her to keep her glasses on and ended up wanking over her tits and face. She then told me I could have her mother as well for an extra 500 pesetas.

As I came out of the room, Steve's first girl was going in with another bloke. The girls were doing a good trade. We met up with the rest of the boys and as we were pissed, we ended up doing a small conga down the street. An American tourist was impressed and took lots of photos of us.

We then went for the metro back to the Bernabeau but as the doors closed, Bill was left behind, and it was the last train that night, we held the doors open but he wouldn't jump in, the local police who witnessed this then started hitting us with their truncheons for our efforts. Everyone shouted at Bill to get a taxi back to the car. He was being a right doughnut!

I arrived at the car just as a tow truck was backing up to tow it away. Luckily Bill arrived in his taxi at the same time, and we jumped into the car as quickly as we could. Even though we were obviously pissed, a copper stopped the traffic for us, and we backed out onto the highway, and drove away, back to the campsite.

The gates of the campsite were locked so we left the car outside and climbed over the gate and headed for the tent.

Monday

We woke up late, with the sun beating down on the tent. I went and got the car and Bill cooked breakfast. Some of the lads had gone to watch Northern Ireland, who were playing at the Vincent Calderon Stadium, Atletico Madrid's ground; we just lazed around the pool all day.

A Spanish geezer hoofed our ball out of the pool area and lost it up a tree. Later we used up the last of our food and beer, and I noticed that the clock in the car had stopped, and the indicators no longer worked, it turned out to be just a fuse, but I didn't know that until I got home, and drove for another three thousand miles with no indicators!

That night we bought chips from the bar and sat drinking with Fat Freddy. Bill went and got his passport, as we were leaving in the morning. This time Conky set his dog on him, and waved the gun again. After he told us this, we went back and told him we needed the passport to change some money and he reluctantly gave it to us.

After we had got the passport, 'El Conky' was threatened by the lads, so he in turn shut the bar down. The Aussie and his lad ended up having a massive argument with Conky and then each other. We decided to call it a night and went back to the tent.

Tuesday

The indicators unfortunately hadn't miraculously started working; I was a bit worried as this was the first problem I had had with the car. We packed up the tent and drove into Madrid. We did get a bit lost, but eventually managed to park up near to the Bernabeau after first filling up with petrol.

We went into the 'Sportsman Bar' and met up with John and Timber. They were nicking Champagne from the supermarket next door; this seemed like a good idea so we went and helped ourselves.

We got talking to a German Forest fan; he told us that he hated Germany! Also in the sportsman bar was the HSV lad, again he was a good lad and ended up buying us some beers.

Some TV cameras from a Swedish TV station and also from the BBC appeared. I shouted at the camera 'hello mum' then we did a conga across the street for the benefit of the viewer's back home. This was the green light for the Spanish coppers to baton charge us, as we ran back to the bar, we got a good hiding for our troubles from the coppers.

I thought to myself, 'I hope my mum isn't watching the news'!

An old woman happened to get knocked over in the melee, I helped her up while the lads behind were goading the coppers, and the locals in general, who had gathered to watch, on the pavement outside, with chants of 'Malvenas Inglatterras', 'Gibraltar is ours' plus we were waving the Basque flags that we still had, while chanting 'ETA, ETA'

ETA were the Basque separatist terrorist group and much hated by the Spaniards.

A while later a group of German skinheads appeared and met up with a load of English skinheads, they all embraced each other and started dancing to the Bad Manners song playing on a portable tape recorder that one of them had. The police and locals looked on in horror.

The HSV Hamburg lad then told me how he didn't like Spanish coppers. At this moment they started to back their horses up to the bar doors. The police then came into the bar with truncheons drawn and forced us to run down between the lines of horses onto the pavement. Here a severe beating was given out courtesy of a row of truncheon wielding policemen.

HSV just launched himself into a copper and ended up whacking him on the nose. He turned to me and said 'good ja'. I grabbed him and we legged it down the road.

I was hit on my back and also round my kidneys and as I was running, with the police close behind and on our tails, I couldn't believe it had started raining as there wasn't a cloud in the sky.

I looked up and saw a hail of bottles going over my head; these were being thrown by the Germans and English lads who were in the next bar down the road. They were being launched in the direction of our police pursuers.

West Ham AWOL grabbed me and my German friend and led the way through the bar and out of the back door, over a fence and into the next street. We had got away for a while.

It didn't take long for a group of Spanish lads to spot us. One with a black flag was their leader; West Ham AWOL ran at him and planted a head butt on his nose. The Spanish scarpered. I then lent West Ham AWOL my Real Sociadad hat so he could disguise himself. Now the police were after 'el skinhead' in particular.

We went into a bar and met up with a group of promotions girls all dressed in really tight blue shorts and orange tops. They had spare tickets so Bill and I bought a couple. We could hear the English fans in the stadium. So we headed up to the ground.

We got in the ground but were in the top tier and it was full of Spanish so we managed to climb down to the English section by getting over a dividing wall.

At half time we met up with some of the boys, they all had similar tales to tell regarding the Spanish and the police. Steve and his mate asked me for a lift to the campsite after the game. As it was kind of on the way to Lloret, where were heading, I agreed to give them a lift.

We kept quiet when we went to the toilets at half time, but a Brummy lad started singing 'England' and was sent flying by some Spanish boys.

In the second half there was sporadic violence all around the ground but mostly at the other end to us. We left the ground and the noise from the match was still reverberating in my ears.

We got in the car and headed for the campsite where we had one more beer with the lads, said our goodbyes then headed off for Lloret.

We drove for a couple of hours, there only seemed to be us and a few lorries on the road. I was really knackered so we stopped for a coffee. We drove a bit further but then I needed a shit so I stopped at a lonely petrol station.

Bill was fast asleep, I went to the car boot to get some bog roll out of the bag, but while I was looking for it, I heard a terrific barking noise and the scamper of claws on dirt, I shone the torch and saw an Alsatian in full attack mode.

I opened a back door and dived in, shutting the door just in time, before seeing snarling teeth and gob that appeared all over the window. Buy this time, and with the running, I had shit all down my leg and had filled my shorts.

I climbed in to the front of the car, and noticed that Bill was laughing in his sleep, and with the boot still open I drove off. At the next lay by I stopped and cleaned myself up as best as I could, using some flat coke that I found in the boot.

I decide to sleep there in the lay-by.

Wednesday

We woke up as the sun rose and I drank the last of the coke. At the first services we saw, I went and cleaned up properly and then had the rest of that shit. We drove to Zaragoza and after a bit of difficulty changed up some more money then had breakfast. It was a long drive to the coast and Bill spent the time opening and shutting the glove compartment.

We had the scarfs out of the windows again, and again got stopped by the police and were told to put them inside. As we were stopped, getting our telling off, a London bus full of Scotland fans went up the motorway in the opposite direction, we gave them the V's.

Eventually after a stop for dinner at some service station, we skirted round Barcelona and headed north up the coast road to Lloret.

We found the Hotel Windsor easily enough, parked up in the car park and went and checked in.

We had a couple of beers but Bill looked pissed already, and he just fell over. He went to the room and had to have a lie down.

Later we sorted out our bags and then went for quick swim in the hotel pool. There was a group of girls from Coventry staying at the hotel and a girl called Gaynor, appeared to be the best of them. We had dinner and had the occasional look over at the girls.

At night it was into Lloret itself. We were having a few drinks but Bill was knackered and went home early.

I ended up drinking with a German girl, she was lovely, but a load of English youths who hadn't even been to the football, started mouthing off about Germans. I stood up for her and they set about me. One of them cracked me on the nose and it wouldn't stop bleeding.

Elise, the German girl, offered to take me to her hotel to clean up. I wasn't sure where my hotel was, so I went back with her. I had a wash then just fell asleep on the bed. Elise climbed in bed with me but apart from a kiss and a cuddle during the night nothing happened. In the morning I felt so embarrassed I climbed out of the window, which luckily was on the ground floor and scuttled back to my hotel, unfortunately I didn't see her again.

Thursday

As I arrived back at the hotel at about 9 a.m. Gaynor was by the pool having breakfast, she gave me a funny look, like I was some kind of dirty stop-out. I went and had breakfast with her and introduced myself. Then I went to see if Bill was all right, he was still asleep.

I looked on the balcony and Bill had covered it in sick. I decided to have a shower then left him to recover. I went down by the pool and spent the morning talking to Gaynor.

We decide to have a walk down to the beach; on the way we started kissing. Typically it was her last day, I couldn't take her back to my room because of Bill and the mess, and she had her mates in her room and they were all packing.

She said she could give me a blowjob in some bushes which she did while I was fingering her. She gave me her home phone number, and I said I would see her when I got home, and take her to Blackpool for a dirty weekend.

Later Gaynor left for the airport and I gave her a kiss as she went. Bill couldn't believe what was happening, as he had just got ready to go out for the night after a day in bed.

The maid had had a right go at him for the mess he had made.

We went out on the town that night and got talking to a girl from Middlesboro who was giving out the club flyers. She was beautiful and Bill and I were in love with her. Later on in the week, she gave me her home phone number, so I could see her when we got home, which of course I lost!

We walked into a hotel bar and a girl was dancing to the music being played by the local DJ. There was something about her and I ended up having a few drinks with her and then decided to go for a swim with her in her hotel's pool. Everything was fine until the manager came and told me to get out, another missed opportunity.

Friday

The days were spent lazing around the pool. There was a geeky young English lad in our hotel, and two Dutch girls who were very nice. One day the English lad just shouted 'I like you' across the pool area to the Dutch girls.

There was an awkward silence, when there was no answer, so he shouted again 'do you like me' still no reply, me and Bill pissed ourselves and kept shouting 'I like you' at him, at every opportunity.

The Dutch girls walked into a bar come nightclub toilet one night and caught me pissing in the hand basin. I thought I was in the gent's toilets but was in the senioritis. The next morning they informed me 'you were very pissed last night.'

Spain v England

I was up very early; Bill had decided he was staying at Lloret. I had breakfast and drove into Barcelona. I parked up the car in a side road and hoped it would be all right, but I was a bit short of time for my train so just abandoned it really.

I walked to the rail station and got a train to Madrid. The journey was 10 hours long and even though I was sitting next to a young American girl it was boring. I had no food or beer for the trip as I was nearly out of money.

I arrived in Madrid early in the morning, and got the metro to the ground. I met up with Steve from Jersey and his crazy mate who he was now hanging about with. We stole some food and beer from a supermarket, and were then spotted by a large group of Spanish lads.

We were hopelessly outnumbered but there were some English nearby and we asked them for help, they didn't want to know, and were off on their toes, when they saw our problem.

The crazy youth Steve was with steamed into the Spanish, his fists were flying but he soon went down, we were then surrounded and were taking a severe beating when some coppers on horseback arrived. One cop, who had leather-riding gloves on, picked up the crazy youth by his hair, and he was nicked. Steve and me got a severe whacking, and had to run off as the coppers beat us.

We met up with some boys we knew in a bar, and they told us that John and Timber had been arrested and were sitting in a cell in Benidorm. Apparently a lad from Brighton was with them in Benidorm, and when they were locked up had managed to get into their room and had stolen their tickets and money.

Fat Freddy Fuckfinder was in jail in Madrid, and West Ham AWOL had been deported and would be doing time for going AWOL in Colchester Military Prison.

The English got together and walked to the stadium. Lads were getting hit left right and centre. We got in and I guess there was about 1500 of us.

After the match, which was 0-0, we went down the stairs onto the street to be met by a hail of bottles. I didn't know what to do, as

I had no hotel, but bumped into Silk, and we went down to the Del Sol area.

It was really dodgy down there with gangs of Spaniards hunting for small groups of English. Two English lads got stabbed that night and according to the British papers ended up having to have emergency surgery to save their lives.

Everyone was sticking together for safety but I decided to get the metro to as near to the campsite as I could, then walk the rest of the way. I ended up sleeping under a hedge near the campsite.

The next day I met Steve. I had breakfast with him; his mate was still locked up. I got the bus into town, then the first train that was going to Barcelona. There were some Manchester United fans on it and a lad from Norway, who has been following England. I had a few beers with them in the buffet car.

At Barcelona I got a taxi to where I had left the car, I knew it was near a bullring, and amazingly, although it was covered in dust and leaves, it was still there and there were no parking tickets on it. I drove back to the hotel where I found Bill sunbathing by the pool.

I went to our room and took some photos of all the truncheon marks on my body by photographing my reflection in the wardrobe mirror. Then I went down to the pool and met Bill.

A German girl had arrived at the hotel with her mum. She was seventeen and after dinner we played pool, and had a few drinks together in the hotel bar. She was from near Munich and was really nice.

We ended up going to my room and after we had slept together, I let her out, just as her mum was walking down the corridor, she was with the headwaiter and they had been all over the hotel looking for her.

'What are you doing' the headwaiter asked me, but the German girl was good as gold and kissed me and said she would dream about me, her mum looked on in disgust. For the rest of the time we were at the hotel, her mum wouldn't let me go anywhere near her.

The next morning we discovered that the car has been broken into and we had lost some money, cameras and other things like sunglasses. We reported it to the local police but they were not interested.

We now had no money left, apart from what we would need for petrol to get home, so the last few days were spent buying Bacardi from supermarkets and drinking in the cheaper shitty bars.

In one such bar I met a girl from Cumbria she was also broke. She said she would sleep with me for five pounds. I said 'ok', but then she admitted she had got a case of the pox and she didn't want to give it to me. I bought her a few drinks for saving me the grief of getting the pox and we said our goodbyes.

We left Lloret for the long drive home, mile after mile with just the occasional diversion, such as when an eagle swooped across the road to catch a rabbit. There wasn't much to break up the boredom and Bill closing and un-closing the glove box was doing my head in. We had to 'Selotape' across the window where it was smashed in the robbery to stop the wind coming in.

At Calais we couldn't afford a drink, so we boiled up some water and used the last tea bag. We boarded the ferry and drove home after we had docked. We were absolutely knackered and completely broke but all in all it was a great world cup.

It turned out that while we were on the piss in Lloret, one of the lads, who we called Big Paul, he had been in the bar with us in Madrid, along with Sprake from Basingstoke had been locked up along with a rough Chelsea fan called Chester who had a swastika tattoo on his forehead.

Apparently Chester spent the whole night in the cells swinging from the bars singing 'Chelsea are here' and 'Maggie will get us out'. They eventually got released after two days.

Greece v England
1982

Saturday

Julie saw me off at the station. I jumped on the early train to London then to Waterloo. I had a couple of beers in a bar at the station then got the train to Folkestone. After it arrived in Folkestone I got the ferry to Calais and then the connecting overnight train to Switzerland.

Sunday

I had breakfast in Geneva, and then got the first train that was going to Milan. The scenery was really nice, with massive mountains covered in snow and green valleys below. I had a walk round Milan to kill some time, then got a train to Rimini.

In Rimini I booked into a hotel and went for a drink, but the place was dead as it was out of season. I had few beers at night, but there were no English about, so ended up going back to the hotel for an early night in a comfortable bed.

Monday

I caught the early train to Brindisi and once there I went to the port to catch the ferry to Greece. An Argentine seaman was by the quayside, and spotted my England shirt. He started shouting 'Malvinas Argentines' at me.

I told him to piss off, and then he just attacked me. The only thing I could do was punch him back and try and defend myself. Before I knew what was happening the port police ran along the quay and arrested both of us. I was taken to the local police station where I was held all day.

I got a phone call from British Embassy later in the afternoon and they told me that the police would release me without charge, but I had to agree to leave the country. I agreed to this, and signed various forms. By now it was too late to make the game in Greece, as I had missed my ferry so I decided to go home.

The Police let me out of my cell and took me to the station in the back of a police car. They put me on the Milan train and stood on the platform watching me, until it pulled out of the station. I was told I had to report to the main police station in Milan the next day.

Tuesday

I found the police station easily enough and waited for the Embassy people to come, and then explained what had happened. They told me that I was to be deported; they stamped my one-year passport, which I later photocopied to keep as a memento.

The Embassy staff sorted everything out and I just accepted it as one of those things.

Once all the paperwork was done I set off to the station and called in for a massive McDonald's dinner. I then jumped on the first train that was going to Paris.

I had no option but to catch this as I had been told I had to get straight out of Italy. I got through customs with no problem and then slept most of the way to Paris.

Wednesday

I got across Paris by using the metro, and then got a train from Gare Du Nord to Calais, then the ferry, and then a train to London. I had a beer in London then got to St Pancras and caught the first train home.

Northern Ireland v England

1983

Julie, my girlfriend, finished with me because I was going to Belfast for the weekend! I said to her 'ok then, I'm still going'. I met Joe in town and we had a few drinks, then we got the train to Crewe, it was packed so we had to stand. We the got the connecting train out of Crewe for Stranrear.

There were loads of England fans on this, including the Belper lads. You couldn't get down the corridor it was so full of passengers. At Preston station, Silk one of the Belper lads, opened the door and had a piss on to the adjacent track.

The transport police came onto the train and tried to nick him. We blocked their way and in the end they had to give up, as the train was due to pull out, and our numbers were too great. One of the Belper lads got into an argument with a Welsh lad and after a minor fight he was arrested.

As he was a knob no one tried to save him! Silk took photos off him getting arrested, as he said it should have been him. Afterwards the Welsh lad was moaning about getting hit, for no reason, but we told him to shut up. Joe was laughing as he tried to sleep.

The train arrived at Stranraer and we transferred to the boat. We got a breakfast from the cafeteria on board, and then went for a couple of beers. In the bar, there were a number of Chelsea fans; most of them were staunch right-wingers and loyalists. One of their group was a left-winger, comie type, and they were all taking the piss out of him.

A couple of Sheffield lads were stealing money from a gaming machine by using a bent strimmer wire. It was possible for them to activate the mechanism that counted the coins into the machine, with it. They more or less emptied it, and none of the staff noticed.

We docked at Larne, and the RUC were waiting for us. They didn't let us go for a wander round, but instead made us get on the train to Belfast. There were some decent Orient lads on the train, and we talked to them on the way into town. In Belfast, Joe and I went off on our own into a number of bars. We were quite careful what we said, in case we got ourselves into trouble.

We talked to a couple of lads and I was saying how we were supporting Northern Ireland when they played in Spain during the world cup. This got a 'sucking in of teeth' type reaction in the bar, but generally we stuck to the city centre pubs and felt fairly safe.

We went into one pub called 'The Morning Star' and met three nice Ulster lads who were going to the match. We tagged along with them, and they seemed to know just about every fit girl that we saw, and there were plenty, many of the girls had the green eyes and red hair that we had heard about.

We arranged to meet up with the lads after the game, but as we came out of the ground on the Saturday night, all hell was let loose. We were getting battered by the Northern Ireland fans; most of who seemed to be enjoying the fight, purely on a football level.

As we were near the catholic area, we were then attacked by the nationalist who were just trying to get to us, any way they could, because we were the 'hated English'.

Most of us had our England shirts on, which earlier we had kept hidden under our fastened coats.

Now we were proudly letting all and sundry see them, while the army were taking up shooting positions, lying under cars or behind post boxes and the like. Meanwhile the RUC were escorting us back into town. They were using the butts of their rifles to stop the nationalists from getting to us. They were hitting them in their faces, as the IRA types poured out of the bars to get us.

Big Paul then shouted at us, as he passed by in the back of an RUC land rover. We were not sure if he been nicked or injured. The Police walked us straight to the station where a train was waiting to take us to Larne. At Larne we slept in the ferry port either on the floor or on the uncomfortable plastic seats.

Sunday

The ferry was at ten in the morning, so to kill some time we had a walk round. All the England fans appeared to have had made it back in one piece.

Once on the ferry we went to the bar and all the Chelsea boys were also there. They were singing songs such as 'a wog is an animal with big rubber lips'. They were led in the singing by a famous England fan nicknamed Nick-a-Zag. My mate Joe was a bit of a lefty, and he didn't like the songs, or the general right wing rhetoric, but thankfully he didn't say anything.

He told me a story about when he was hitch hiking to a bike race in the Isle of Man and how he never got a lift while he was with a black lad he had met. He had to say to him 'sorry mate can you try hitching thirty yards down the road', as soon this happened he got a lift more or less straight away. For some reason Joe sounded surprised as he told the story.

At Stranraer we tried to go into a pub, but as soon as they heard our English accents they refused us entry. We ended up going to an off licence and bought some cans of lager. Later we met John and Timber outside the 'offy'. They had been out nicking what they could.

John had also met a local Stranrear girl and gone and shagged her on the beach.

We had a game of football but it was pretty violent. It started out as a kind of a North versus South game. A few local Scots then turned up hoping for a game, but some of the boys chased them off for a bit of sport, that they preferred, though I don't think any thumpings were handed out.

We got the train to Glasgow then had to change for the Crewe train, finally arriving back in Matlock at about 9 p.m.

Hungary
1983

Monday

I took Lynn, the girl I was seeing home, and she made me miss my train, as she was slow to get ready. I caught the next one anyway; In London I got the tube to Victoria and then the first train that was going down to Dover. There happened to be some Wolves lads and a Manchester lad on the train who were also going to Hungary. I said 'hello' and ended up having a drink with them.

We got on the ferry at Dover, and sailed across the channel. I went to the bar and the boys from the train were there, so again I joined them for a few beers, then at Oostende we all caught the overnight train heading towards Vienna. I found where my couchette was and checked that it was an empty compartment; otherwise I would have tried to find another one.

I dumped my bag on the luggage rack and then went and had a drink with the lads from before. They were now drinking with a German bloke, who was in their compartment. One of the Wolves fans, he was from Shrewsbury, was dead smelly, he had a real body odour problem. We had a drink for a couple of hours then I went back to my couchette and had a good night's sleep, which you often do as you're travelling across a country on an overnight train.

Tuesday

I woke up and it looked like I was in Austria. During the journey some people got on the train at a German station and came into my compartment. Luckily neither of them were loud snorers. As we neared the final destination of the train, in Vienna, I went and had a wash and cleaned my teeth. On the way down the train I saw the lads but they were still asleep in their bunks.

Their compartment door was open, probably because of the smell. At Vienna I got off the train and the Manchester lad met his mates. He had told us that they had gone on, ahead of him.

I ended up going for a couple of drinks with them, to kill the few hours that I had to wait for the Budapest train. We had some drinks in various bars around Vienna, but I ended up in one bar with the smelly Wolves fan and his mate. I decided to head back to the station.

The Budapest train was soon ready to board. I got on the train and found a seat. The Wolves lads had gone for some food in the restaurant car, so I read my book for a bit, and then decided to have a walk down the train.

There were quite a few English fans on this train now.

I said hello to a couple of lads, then in the next carriage there was a compartment full of English boys all drinking the local ale. They introduced themselves and amongst them was Rich from Oldham, Steve a Man City fan, a Portsmouth lad called Jeff, a Sheff Utd lad who was wearing a Fila tracksuit and a couple of others.

They seemed to be good boys and I ended up standing in the corridor having a few beers with them until we reached the Hungarian border.

Three lots of security checks were made at the border, that wasn't a problem but the ticket inspector who was with the border guards reckoned that I hadn't got the right train ticket. After a bit of explaining and pleading about not knowing which train I should have been on, he let me off.

I went to buy some more beers from the buffet. As I waited to be served I looked out of the window at the countryside we were passing through. On the roads there were tanks, and old Lada cars, we past large mine workings, in the village's, people were still using horses and traps and very old lorries.

We arrived in Budapest, at Keletti Station. I disembarked and said I might see the lads later; I jumped into a taxi at the taxi rank outside the station and gave the driver the address to the hotel I had already booked. On arrival, at the hotel, I was pleased to see some English flags hanging from a couple of the balconies.

The receptionist gave me the keys to my room, after I had presented my passport to check in. I went to the room and went in, but someone else's clothes were hanging up in the wardrobe.

For a minute I thought that they couldn't expect me to share the room with a stranger. I hadn't been to Eastern Europe before, but then I said to myself I can't be sharing so went back to the reception area. This time they gave me the correct room key.

I went to the new room, which was sparse but clean enough. I had a good wash and then checked my room for any 'bugs' like I was 'James Bond' or something. Once I was sure I wasn't being spied on, I decided to go and have a beer.

The hotel was a long way out of central Budapest so I got another taxi into the town centre and had some drinks in a bar that didn't look too bad. The locals including a number of women were staring at me, I wasn't sure why, but presumed it was because they could tell I was a foreigner.

I decided to leave and went across road to another bar, which looked a bit more westernised. In there I got talking to a fit Hungarian girl, but I think she was only talking to me to practise speaking English.

It was pouring with rain so I didn't want to walk too far. I tried another pub, this time it was a more modern bar, but it was full of dark skinned Roma types so I had a quick drink and then hailed another taxi to go back to the hotel. At the hotel I went to my room, read my book for a bit, and then fell asleep.

Wednesday

I woke up quite early and went for a rubbish breakfast in the hotel's dining room. It consisted of stale bread, plastic cheese, and fatty ham along with cold coffee that was served with horrible warm milk, with skin floating on it.

I said hello to three other English lads staying at hotel but they weren't very friendly and didn't really want to talk to me. I decided to have a walk up the road and managed to buy a couple of programmes, for the game later that day, from a newspaper stand.

I walked back to the hotel and booked a taxi. At that point a lad from Belper called Silk appeared. As it happened he was staying at the same hotel as me, along with Rob Jones and some of their mates.

They told me they were all on the piss the night before in Budapest and between them had lost a couple of cameras during the session, got pissed up and a couple of them had bought whores back to the hotel. Between them they all looked a bit hung-over.

Rob went to change some money at the hotel front desk. The girl behind the counter gave him loads more than the official rate and he was made up. We had heard that this could happen so the other lads all had a go but they just got the normal rate, it turned out that she had just made a mistake.

Rob wasn't about to tell her about it.

I sacked my taxi off; apparently they charged you more if they picked you up from a hotel. We walked up the road to where their seemed to be a taxi rank and after waiting ages we got a number of taxi's to the Duna International Hotel. I jumped in with the Belper lot and some of them weren't too happy about it.

In the Duna there were about forty English fans in the foyer. Bobby Charlton, the ex-footballer must have been staying there and he was standing, with some of his friends, in the foyer too. Rob went up to him, and asked for his autograph, which to be fair he did give to him.

Ted Croker, the hated F.A secretary, then walked out of the lift area. As he came into the foyer he told us all to behave. He spoke in a manner that suggested he thought he was in charge of us. Basically the response from the boys was 'fuck off'.

We managed to buy some match tickets from the hotel receptionist. Where she had got them from we didn't know, but they were presumably from an F.A source. The F.A had also left some free badges on various tables in the hotel, as a good will thing, so we took those as well.

A lad came into foyer and he was really happy. He announced to all that he had got a great rate when he was changing some money on the street corner, outside. As he looked at the wad of money that he had in his hand, it turned out that he only had a bank note on the top, and one on the bottom of the wad, and the rest had been switched and was just newspaper cut up to the right size. His face really dropped and everyone took the piss out of him, even Bobby Charlton could be seen laughing to himself.

Across the road was a pub. I went across to it and in here I met up with Henry Powell from Glossop and the Southampton lads. There was some food available in the bar but it looked really horrible so again, I didn't eat anything.

I ended up pissing it up with the Southampton lads. These were the boys I had I met at the World Cup, who although from Basingstoke followed the Saints, along with a massive lad called Big Paul, who was from Watford. I had bumped into them for the last few England home games and they were a good crack.

We seemed to be forming a bit of a group and had arranged to meet up in Budapest, though no one quite new where. This was, to later be called 'the magnet effect', this being, it didn't matter how shit the bar or the town was, if you stayed long enough, other people you know would come in.

The word on the street was, that apparently Legg was in town. He was a famous Chelsea boy, who had the knack of being able to organise football fans when the fighting got nasty. The last time England played here, according to the lads and the press at the time, there was loads of trouble. It was decided we needed someone like Legg to turn up; otherwise there was a good chance we were going to get turned over by the Hungarians.

We were all on the piss in the pub and had had a good session especially as the beer out there was very cheap. Then as usual someone started singing 'God save our gracious Queen'. Most of the English boys in the bar joined in.

The bar manager then decided to shut the bar as it was getting too noisy and we were getting the attention of Hungarian youths who were now hanging about outside.

As it was about four in the afternoon by then, we decided to make our way up to the ground.

We went down some steps into the underground and waited on the correct platform for the tube train to the Nep Stadium. When the train pulled in Legg and his Chelsea firm were on it. We were now a large firm, mainly Chelsea but there were boys from Manchester City, Southampton, Hull and Villa as well. There must have been about fifty to sixty of us.

As the train pulled into the station that was nearest to the Nep stadium, we all got off together. As we walked up to the Seventies-style concrete structure, which was a bowl of a stadium, we all stuck together, ready for any Hungarian attack.

Legg decided it would be a good idea to attack the Hungarians first, so as we entered the ground, we attacked them in their stand rather than going into our allocated English away fan section.

We entered the area the Hungarians seemed to be congregating in. As soon as we were in, we charged across the seating spreading Hungarians near and far. Not only did we have the surprise factor, Legg had led us in from the top so we had the higher ground.

We had soon cleared that section of Hungarians, they either jumped onto the pitch or over the fence to the next section, not many stayed to fight. We then decided to position ourselves right behind the goal.

We had a good firm including three East German lads who followed England whenever they played behind the iron curtain. The Hungarians were none too happy with what had just happened and within a couple of minutes we were being bombarded by a hail of missiles.

We were singing 'ria, ria, diahorea' as they were singing 'Hungaria'. Big Paul had a wad of notes in his hand, and was taunting the locals in the next section by waving it near their faces and shouting 'loads of money'.

When John Paul later turned up, he had got a local Hungarian girl with him and she was quite nice looking. Everyone grouped together, and Silk and his mates stood near us.

The police then moved into our section and a couple of English lads got kicked out for throwing bits of concrete back at the Hungarians. Paul was singing 'steam in regardless' which we all joined in with. The police were initially thrown off guard, as they were expecting us to be in the designated England section.

After England won the game, we waited at the end while the England players came over and gave us the 'thumbs up' and a bit of applause.

By now there was about one hundred and fifty of us and we left en mass, to walk the short distance to the tube station. The Hungarians were on the other platform, they had pre-armed themselves with rocks and bottles and again a rain of missiles came at us.

We charged over the connecting bridge and onto their platform, where after some viscous hand-to-hand fighting, the platform was cleared. We walked back over the bridge and some Hungarians were just getting up, after the first beating that they had received, in time to be slapped again.

Some of the English boys had taken some injuries, and a lad called Lane from Sheffield, had a big cut on his face. I saw that Baz Smith, a lad from Stoke, had hit a Hungarian over the head using his flagpole, and the Hungarian still seemed to be down and out cold.

As we returned to our correct platform, the police decided to baton charge us. A couple of the fat Chelsea fans and a villa fan called Frank were too slow to get out of the way, and they get a royal beating off the coppers.

It didn't take long for the police to catch the rest of us, as there was nowhere for us to run. Once they had caught us, I took a few thumps to my back and lost my hat as another copper hit me over the head with his truncheon. Luckily for me it was only a glancing blow. We had nowhere to go and the coppers were just wading into us until they had had their fun.

By now the Hungarians on the other platform were back and were adding to the pandemonium by throwing anything they could get their hands on at us.

Their train then pulled in, once they were all aboard, some sort of order was established and the police seemed to have had enough of beating us. Our train then pulled up and we all piled on, no one wanted to be left behind. As the train moved to the next station a lot of the lads were laughing and talking about the massive tear up we had just had.

As the train pulled into Keletti Station, before we knew it, we were ambushed by another group of Hungarian lads. Every window on the train was smashed, and put in by various rocks and missiles. As the doors opened some of the English got off the train and there was a big roar as the Hungarians gave the first few a good beating.

We decided to jump off as well to help them, but our numbers were split as many of our group carried on to the next station. By now there was only about fifty of us left in the mob, but when you looked around, there were some really handy boys.

There was a massive fight at the bottom of the escalators and we were slowly gaining the upper hand and some ground. The last Hungarians that were still standing to fight legged it up the escalators and we followed.

They knew what they were doing and they hit the emergency stop button, which stopped the escalators dead, in turn making us all fall over. Next a large number of bins were thrown down at us; Big Paul managed to kick one on the volley back towards them. We eventually reached the top concourse, where it was hand to hand fighting again.

I was alongside a Chelsea fan; he was losing his fight with a couple of Hungarians. I smacked one as hard as I could, and he went down, the other backed off. The Chelsea fan smiled, said 'thanks' to me, and we pushed on towards the next Hungarian who was waiting for us.

An American, who apparently was a journalist for the 'Washington Post', was in the middle of the melee. He shouted out 'you boys are crazy, that's the god dam Russian army you're fighting!'

Next, he was lifted by a couple of coppers and was dragged away. As he was bundled away, he was shouting 'I am an American citizen' and 'get your god dam hands off me'.

We decided to go back to the platform, but then Legg took charge. He shouted at everyone 'no fucker runs or you will have me to deal with tomorrow, now group up, were going out onto the street!'

As we got out onto the street level in Keletti Square, a Russian army unit was quick marching towards us. Legg shouted again 'no fucker runs, the first fucker that runs I will kick their fuckin heads in.'

We looked at each other, and followed him as he led us down a side street. Loads of local Hungarians were after us, plus the police, and now it seemed also the army! There was about forty of us left by now, as some lads had actually gone back for the next tube. Half way down the street Legg shouted 'right get moving, were going to run round the block and take these cunts by surprise'.

We were on our toes and running as fast as we could. There was the odd rock being thrown in our direction, and on the whole they were coming horizontally at us, as they were being thrown that hard.

As we turned the last corner of the block we surprised their mob, who on the whole had been hiding behind their army and police.

We ran into their firm and literally kicked the shit out of the ones we caught. Some of them tripped as they ran, and groups of England lads could be seen kicking the fallen yobs.

In the major fight we had all got split up, Big Paul and the East Germans were having the time of their lives and were covered in blood, both their own and Hungarian. Most of the Hungarians had now dispersed and there was just a load of police about.

A few of us got together, and decided to go to a bar that we could see in the distance.

A Hungarian mental lad came at us but one of the East Germans decked him with one punch. This was seen by two coppers in a Lada police car. They aimed their car at us, and mounted the pavement trying to run us over. We were then off on our toes again as the coppers tried to run us over and chased after us.

We turned down an alleyway; it was so narrow that they couldn't drive down to follow us. The alley opened out onto a main road. This had lots of nice shops, and the big hotels and banks on it. We headed towards the hotels.

We reached the 'Sheraton Hotel' and the beauty of being in Eastern Europe was that we could afford to drink in it, so we went to the bar and ordered drinks. The bar and the hotel in general had got lots of fit prostitutes in it; we started talking to a couple of them.

They wanted £100 a go, which was way out of our league; but one of them, told us she has been with two of the England players. We were enjoying the chat when another fight erupted outside the hotel. We went and had a look at what was going on. It was another group of England fans doing their best, and doing all right, against a small group of Hungarians.

After a while Rob and his mates came into the hotel. After a beer they decided to call it a night, but left Silk, as he had fallen asleep at the bar. They got taxis back to their hotel.

I went and woke up Silk and he said he wanted a beer. The bar manager, had by now, decided that we had had enough and wouldn't serve us anymore. He then went a further step and we all got asked to leave!

By now, we were about twenty strong and we jumped onto a tram that was going to a place called Margaret Bridge. This was an area where Big Paul and the Saint's lads had had a good night the night before. After a bit of trouble finding the disco that they were on about, we paid our entrance fee and went in.

The bouncers allowed us in, they were big lads and I presumed they thought that they could handle us. We went down stairs to the dance floor where a folk band was playing. We got a round of beers ordered, then started to take the piss out of the folk band. They finished their number and vacated the stage.

This meant that they started the disco. It was one of those, where the floor squares had lights under them that flashed different colours. The waitresses in the place were also really pretty. We hit the dance floor when the first song started; it was Rod Stewart's 'Baby Jane'.

A group of Danish girl tourists were also in the disco, and they got up and joined in. Things were looking up, as they were the usual blonde, blue eyed, Scandinavians, who could also speak very good English.

Then Big Paul decided to hang his Union Flag up, as he reached to tie one end he fell over and landed on the dance floor. As he lay there we all jumped on top of him and he was squashed under a group of about ten lads.

The bouncers looked on, they could tell we were just having a laugh, and were not causing any trouble, the atmosphere was still good.

We had a good night until closing at about 2 a.m. We were talking to the Danish girls and the waitresses, then as some of our lot started to leave, there was trouble on the stairs with the bouncers and a couple of the England boys.

Two of the lads were thrown out with a 'clip round the ear'. After what had happened earlier one of them decided to throw a brick through the plate glass front window. As soon as this happened the bouncers got showered in glass.

Now the whole place turned ugly. The bouncers had us trapped, and were after our blood. At the time I was getting on really well with a waitress and didn't want to get involved, but I didn't dare risk being left on my own in the place.

We managed to fight our way up the stairs, across the entrance and out onto the street.

Outside someone smashed a portable road sign across a bouncer's back. We decide to do a runner, but Big Paul was in a violent mood and picked up some brick ends and smashed two parked car windscreens as we went down the street. A lad called Pat then picked up a concrete bollard and smashed another windscreen.

All of a sudden we had about eight coppers on our tail. Silk dived under a parked lorry and hid. He got away with it, as the police just ran past where he was hiding. Me, Smoke, Rich, John and Stevie dived down another alley.

We were losing the police who were behind us, but up in front, under the pool of light that was emitting from a street lamp, stood a copper with a sub-machine gun. We charged at him, but he shouted 'halt' and then made a noise as he cocked his gun.

We kept running, straight at him, but next time he shouted, his voice was dead shaky. As he shouted 'halt' and levelled the gun at us, everyone came to a stop. In no time at all, our pursuing coppers caught us up and flung us against the wall.

Personally I was shitting it, as I knew we had caused some damage and cracked some heads. We were not allowed to talk or look round and every time any of us moved our hands, which were in the spread position against wall, they were whacked by police truncheons.

After about ten minutes we were walked back at gunpoint to the main road. We were all lined up along the pavement while they picked up any other English stragglers still coming out of the various clubs and pubs.

Smoke, who was next to me, managed to get rid of a small Hungarian flag, he had stolen earlier, by pushing it down a street drain. We said to each other that we hoped we would just get a beating and not a night in the cells.

One lad from Oldham was taking none of it; he was really lippy and kept telling the police to 'fuck off'. He got a good whacking for his troubles. A police interpreter was then presented to us. The first thing he said to us, was: 'today you have won, you have been celebrating, you are happy, but you have caused a lot of trouble. I have lost, and have had to come out here, I am unhappy, and I am going to make your lives as bad as I can'.

This was turning out to be a bad situation. The last tram of the night then trundled past down the street, John Paul and Duggie were on it, I wished to myself that I was, then they made the mistake of doing a Sieg heil at us, as they went by. The tram stopped at the next corner and a load of coppers got on and bundled them off to join us, against the wall.

Meanwhile we could see Big Paul, who started most of the trouble, explaining to the interpreter that he had hurt his head. The interpreter told the police, who told him that he must go to hospital. He said he didn't want to go, so they just let him walk off! He then stood in the shadows down the road watching the proceedings.

The cops had now got it in for John Paul, once they had got him off the tram they had put him against the wall and had kicked his legs as far apart, as far as they would go, while he was holding onto a railing. Next a cop came up and gave him a massive boot in the balls; meanwhile another copper was whacking him about the head with a truncheon.

The waitresses and bouncers were bought down to where we were standing, and there was an impromptu identity parade. I hoped the waitress that I was talking to didn't have the hump with me, and pick me out. Two of the Oldham lads, who had ruined the folk singers performance, were picked out, one who was the lippy one, and they were bundled into the back of a police car and taken off to the cells.

A number of ambulances arrived and the injured bouncers and a couple of English lads were dispatched to hospital. A copper noticed Big Paul still standing down the street and he was dragged back by the cops. They then told him to run, and he has too keep running, this he did and he disappeared down the street not to be seen again that night.

It was about 4-30 by now, and a taxi went past and I saw that Silk was sat in the back; at least he had got away. The police checked our passports; all but two of us had them with us. Details were taken and then we were released and told to go to our hotels.

Stevie and Smoke were the two without their passports.

They were bundled into the back of a police car. We were all told to run to the corner, which we had to do in a jogging type run. Luckily there was a taxi rank up the street so we jumped into taxis and went to our various hotels. The taxis ended up having a race with each other as we went down the deserted roads!

Thursday

It turned out that Stevie and Smoke were driven to a forest on the outskirts of Budapest, told to take their shoes off and leave them in the car, then told to get out and run. While they were running the cops tried to run them over. The next day they had bleeding feet from all the thorns and the long walk to find a taxi, that got them back to their hotel.

They also had to climb over a barbed wire fence at one point and their clothes were torn.

I went for breakfast and the lads in the Hotel were surprised to see me, as Silk had told them I had been arrested. I told them the whole story of what had happened.

Rob went to change some more money up and again managed to get extra again! We ordered taxis, cleared our rooms and checked out.

We went back into Budapest, and went into a bar and drank all that afternoon. One of the Chelsea fans, who was also in the bar, had bought a suitcase with him. Legg took the piss out of him, and asked him if he was dressing for dinner. From that day he was known as Freddie the Case.

The doors to the bar were slid open to give an open aspect to the pavement. Dave Sexton, the Manchester United manager at the time, walked by and I shouted at him, above the music from the jukebox, 'Birtles is a wanker'. Birtles was a player he had spent a load of money on, but he had hardly scored for United, though he had scored loads of goals for his previous club, Nottingham Forest.

A few minutes later Sexton came back with a couple of his mates. He was red in the face, and obviously angry, he stood at the open doors and asked the whole bar 'who said Birtles is a wanker'. Silk said 'hang on a minute' and turned, he shouted to the rest of the bar 'who said Birtles is a wanker'. After he did this, he was laughing into his beer and looking at me as he new I was the one who had said it.

Rob, who was oblivious to what had been happening, spotted Sexton at this moment and stepped forward. Having missed what had happened earlier he put out his hand, his arm had red devil tattoo on it, and said 'hello Dave, I go to every match'. Sexton just gave him a hard stare and stormed off. Rob couldn't understand what was up with him.

Silk was still laughing at me, but he didn't tell everyone what I had done.

The Saint's lads came into the bar and we pissed it up for the rest of the afternoon. We were chatting up the local girls, most of who were friendly and fit and seemed to be making this bar the place to be for an afternoon drink.

We popped to the supermarket up the road, and bought a load of beer, then we went to catch the 4:10 train to Vienna. Meanwhile the police were at the airport to re-arrest us all because of the events of the night before. There was only one of the named fans at the airport so he was held. Eventually he was released two days later with a two thousand pound suspended sentence hanging over him, as did the rest of us, as we were tried in our absence.

I sat with the Belper lads for a bit, but they were a bit miserable and were just sleeping or reading, so I went down the train and sat with the Saint's boys. Every bit of the overhead luggage compartment had a bottle of beer stored in it.

A Stockport lad who was also a big Rangers fan, started teaching us some loyalist songs, and as we learnt the words as we got completely wrecked. We changed trains at Vienna and were soon moving across Germany. As the train crossed some major roads the lads were throwing out the empty bottles at the Germans driving along the road. Due to the amount of ale I had now consumed, I could feel that I was going to be sick; I headed for the toilet at the end of the coach.

I didn't make it and was sick all over the corridor. Two plain clothed German coppers appeared from nowhere and arrested me. They said I must pay a fine in Deutschmarks or else they would put me off the train at the next station.

I didn't have hardly any Deutschmarks but Jerry and some Chelsea boys threw a load of coins at the cops, there was enough change to pay my fine and I was released. This was near a place called Passau.

We carried on drinking but I had sick all over my jeans and must have stunk. Luckily I had another pair of jeans in my bag, so I went back to the toilet and changed. The guards came down and Gary, an arsenal fan, that would later do time abroad for drug smuggling, plus time in England for armed robbery, came into our compartment and hid under the seat.

The inspector, who we were calling Hector, came into our compartment and found him. He had already found Gary's mate, who had been hiding in the toilet, also with no ticket. They both got kicked off the train at Brussels, not a bad jib from Budapest to Brussels.

Gary was at this time sporting a broken nose from the earlier fights. We arrived at Oostende at about 9 a.m. and the ferry was already in port. We got on the ferry and we all hit the bar.

As we were basically just topping up on the day before's drinking, it wasn't long until there was a raucous atmosphere in the bar. As we sailed across the Channel, the boys were singing 'Rule Britannia', 'tits out for the lads' to the female passengers, and some lads ended up having a biggest dick competition in the bar.

We ended up doing the conga around the ferry, while singing 'if you all went to Hungary clap your hands'. Mick from Southampton knocked back a bottle of Blue Nun wine in one go.

Of course all of this meant the British cops were waiting for us as we disembarked. Again the police took our names, before we were allowed onto the train to London. As we pulled into London the actress, Paula Yates was on the platform. Some of the lads made crewed comments to her. We were all singing 'we all ran the commies' as we walked down the platform.

I said my goodbyes to the Saints boys then went to the Shires pub at St Pancras with the Sheffield and Derby boys. The train from London was a continuation of drinking all the way home. At Matlock I got off the train and Lynn was waiting for me on the platform.

Luxembourg

1983

We set out on a Tuesday night; I was travelling with Joe Smith. On the way to London we had time to sort out our European Train Tickets. We had got dodgy European blank tickets a friend had stolen from a travel firm. By forging them using a pin to punch the required holes, and a replay pen, they looked pretty realistic.

We had some beer on the train, then crossed London to Victoria Station. At the station, we met up with Mick and some of the other Saints fans.

We got the train to the port, it was packed with England fans, there also loads of Chelsea boys on board.

The Chelsea boys were all singing 'ten men went to mo.'

We got on the ferry, and got talking to some Arsenal lads. There was quite a lot of Derby fans on the ferry too. One of the Derby lot, was a lad called Glen, and he sometimes drank in my pub in Matlock.

Wednesday

The coppers had decided to shut the bar on the ferry, so we got a bit of shut-eye. At Oostende we transferred to the Brussels train. At Brussels station there were loads more England fans waiting for the Luxembourg train. They must have come over the day before, and had a night on the raz around Brussels. They included a deformed Spurs fan who seemed to be quite famous. We decided to jump on the first train to Luxembourg, along with a lot of other England fans.

It started to snow as the train moved across the Belgium countryside. The ticket inspector was approaching and this was to be the test of our dodgy tickets.

Four England fans in front of us panicked and decided leg it up the train, as they had no tickets at all. Then about six more behind us did the same thing. The confusion probably helped and we got away with our forged tickets.

The train pulled into Luxembourg and Big Paul and Duggie were at the station waiting for us. We got off and they took us to a bar where we met up with Sprake and some other Hull lads including Harry.

The Hull lads told us about a scam they were doing. It turned out they were all signing on in Hull, then working on a trawler, which went up the East coast to Scotland. This meant they were then signing on again, the following week in Scotland, then working the trawler back!

We went to their hotel and had some cans of beer, then went for a walk across the river bridge to the old part of town.

We took some photos of the lads all at the gorge bridge, and then tried to find a bar. A few of the bars apparently had got wrecked the night before. It turned out that Duggie and Harry were involved and had already been locked up for four hours.

We found a pub near the old square and went in. The bar staff seemed to like us, so we settled in for a decent session. Brian Clough, the Nottingham Forest manager, was seen in the next bar up the road.

John from Rotherham turned up. He was using this trip to shoplift as much casual sports gear as he could, but while he was in that mood, he managed to sneak upstairs at the bar and stole some money from a purse that had been left up there in the staff area, and a couple of bottles of spirits.

By mid-afternoon we were pretty pissed, our flags had been put up and we were having a singsong. The songs at the time were mostly 'steam in regardless' and 'God Save the Queen'.

Some West Ham boys came into the bar and they were looking for trouble. There was a bit of a stand off between them and us, then a punch was thrown and before we knew it the police had arrived and the bar was shut and we were out on the street. The West Ham boys then decided to put the bars windows in. We went down the street and found another bar. We managed to have a load more beer by keeping a low profile, we told the boys not to sing or to bring attention to the bar, so no flags were put up.

At about 6 p.m we left the bar and headed towards the ground. There was a fight going on in the park between various England fans, the police and the army.

A lad called Benny had run through a local nunnery, singing 'No Pope of Rome' and apparently the rosary beads that the nuns had hit him with, were now spread all over the place.

There was a bloke standing next to his Mercedes, he was just a Luxembourg resident, but he was holding a hammer and trying to protect his car, as it was parked on the street, outside of his house.

We brought some more beer at a shop near the ground. Paul tried to phone home to see if we were knocked out the finals yet, as another game was being played earlier that afternoon, the result meant we had a chance, or we were out of the European Championship finals in France.

The pubs near the ground were too full to get in.

We were searched on entry to the stadium and as we got in the ground, West Ham fans were attacking any northern team's fans. We moved to a safer area away from the Hammers fans.

As the match progressed some lads started tearing the stadium toilets to pieces. One lad then skimmed a toilet seat, like a giant frisbee, at the police who were standing on the perimeter of the pitch. It hit a cop clean on the chin and he went down nursing a big gash in his face.

Word got around that we had been knocked out as Denmark had won their game. At this point the whole world went crazy, lads started ripping out the seats to throw at the police, lads climbed the fences to get on the pitch and the fences started to give way.

The cops around the pitch were being bombarded with coins, seats and smoke bombs. A big fight mushroomed out in the middle of the terrace at the other end, as some English boys turned on other English boys.

After the match we were locked in, but the lads at the front smashed down the gates. The English from the other end of the ground were already out, and from our vantage point we could see that they were systematically turning cars over in the street.

We got out and ran up the street; a policeman on a motorbike was kicked off his bike. Two Scouse lads then picked him up. Put him in a headlock and then ran him towards a shop window. They used him as a battering ram and charged him, helmet first, through a fur coat shop window.

After the window was smashed, and with the copper lying dazed in the broken glass, they stepped inside and helped themselves.

An ambulance soon reached the cop, he was still lying on the pavement by the broken glass; he was put into the back of the ambulance on a stretcher, and as the ambulance went to pull away, a load of the England lads started rocking it from side to side. The ambulance, within a couple of minutes, was on its side. This was not one of the coppers better days!

A woman and her kid were caught up in a traffic jam further up the road. She was pleading for mercy, but the lads just turned the car onto its roof and the woman and her kids were all hanging upside down, held by their seatbelts.

A horrible Scaly then came up; he had a cigarette lighter and he tried to set fire to the fuel line. We told him to 'fuck off', and he looked at us, as if we were in the wrong.

The bloke who was earlier standing with a hammer protecting his Mercedes, before the match, was now on his knees, blood pouring from his nose, and the hammer had been used to remodel the car and smash its windows. It was now lying forlornly on the back seat.

A load of English fans then started chasing a group of police down the street. They managed to catch a slow copper, roughed him up a bit and then for a bit of a laugh, the lads turned him upside down and dangled him over the ravine bridge. He was hanging by his ankles. He was then hauled back up, but was obviously shitting himself; it must have been a two hundred foot drop they were hanging him over.

All the bars were by this time shut, just about every shop window had been put through and the lads were now busy looting the place. Joe and I went for a meal to get out of the way as much as to stave off the hunger. Word got out that the French army has been drafted in, and a train, due to leave at midnight, had been commandeered to get us out of town.

We went for this midnight train; no actual tickets seemed to be required which helped us with our forged ones. At the station we all had to enter in single file and go into the ticket area where the police searched everyone.

If you had any stolen goods, jumpers still with labels on and the like, on you, or in your bag, you were arrested and taken away in police vans that were parked outside. Loads of lads, particularly Scousers and Manchester lads were arrested. A lad from Derby called Steve Power came along the road outside, pissed up and very wobbly, he tripped up on the pavement just outside the station, plus, when questioned by the Gendarmes he had lost his passport. He was arrested as well.

Big Paul asked a policeman if he was scared, he replied 'yes, I was very scared'

We got back to Oostende and it was a really rough crossing back to

England. I tried to sleep by lying on the floor of the bar as all the seats had been taken. At Dover we were met by the usual gaggle of British Coppers and also the BBC and ITN news cameras.

We then got the first train back to London, the tube across London, and then the first train to Matlock. We arrived home at about five in the afternoon.

France
1984

I set out on the Sunday afternoon before the game that was scheduled for the following Wednesday. I met up with Bill, my cousin, at St Pancras and had a drink in a bar on the Euston Road. Then we crossed London to Victoria Station and met up with the lads. There were a few other fans that I had seen before in the bar at Victoria.

I said 'goodbye' to Bill, as he wasn't going to France, and we set off on the train for Folkestone. We ended up walking to the ferry port, as the train didn't go that far along the sea front.

We boarded the ferry, and we played cards as we sailed across. We had a few more beers then arrived at Calais.

Monday

There was no connecting train and it was freezing cold. We ended up wandering around Calais but the place was dead, and it was about four in the morning. We broke into a parked car but it was no warmer in there, so John Paul pissed on the seats to piss the owner of in the morning. We ended up in a park trying to sleep on a bench, but it was just too cold so we kept on walking.

Big Paul wrote 'England' all over a white Volkswagen Golf in indelible pen then graffitied a statue. A police car drove down the street so we ran off down an alley. Someone decided to light a fire using a few cardboard boxes that we found stacked by a shop. Unfortunately they had flammable stuff in them and the flames shot out up the building wall. The next thing we knew was that the alarm of the building had gone off and the sprinklers were spraying the inside of the shop next door. We decided to scarper back to the station. Luckily there was a slow train to Paris waiting at the station so we jumped on it, and arrived at Paris at about eight o'clock.

We came out of the Gare De Nord station and booked into the Hotel Nord just down the road. It was a bit of a dump but it was all right as a base. We dumped our bags and went for a look around.

There were a few Leicester lads with another lad called Paul Parrot in a café up the road. They had been over in Paris for the Tony Sibson boxing match the previous Saturday. They told us that there was a bit of trouble at the fight and in the end a load of West Ham fans attacked the CRS (Commando Riot Squad) outside the stadium. We had a few beers with them then headed back to the hotel, it turned out that Parrot was staying there as well. We got some beer and went to one of the rooms we had booked, and carried on drinking while Parrot and his mates went out shoplifting.

There was a cockney lad who was also drinking with us in our room, he had a massive scar across his face and apparently it had been done with a credit card in prison. It happened, after he had blinded someone, in an earlier fight.

Some workmen were decorating down the corridor, so he just went and stole their radio. He was on the whisky and was a bit of a handful. Parrot and his mates came back. They had robbed some designer clothes and taken a screwdriver to the left luggage lockers at Gare De Nord, their pockets were now full of five-franc coins.

We decided to go out for a beer, but in the first bar we were already pissed. For some reason it got surrounded by Algerian types. They seemed to want to fight us and we were lucky to get out without getting done.

Big Paul was not feeling well, he decided to go back to the hotel but as he went he couldn't help but slap an Algerian in the street. John Paul and I decided to catch the metro to the red light area, which was called Pigalle. For some reason we had all got split up, and it was just the two of us on the piss.

We ended up having a load of beer in various pubs and started getting to talk to various prostitutes in the cheaper bars, a lot of them turned out to be transvestites. In one bar, John was really pissed; he dropped his glass of beer as he had fallen asleep while standing up.

We were asked to leave and as we went out of the bar, a Frenchman had broken down in his Mini. John and I gave him a push start and he offered to give us a lift to another, better area, that he reckoned had better bars. We got in his car and he dropped us off in a completely different area but we were hammered. We only had one more beer then called it a night. Unfortunately the metro wasn't nearby, and we couldn't see a station, so we had to get a taxi.

The taxi driver was asking us if we wanted to screw his sister. We said 'no' but it seamed like he was taking a long way back to the hotel.

On arrival he wanted one hundred francs. We offered him ten francs, but he wouldn't take it, so we threw some change at him and got out.

John started to kick his door in, and the taxi driver ran around and tear-gassed us. Our eyes were really stinging as we ran off.

John couldn't see where he was going, so I grabbed him and we worked our way back to the hotel. We tried to wash our faces when we got back, but it made our eyes sting even more. John's face was starting to blister. We told Big Paul what had happened to us as he was sharing our room as well, and then I collapsed into a drunken sleep.

Tuesday

We woke up and went to the local supermarket and stole some food for breakfast and a big glass jar full of orange-juice. Then we went back to the room and I drunk half the orange as I had a throat as dry as the Sahara desert. I decided to save the rest for the next morning, as no doubt I would feel the same. After a while we went out and went to the same supermarket, this time we stole a load of Champagne.

After drinking the Champagne in a park, we decided to go to the French F.A. to try and get some tickets for the match. This involved walking up the 'Champs Elise' and across the road at the 'Arc De Triumph'.

Every time we used the metro we were just jumping over the barriers. Sprake kept saying things like 'morning ethnic' to any Algerian type. We managed to get some tickets from the French F.A then went out on the piss. In one bar we bumped into Chris from Manchester who I had met in Hungary.

We kept moving from bar to bar and when we came across it we tried the London pub, which was across the road from the Moulin Rouge. It was too expensive, so after one beer, we tried some cheaper bars a few blocks back. One of these had a load of wine stacked up in creates next to the door, so we helped ourselves and necked a bottle each as we walked to the next bar, Chris was promptly sick.

We saw a wig shop down the road and we called in. Big Paul bought himself an Afro wig and a false moustache. Next-door was a music shop, we went in and some of the boys started playing various musical instruments. The owner of the shop, who was dressed as a punk rocker, was getting all upset and asked us to leave.

After a while we did, and as we left the punk locked up the shop and walked off up the street. Big Paul picked up an egg from a grocers display, which was on the pavement outside a shop, and launched it at the punk.

From about forty yards away, it landed smack in his Mohican haircut, we all cheered. It was then decided to bunk the metro back up to Pigalle. We were starting to know our way around by now, and it was only a few stops on the green line.

We went into a few sex shops and stole some hard-core porn books. As we came out of one shop, Big Paul was nearly run over by a coach that was coming down the road. He went over to the driver's door and thumped the coach; the driver was just staring at him. As this was happening a taxi came by and just clipped him across his arse with its wing mirror.

The taxi carried on without stopping, straight across the junction. Big Paul, who had been rubbing his backside, threw his bottle of beer, in a beautiful arc, across the junction. It landed straight through the taxi's back window.

Paul walked across, to the now stationary taxi, and the driver got out asking 'why' in a typically French way, with his shoulders scrunched up and hands waving in the air. Big Paul ignored him and then proceeded to kick both the taxi's headlamps in. The taxi driver just looked on in amazement.

We drank our way back to the Gare De Nord where we were meeting some more of the Hull boys. We arrived just as their train pulled in. About fifty English fans piled off the train and started hitting and kicking any Frenchman or black bloke they could find.

As we watched what was happening, some women actually retaliated and whacked one England lad with their umbrellas. On the whole most people appeared to be running for their lives in various directions.

As the boys stormed past the ticket inspection point I saw that Timber was one of the newcomers. He said to me, that he didn't want to get nicked, but was still lamping any French git he could catch. We all joined in and attacked as many French as we could who happened to be on the station forecourt; this was becoming a bit of a riot.

As we spilled out of the station, across the road there was a restaurant, which had floor to ceiling massive plate glass front windows. At one of the tables by a window, were sitting two black blokes and their black wives.

Big Paul ran across the road from the station and just kicked the window in. The blacks jumped out of the away but were still covered in a shower of glass. All of a sudden we were surrounded by police cars. The police managed to arrest about fourteen of us in all.

We were handcuffed and marched back to the station and taken up some stairs to a police station within the station building.

We were all individually questioned, then put back into some holding cells. Meanwhile somehow, big Paul had got rid of his Afro wig and false moustache. He must have done this after kicking in the window, but before the police arrested us.

After a few hours all seemed calm and it appeared as though we were being released, but as we got outside, we were bundled into the French equivalent of black Marias and were soon travelling at speed to another police station.

It was about six to a van and we were all laughing, and pissing about, which was winding the coppers up no end. One of the lads had noticed that another group of England fans were being held in a 'corralled area' outside the station and in their numbers were Duggie from Hull and John Paul.

At the next Police Station, the police made us remove our shoelaces and belts and then we were put into proper cells.

These had thick glass walls, and our cell already had a number of black drug pusher types in it. On our entry they were beaten up by us, the police responded by filling the cell with tear gas. They did this by using some designated holes in the glass, where they could put the canister nozzle through and the gas just came into the cell.

I stood near the door and tried to get some fresh air as my eyes and lungs burned again, for the second time within twenty-four hours! Chris was already in the cell and he took a photo of what the coppers were doing. They took his camera off him, opened the back and destroyed his film.

We were not allowed to go to the toilet and I was bursting for a piss. Each of us were being taken out one at a time, to be interviewed as the coppers tried to unravel what had happened. The police took our names and passport numbers, from those of us that had passports with us.

Each copper was asking about the whereabouts of 'le grando avec le moustache'. You had to laugh as big Paul was six foot ten tall and weighed about twenty stones and was sitting in the cell, large as life, except for the wig and moustache.

Next we were taken back out of the cell, this time for an ID parade. Various old women, women with umbrellas, injured Frenchmen, injured black men and black men who had been covered in glass were bought down the line of England boys to look at us.

Duggie, who had now joined us at the police station, courtesy of a lift in another cop van, and Timber were picked out as they had skinheads, plus perhaps because they were guilty. The rest of us were put back into the cells. Some of the French who were there to pick out their attackers were quite severely injured; one in particular had his ear hanging to his head by a thin piece of skin.

We sat in the cell; occasionally a copper would ask us 'where is the big moustachioed one'.

Then to brighten the evening up, the cops dragged in a Scottish lad.

It turned out he has been mugged in a bar, but then mistakenly tear-gassed by the bar staff, before being arrested by the local cops who thought he was an English troublemaker.

He was crying his eyes out as he was shoved in our cell and started shouting 'I'm not an English hooligan, I'm Scottish'. We all cheered when he said this and one of the lads gave him a good thumping to boot. As he was receiving this further punishment he was screaming out, through his tears, that he 'didney' like football.

We all started laughing at him, and fair play to him, he started singing 'flower of Scotland at us'. At this point we all laid into him, and he was just a mess on the floor. The police came to his rescue, and we didn't see him again.

All of a sudden a French detective came in, and in very good English, said 'You are going to be released'. He then said if we got caught again we would get our 'fucking heads kicked in'!

I thought this was a strange thing to say, as it must have been very late. But, as we were putting our shoelaces back in, I asked Alf what time it was and he told me it was only nine-thirty.

We headed back to Pigalle laughing about what has happened. Meanwhile Duggie, Smoke and Harry had still been held at the police station. The police ended up taking all their money from them and then also from their hotel rooms, but at least eventually released them, a day later.

It turned out that we were held just outside Charmattin station. About eight of us went into a strip club, and we had a good laugh, and ended up sitting at the front, plus we didn't get too ripped off by the bar prices.

Once outside the club, the area we were in was the usual mix of prosses, some expensive, some cheap, mostly black and some very dodgy regarding whether they were male or female. We were not interested and Stevie, Alf and me had a few more beers before getting back to the hotel at about 2 a.m.

I knocked on the bedroom door and Big Paul let me in, John Paul was fast asleep pissed up, but the room was wrecked. We were on the fifth floor but my jar of orange had been thrown out of the window at some passing Algerians, followed by various light fittings, the table lamps and other bits of furniture. For some reason the wardrobe was on its side.

We couldn't draw the curtains as apparently the curtain rail and curtains had also been dispatched out of the window.

Wednesday

In the morning we saw the mess we had made of the room, so decided to check out and move to another hotel up the road. We tried a few budget type hotels but not one had any spare rooms.

In one as we were waiting while the receptionist checked for any vacancies, a lad we didn't know got his foot trapped in the old style scissor action lift door. He was suspended upside down by his trapped foot; you could hear the snap as the lift broke his leg, before anyone had managed to hit the alarm, to stop the lift.

He was wailing and screaming until his mates managed to free him. He was still in a lot of pain as he waited for an ambulance. It was quite a horrific scene as his mates helped him down, but there didn't appear to be much blood.

Sprake had earlier lent Parrot 50 francs and was unsure as to whether to ask for it back. I told him he had to, so he did. Parrott said to him 'sorry, I forgot all about it', he pulled out his screwdriver from his pocket, and went off to prise the coin return of a left luggage locker or two. He was back within ten minutes with Sprake's 50 francs.

We decided to leave our bags at the left luggage, hoping Parrot wouldn't knacker the locks, then went for a beer opposite the station. Big Paul was a bit quieter today. The other lads, who had been arrested the previous night, had now been released and met up with us.

We found a quiet bar, out of the way, and pissed it up all day. The barmaid was pretty fit and on another day she would probably have been available, but today was match day, so although she kept talking to me, I didn't leave with her when her shift finished.

We stayed in the same bar all day, until near kick-off, when it was decided we should move nearer to the Parc De Princess football ground.

As we got nearer to the stadium, we couldn't get in the bars as they were packed. We bought some more beers from a shop and drank them on the street. Some of the lads we ended up talking to, as we drank, were telling us all about the trouble on the various ferries on their way out.

The police for no apparent reason then baton charged us. It was difficult to tell what the reasoning was, but it dispersed us all and we finished our cans down a side street and then went to the stadium.

As we got into the ground the atmosphere was one of violence. We went to our seats, when we found them we looked behind us, just as Ken Bailey, the England mascot at the time, was battered to the ground. He was about eighty years old, but as most of the lads thought he was a sex case, not much was done to help him.

As he got up he said 'ey up mate' to me and I replied 'hello Ken' much to Sprake's amusement.

In the stands above and below, fights were erupting all over the place. One English lad did particularly well. He had his back against the fence, and he had nowhere to go, he stood his ground and knocked down about four French youths who were attacking him. At one point he seemed to be loosing, but he got a second wind, and won before other England fans came to his rescue.

The group of Leicester lads we met earlier in the week were taking a right battering from the French, and the police, in another section.

Meanwhile the Blackburn boys with the Blackburn NF flag, they had hung from the fence below us, appeared to be getting swamped by an attack launched from down the side of them.

We lost the game, and as we came out the ground the England

boys, (most of whom had travelled on a special Persil promotion that was running at the time. It was for the ferries and train, two could travel for the price of one to Paris), went on the rampage.

Cars were being turned over up the main street. At one point a Porsche 911 slowly spun on its roof. A large van was on its side, while a number of lads were bouncing a truck to about 45 degrees trying to turn it over. Each time it came back to rest on its tyres it was amazing nobody got squashed.

All the shop windows were going through and, unlike Luxembourg, this was a riot with an edge to it as we were involved against not only the French and the blacks, but also the police and the dreaded Paris Commando Riot Squad or CRS as they were known.

England basically had the French on their toes, and as we chased them down the road, some of them were taking proper beatings. At the metro station we decided to get back towards Gare De Nord, but as we got on the platform there was a proper four-way fight going on. This was highly enjoyable and the adrenalin, plus the shitting yourself, in case you got nicked again, made the fighting keenly contested.

We managed to give some Moroccan types a good beating, then a train pulled in so we jumped on, making sure no one was left on the platform, with our antagonists. Next the CRS, with batons drawn charged down the stairs. They were coming at us so we went back onto the platform.

'Stand your ground' was the shout you could here in cases like this, usually from someone behind you, but we didn't stand a chance. Yet again I introduced my body to the pain off a baton beating.

We retreated onto the train, the doors closed but the train didn't move. In our carriage we seemed to have the main England crew from the previous battles. The police obviously had the same opinion. They opened the small windows at the top of each window, the ones used for ventilation when the train was moving. The police then liberally sprayed us with tear gas from through the small windows.

The train pulled out of the station, we tried to smash the windows but for about three minutes, until we reached the next station, all we could do was fight for our breath. The best thing to do was get next to a gap in the windows or doors.

At the next station we all piled out. Ordinary French commuters had also been gassed and everyone was wheezing, and there lots of people with stinging eyes. Rob and the Belper lot were in another carriage and hadn't been touched.

We got back on board, but in another carriage and arrived at Gare De Nord. We collected our bags from the left luggage lockers and went to get some beers until the bars shut. Big Paul came into the bar and told us that he had managed to get a room in a hotel around the corner; he said we could sleep on his floor so when the bar shut we went back to his hotel.

After about an hour the hotel was raided. The manager must have been concerned at having about ten blokes in one room, and at about four in the morning we were all kicked out, including Big Paul. We stood outside the Gare De Nord station in the freezing cold waiting for it to open at six.

A group of French lads who fancied their chances came up, and started having a go at us. We were about twenty strong. There was about twenty police who were sat inside vans, watching us from the road that ran alongside the station. One of our lads hit one of the French gang and the police did nothing. They obviously didn't like this gang of French boys anymore than they liked us. Soon one of the Oldham boys was attacking the French from behind. They took a bit of a beating before they scarpered.

The station eventually opened its doors; our train was already at its platform, so me and Sprake went and sat in a warm carriage compartment. We managed to sleep all the way to the ferry terminal at Calais.

We got a beer at Calais, at one of the bars outside the station. In a compound by the port we saw all the brand new, wrecked cars that had been smashed by England fans in the previous days.

The ferry sailed on time and we were aboard. There were loads of British coppers on it, the bars were shut.

Once we had docked, we went through customs, we were picked out and searched and the customs officers found the hard-core porn books we had stolen. 'Is this for your own personal pleasure?' one asked me in front of everyone. 'Yes' I replied, trying to make out it didn't bother me, so they let me keep them. I later sold the more extreme magazines for a tidy profit.

We grabbed some fish and chips from outside Dover station, then caught the train to London and then the train home.

England v Wales
Wrexham 1984

I skived off from work and went to the Bridge Inn. I had a few beers then drove to Crewe. At Crewe I bought some cans and then jumped on the Chester train. There were lots of Manchester United fans on the train, and one Welsh fan who seemed to be keeping quiet.

At Chester I had a walk round, but ended up just buying four more cans of lager and then got the next train to Wrexham. At Wrexham in the first pub I went into, I didn't know anyone, I tried the next one down the road and got talking to some Wolves fans. As we were talking, Fat Freddy walked in to the pub with some Arsenal boys.

We were talking about the World Cup and a group of Welsh lads were listening in. One of the Arsenal boys said 'fuck off taffy' to them.

There was a bit of a stand off between the Arsenal boys and the Welsh fans. In the end the Taffies did 'fuck off'.

We paid on the gate to get in the ground, and stood near the half way line on the terrace. Most of the English fans were behind one goal. Loads of flags were on display on the perimeter fence, Blackburn and Hull City to name a few. I then bumped into Big Paul and John Paul and we tried to get in the main England end, but the coppers wouldn't let us transfer across.

We were singing 'on the pitch' as the match was going on. A group of Derby fans reckoned that I wouldn't get on because of the tall fence between the pitch and the terrace. At full time we were straight over it and Big Paul, who got over at the same time as me, ran across the pitch and punched the Welsh full back.

This was all on the television highlights later, when I watched the video recording I had made, I could see myself running across the turf towards the Welsh end.

The police then charged at us, as we had got quite close to the fence between us, and the Welsh, in their kop.

The police charge seemed to do the trick, and it was a quick turn around for us and then back over the fence on to the original terrace. This was far easier to do from that side, as the pitch was about three feet above the bottom of the terrace. We then got out of the ground as fast as we could, and before Big Paul could get arrested.

The Police and bar owners wouldn't let us in to any of the pubs after the match. A local lad knew a back way in to one of the pubs and took us in so long as we promised not to cause any bother.

There was a bit of singing, but no trouble, and we drank up and went for the last train to Crewe. The Arsenal lads pulled the communication cord, which in turn stopped the train and they all jumped off the train as it approached Crewe. I never did find out why.

I got to my car and wound down all the windows and chewed on some mints. This I thought would give me a better chance of passing the breathalyser test, if I was over the limit, which I wasn't too sure about.

There were police parked on every traffic island to start with, but they were just making sure the traffic was moving, as a lot of England fans were driving home that way. I arrived home at 3:30 in the morning.

Scotland v England

1984

I got on the train to Crewe and then met up with a few lads and went for a drink. We caught the overnight train to Glasgow. I managed to climb up and into the overhead luggage rack, as the train was full, and slept there after I had had a few more beers. The train had loads of Everton's mob on it, you had to be a bit careful, or else they would steal all your money out of your pocket while you slept.

The train arrived at Central Station, Glasgow at about 5 in the morning. We hung around for a while at the station, as another train was due in. This one had originated at Wolverhampton. Legg and Villa youth were on this, and they apparently knew of a bar that opened at 6 a.m, I went along with them.

There was about sixty of us in total, about half tried various cafes for breakfast while the rest of us went to the pub. Once we got in the bar, the owner had sorted a porn show on a side stage. I got myself a beer, Barry from Stockport came in. I ended up having a couple of beers with him.

I felt a bit faint at about 9 a.m. so I went outside and nearly collapsed. I decided to stop drinking for an hour or two and went for some food. I met up with some more lads I knew, as they walked down the street, past the café I was eating in. Included in the group was 'The Tinman' and Benny, two famous England fans.

We went across the road to a bar, as kick off time approached Benny and The Tinman stated that they didn't want to go to the match, just stay in the bar drinking. In the end, they decided to go, a taxi was summoned and we were all on our way to Hampden Park, they reluctantly got in.

I had a Bulldog Bobby flag with me that I had made. As we got out of the taxi loads of Scots that were getting off various buses and coaches and were staring at my banner. Benny and The Tinman were not fazed at all and were up for anything that they decided to do to us.

We got to the ground and I lost the lads. I went onto the terrace and the England fans had got our own little section. Barry from Stockport was asleep on a bench. When England scored, I saw Big Paul and

Sprake fighting in the main stand before being ejected by the police and stewards.

It started to pour with rain, we were getting soaked on the open terrace, some of the lads near me, used my Bulldog Barry banner as a cover. Unfortunately the colours started to run, people sheltering under it ended up with blue and red hair.

We left the ground at the end of the game and our little mob of about twenty, were surrounded, but unknown to me, our mob included some hardened hooligans and they just stood their ground. The Scots didn't know what to do, as every time some of them attacked us, they ended up getting beaten.

After getting nothing more than a beating for their troubles, they started throwing half-bricks and concrete at us. One half brick hit 'Oo Oo Frog' on his head; I said to him 'sorry mate, I could see it coming, but was too slow to warn you'. He just picked up the half-brick and threw it back at the Scots, shrugged his shoulders, and said 'don't worry about it mate, that's football'.

We just walked through the Scottish mob, and then walked back to the station, while kicking the shit out of any of the Scots who dared to have a go. This was a proper firm. A train to Euston Station, London, was at the platform and as we boarded the train, the Scots attacked again.

The train journey home was uneventful, a few cans of beer. I ended up having to change at Manchester and Sheffield before arriving home at one in the morning.

Brazil v England

I went for a beer at the Half Moon pub with my cousin, then went home to get my bag just as my dad arrived home at dinnertime. He saw me with my bag as I was leaving the house; he hated me going to football.

He said to me 'you're not going to football again are you?'

I replied 'yes, just for a few days'.

He said 'where to this time?'

I said 'Rio de Janeiro'.

His face was madder than hell, and I guessed my board would be going up when I got home. I had to smile to myself, as I walked to the bus stop, to catch a bus to the railway station.

Bill, my cousin, was waiting at the bus stop and after we got to the station we caught the London train. We had a few cans of lager on the way down. I was stopping with my cousin for the night at his place in Tooting.

We ended up going to a party, it was a good do, one of Bill's workmates was throwing it. I was there until the early hours, and then went back to Bill's house for some sleep.

The next day I was up quite early and on the first train I could catch that was going to Gatwick. I arrived in plenty of time to catch the British Caledonian flight I had booked to Rio.

On the flight I got talking to some of the aircrew. As the flight wasn't full they kept supplying beers to me whenever I wanted one. One of the stewards was a football fan, and as he had been to Rio often, he gave me some tips about getting around.

After a short stop in Recife, we landed at the airport just on the outskirts of Rio and I disembarked the plane, and went through customs. The entry stamp into Brazil was very plain; I was hoping it would be a big colourful one, to make my passport more impressive.

Sunday

Outside the terminal I jumped onto a bus that's destination board said it was going towards the Copacabana. This was what I had been told to do by the cabin crew, and then to get off when I saw the beach. The bus passed through some slums on the way to the beach, but I had no bother from anyone and eventually arrived at the Copacabana.

I got off the bus and, after a short walk, I found my hotel and checked in, it was all right but a bit tucked away down a side street.

I went and changed up some money in the reception area, there was a Fulham fan standing in the foyer, he was also staying at the hotel. He told me that he had just phoned home, he reckoned it had cost him Thirty pounds to do so!

I then got the bus from outside the hotel to the Impanema Beach. Once I was at Impanena I got off outside the Intercontinental Hotel. Some people on the bus had told me that it wasn't safe for a single tourist to travel on public transport, but I felt safe enough.

The hotel was where the England team were staying. I was hoping to pick up a match ticket for that afternoon's game.

The Football Association had already refused me a ticket, when I wrote to them. They stated to me in a return letter, that they had not requested any tickets for England fans. I had travelled down in the hope that some might be available.

A West Ham couple were in the bar, and a few England players were hanging around, these included Ray Wilkins and Kenny Sansom. They were good enough to have a photo taken with me, along with another player, called Alan Kennedy.

While I was having my photo taken, Ted Croker, the FA 'Secretary' walked across the foyer holding a squash racquet, obviously on his way back from a game.

'What are you doing here' he bellowed at me.

'Well I've just got off the overnight flight and thought there might be some tickets down here' I replied.

'We don't want your sort with us' he said and stormed off.

Trevor Brooking, the ex-international player, who was in Brazil on a corporate event, came over and asked 'what was his problem'.

I replied 'I don't think he likes me'.

Trevor said to me 'come on, I will buy you a beer' which he did in the bar of the hotel.

Bobby Robson, the England team manager then came into the bar and I had a photo taken of myself with him. A hotel worker walked past, he had a fist full of complimentary tickets and I eventually manage to buy one from him.

I decided to head back to my hotel, have a wash, then head for the 'Sugar Loaf Mountain' which was a short taxi ride away. Once I had arrived there, I had a beer at the bar at the base, but it was deemed too windy for the cable car to run up to the summit, so I got another taxi back to the Copacabana beach.

The hotel I was staying at was running a bus to the stadium so, an hour or so after sitting on the beach; I got onto it and arrived half an hour later at the Maracanna Stadium. I popped into a local bar, had a quick beer but there was no one I knew in there and no England fans about. I then made my way into the ground.

The stadium was about half full, I could see a small group of England fans on the other side of the stadium. It was possible to walk right round the stadium, using the concourse. This meant I was able to walk round to them. When I got to where their seats were, I noticed some of the usual faces. Amongst the boys were Rich, The Tinman, Benny and a few other boys I recognised.

Later when England scored, the cheer sounded quite loud, which pissed the lads off. This was because there were only about twenty of us who had made the trip, the rest who were cheering were the British Embassy staff, who were sat in the posh seats, and some ex-pats.

Benny and The Tinman looked up to the stand above us, and both performed Nazi salutes, at the black Brazilians who were taunting us from their seats. They were then covered in piss from bags that the Brazilians had urinated into and thrown from the stand above. As they got hit they just wiped their faces and carried on.

Stuart Hill, a Manchester City fan, had managed to pull a nice looking local Brazilian girl the night before. He had bought her to the match with him.

When the game finished, we left the ground with no trouble as the police kept the Brazilians from us. We then flagged down some passing taxis; I went back to the Copacabana with the lads and shared the fare with the boys I rode with.

I didn't know all of them, but amongst the ones I shared a taxi with, was a couple of Sheffield lads that I had met before.

We went on the piss and later Benny, The Tinman, Frank and myself ended up in an English themed pub. Even though it was winter the lads were complaining because it was too hot.

Benny and the boys were proud to be white, various pub umbrellas and other shade was used to keep the sun off them for the next few days.

In the bar, we were surrounded by prostitutes. Presumably this was not for our looks, but because there weren't many tourists about; it was out of season and I think we were viewed as a potential paycheck.

Some of them were really pretty, at one point I was talking to Frank, as one of the girls was sitting on one of my hands and squirming as I fingered her, and another fit blonde was playing about with my cock, by putting her hands down my shorts, this was in the middle of the bar.

I bought the girls a drink and they were happy with that.

Once the pub had closed, we moved on and ended up having something to eat in a restaurant down the road. We ended up all falling asleep at the table; the waiters woke us up and kicked us out. We headed back to our various hotels.

On the way back, I found a really nice Brazilian prostitute waiting on a street corner. I decided to take her back to the hotel with me. I had to pay extra to get her into my room, but she stayed for most of the night and was very noisy!

Monday

I met Benny and The Tinman at a beach bar. They had been drinking for a while at this particular bar. This meant I had to be careful and watch them, as they would do a runner at a moments notice, if I got caught they wouldn't pay towards the cost. It was just a way of life for them.

The previous night, after I had left them to walk back to my hotel, they had got arrested for not having a hotel. I didn't realise that they were just dossing on the beach. They had spent most of the night in the local police station, another normal occurrence for these two.

They spent most of the dinnertime drinking session talking about the goings on in the TV programme 'Coronation Street'.

Stuart Hill then appeared in the bar, he was with his Brazilian girl. Soon the rest of the lads turned up. It turned out most had been with one pross or another.

Benny ordered some food; he had drawn a picture of two eggs and a saucepan and gave it to the waiter. When the eggs arrived, he cut into them, but they smelt really bad so he went without.

It was decided we should have a North v South football match on the beach. It was hard work as it was very warm and the sand was soft. The Tinman was in inspired form in goal, making some great saves, and Hill scored a hat trick in a 6-1 win to the North.

After the match we went for a swim but the current was too strong. The Tinman ended up getting bowled over by a big wave; his socks got sucked off his feet by the power of the sea.

Benny and 'Sheffield Dave' were both struggling against the undercurrent. Eventually they managed to get back to the shore; they just lay on the beach panting while they got their breath back.

It was decided it would be a good idea to go and find Ronnie Biggs bar and beat him up. Off course, after a few more beers the idea was dropped.

A strange thing I noticed was that the TV presenter, on the news programme showing in the bar, was smoking a cigarette while on screen. This, even in the eighties, seemed to be a bit surreal.

It was the lads last night, before they were going on to the next leg of the South American tour, which was in Uruguay. They were hitting the beer hard. A younger Chelsea lad had downed a bottle of spirits in his room; he ended up collapsing in the bar, and was carried back to his hotel.

A group of prostitutes, that had been hanging about, the previous night, came into the bar. One was as black as night, she sat opposite Dave from Sheffield with her legs open, exposing her pubes.

Dave said to her 'thar's black and I'm white, now fuck off' this didn't appear to go down to well with them and a few of the girls moved off.

I was sat next to a really sexy girl; she was wearing a very short mini dress. Another girl from the previous night came up to us, she said that a lad called Andy, and pointed at him as she said it, was crap in bed.

All the prosses took the piss out of him, as did the England boys and there wasn't a lot that Andy could do or say.

Stuart Hill's girl turned up, as she was doing sex for free, she was not popular with the prosses. The other girls started shouting at her, she shouted back and then a fight started.

Stuart's girl, she was called Sheila or its Portuguese equivalent, and a hooker were rolling around on the pavement, we were saying 'put a bucket of mud over them to make it more interesting'. Stuart watched on laughing.

The police arrived and arrested the two girls. Stuart's girl told him to come to the police station with her. He said 'you can fuck off, I aint going anywhere near one of those places out here'.

He thought it was funny, and said that they were fighting over him!

Stuart had a nervous, turrets type twitch, and at the same time did a cough type thing as well. Because of this Benny called him 'Coughing Stu'.

Before he came out to Brazil, Benny had phoned Stuart at home, and asked if that was 'Coughing Stu', to which he had got a sharp reply of 'no it fucking isn't'.

After all the fighting, and the police, it had bought us to the attention of a local gang, one of whom wanted to arrange a fight. He was fairly small, and I was fairly pissed, so I stood up from my chair, and in one punch hit him square on the jaw, he staggered backwards.

I was wondering if this would cause a problem, but he just said something in Portuguese, and he and his mates went off. Later on in the night The Tinman was happy, because one of the lads produced a new pair of socks, with which he could replace the ones he had lost earlier in the sea.

Tuesday

The next day, I went down to the front. The rest of the lads had left; there was just Stuart, Dave and myself left in Rio. Stuart was staying for a week and Sheila had been released from the police station and was back with him.

Dave had a 'Varig Airlines' flight home later on that day and, as I was off work, having phoned in sick, I decide to go up to the airport to see if I could transfer my flight to his.

Amazingly, the girl at the Varig information desk said that it would be possible to transfer me, and produced a boarding card for me, after a bit of sorting out on the computer.

I got the bus back down to the beach and had some beers with the boys. I checked out of my hotel, but by now we had left it a bit late to get back to the airport so we got a taxi.

On the way, the taxi we had hailed, it was a VW Beetle with only one front seat, was held up by a large crash ahead of us. Then the taxi ran out of petrol, the driver had to coast down the slip road to the terminal.

We made the flight with a few minutes to spare. I sent some postcards to the lads back home, which pissed them off, as they hadn't made the trip. The post cards didn't say much and one just had the score written on it!

Once I got to my turn to check in, the check in girl, who was the same girl I had spoken to before, had now changed her mind. She said I couldn't board the plane.

I told her I had come all way back to the airport, and had cancelled my hotel. In the end, as the plane was only half full, she let me board.

I sat next to Dave and we had a few beers and a good steak meal, then I slept as we flew across the Atlantic. On reaching Europe our first stop was in Lisbon.

We stayed on the plane as other passengers got off, and then new ones got on. Then it was a short flight home, through customs and then we went into London for a few beers. After a couple of pints we caught our trains home.

Turkey v England
1984

Tuesday

I met up with John Paul at 'Moriaties Bar' in Baker Street. We had a drink then got the tube to Heathrow. The train ahead had been derailed and everything was really delayed.

We ended up having to run into the terminal from the tube station and up to the check-in desk. We just caught the plane with minutes to spare.

Some Pompey lads, plus Ken Bailey, the England mascot, were on the plane to Istanbul. We said 'hello' and noticed there were some other England boys on the flight that we didn't know.

We ended up drinking the plane dry. 'It's just like any normal flight' John said, as the stewardesses couldn't believe how much beer and wine we had consumed.

We arrived at Istanbul and John was pissed. He did the old Nazi salute in the arrival terminal but luckily nothing was said by the on looking police and customs officials. A busload of England fans, were waiting outside the terminal. They were from an earlier flight from Manchester; we jumped on their bus for a free lift into Istanbul.

When we got into the town centre we got off the bus when it stopped at a red traffic light. The rep on the bus looked at us 'gone out', she must have wondered why we weren't going to the designated hotel.

We stopped a taxi in the street and told the driver to go to the hotel the rest of Saint's lads were staying at. A car full of Turks, which had Turkish flags flying out of its windows, started following our taxi. Our taxi driver appeared to keep slowing down which allowed them to keep up. At a set off traffic lights, we opened the taxi's rear doors and we did a runner.

The carload of Turks saw this, but they were stuck in the traffic so couldn't get to us. Luckily as we ran round the corner, to get away from the taxi driver and following car, half way down the next block, was the Saint's lad's hotel.

We went for a drink in the hotel bar and then asked if they had any vacancies. Unfortunately the hotel was full. Across the road, we could see that there was a dossy hotel. It didn't have a bar and we had to go up some steps, which led to another flight of steps to the reception. The cost of staying a night at this hotel worked out at about forty-five pence a night.

We booked in at the reception, but when we saw our room, we found it had metal bunk beds and it stunk of urine. John had a piss in the sink that was in the corner of the room as there was no toilet. We dumped our bags, then went back to the bar in the lad's hotel across the road.

They arrived in the bar just after 9 p.m. They had been to watch the under twenty-one team play in a place called Erdu. We told the boys how shitty our hotel was and they said we could sleep on their floor. We went back to our hotel and got our bags. It was better and more comfortable to doss in with the boys in their room.

We had a few beers in the hotel, the under 21 game sounded good, as the lads had sat in the press seats and to add to the atmosphere the locals had made fires on the terraces. Apparently there had only been one shop in town, the boys had bought all off its beer, which apparently wasn't a vast amount.

That night, we just went out around the local area. We ended up in a belly-dancing bar. It was what the local Turks used, and the belly dancer was nothing to shout about.

A group of West Brom lads were already in there and they were causing trouble. The locals rounded on them and we all had to leave together.

At the next bar we went to, Big Paul went to the toilet and ended up being threatened by a Turk chef who was holding a meat cleaver. We left that bar after he told us, and found a bar we could have a few drinks in without bother, but when we started singing we attracted a gang of Turks who stood outside the bar.

As we left the bar we chased the Turks up the road, but loads more locals came out of various alleyways. We were well outnumbered, but luckily we had run in the right direction towards the hotel. After a quick sprint we were through the foyer doors.

In the confusion the staff didn't do a head count, so we went to our rooms. I slept on Big Paul's floor using a spare pillow and a spare quilt, which were handily left in the wardrobe.

Wednesday

I was woken at about six in the morning, by some 'Mullahs' calling the Turks to prayer. Duggie opened the window and shouted out 'shut the fuck up, were trying to sleep'. Eventually they stopped the racquet from the various mosques and we got a bit more sleep.

Me and John hadn't got tickets for the match, that was later that day, so after we had smuggled into get a breakfast we got into a taxi that was parked outside the hotel.

It took us through the old town, past fruit and fish markets to the Sheraton hotel. This was where the England team were staying; it took ages to get there in the taxi, but at least it didn't cost too much as things in Turkey appeared to be cheap.

At the Sheraton, there were loads of England fans milling about in the main concourse.

I got talking to Gary who I had met in Norway, and Ray, a lad who followed Leyton Orient.

Ted Croker, the F.A. Secretary walked into the foyer and started complaining about us being in there. The lads told him to 'fuck off'; they told him that without fans like us, he wouldn't have a job.

He then asked why some of the lads were wearing England scarfs, as it might cause trouble with the Turks. We told him it was the F.A. that sold them, and they were the ones making money out of it.

John had arranged to meet Mark Wright, the young England reserve centre half, at the players hotel, before we had travelled to Turkey. This was in the off chance, he could get some spare tickets from the F.A. John went to the receptionist and tried to phone Mark's room but got no reply.

Some of the lads had taken a walk to the nearby Inonu Stadium, where the match was to be played; it was just down the hill from the Sheraton. They told us that it was already full, four hours before kick off, and when they tried to buy tickets at a window, an angry Turkish mob nearly lynched them.

As there was not much going on in the hotel, we got another taxis to the town centre. Our taxi ended up going over the Bosphurus Bridge at one point so we had to turn around, wasting valuable drinking time. Meanwhile the taxi that Sprake was in ended up having a minor crash.

We found a bar, but it was no good, the beer was warm and the bar itself was filthy, so we worked our way back to the Sheraton by calling in at a couple of equally shitty bars. When we arrived back at the Sheraton, we could see the England team getting onto their coach, which was going to take them to the nearby stadium.

John saw Mark Wright, just as he was about to board the coach. He shouted to him 'is there any chance of a ticket?'

Mark replied 'yes, I've been looking for you, but I could only get twelve'!

He brought them over to us. They were really smart tickets, they were embossed with gold writing on them, plus they were for the best seats. This happened to be where the under twenty-one's should have been sitting. As we had a few spare tickets we just gave them out, for free, to the rest of the English lads who were standing nearby.

Some lads had managed to get tickets from various outlets in Istanbul. Then the old guard, like Legg, Steve, 'Oo Oo Frog' and Jerry turned up.

After a couple of beers in the upmarket surroundings of the Sheraton bar, we started to walk to the ground. As we approached the stadium the noise was unbelievable.

We got to the turnstile to get in, and a load of missiles were thrown at us from the back of the stand above.

The police came and protected us with their shields. They probably thought that we were important, as we were using that particular 'VIP' entrance, not just England fans. The under twenty-one's were now standing with us, and we were shepherded by the police, into the main stand.

We sat down in our seats while the under twenty-ones' had to stand. To make matters worse they had two black players in their number. These players' names were Fairclough and Wallace, and they had to take a lot of 'banter' from the England fans.

Behind one goal, in the massed ranks of Turkish supporters, a King William of Orange flag, was making its way down the terrace. It was proudly held aloft, by The Tinman and Benny. There was just the two of them in that stand along with ten thousand crazed Turks.

England won the actual match eight goals to nil. This included missing a number of 'sitters'. We got fed up of having to stand up at every goal we scored.

At half time Legg went for a piss and pushed his way past one of the under twenty-one's, who was standing in the stairway. 'Sorry mate, am I in the way' the player said to Legg.

'No' he replied, 'but I'm in your seat, you cunt'.

In the second half, the Turks lit fires all around the terraces by using scrunched up newspapers. Benny and The Tinman were escorted round the pitch, by armed police, to our section and were welcomed like long lost brothers, and, the King Billy flag was joyously displayed in front off the F.A. bigwigs.

At the end of the match, the police forced us to stay in the stadium. A lot of the Turks were staring at us, and we gave them a good rendition of 'No Pope in Rome'.

As we were let out of the ground, onto the road outside, we were met by a barrage of missiles.

The Turks had the high ground, which was near the Sheraton, and we were sitting ducks. However, the Turkish police, who were watching us, were also getting hit by various missiles. It wasn't long until they had had enough of that, and they were off after the Turks. They started chasing them up the hill, and when they caught any of them, they gave out severe beatings with truncheon and boot.

Bricks, bottles and green house type thin sheets of glass were being thrown or skimmed at us. The sheets of glass were particularly nasty to deal with as they changed direction in the wind all the time, and the sun glinted off them as they spun towards us.

We were about two hundred strong, and a chant of 'oo oo' went up as we started to move up the hill towards the Turks. After a bit of a walk, we broke out into a run and then a charge. The Turks stood their ground for a bit. As we were chasing up the hill to get into the Turks, the police then ran at us, batons drawn, and told us to stop running.

Even though they had their batons drawn, we ran past them as they hit out at us. Some of the English lads were going down, as they were hit by stones and bricks.

At the top of the hill, we regrouped and then charged at the Turks, but they legged it. Hardly any of them got a slap. This was a bit of an anti-climax, but it had still been fun.

About eight of us decided to go for a drink in the Sheraton; we had one in the foyer bar, then got the lift to the panorama bar on the twentieth floor. We ordered beer and were given free appetisers, which we consumed.

I had booked to stay for a few extra days in Istanbul. I got talking to Benny, Steve and Gary in the bar. I arranged to meet Gary at his hotel the next day and told him I would book in there.

The sunset over Istanbul from the panorama bar was amazing, especially when you looked at the horizon and all the minarets. When we looked down at the roads around the hotel, we could see that there was a mob of Turkish fans. They were basically outside the hotel, and they had just jumped some lone England fans as they had left. We decided to go down to see what was going on.

We got the lift back downstairs; there were loads of Turks outside the hotel. Ray Wilkins, the England player, was at the bar on his own. He had a flight back to Italy later that night as he was playing for 'AC Milan' at the time.

He was good enough to buy us all a drink and, as we were downing it and having a chat, a load of missiles smashed one of the front windows of the hotel.

The doorman, dressed in his top hat and tails, was fighting the Turks off to the best of his ability. He was kind of trapped, in the revolving door. Wilkins said to us 'we have done our job, now it's your turn'.

We were about ten in number; we all vaulted over the leather sofas in the foyer area, and smashed each Turk as he managed to get in. Women in the hotel were screaming, as we kicked the shit out of any Turkish fans that had got into the foyer. They were now trying to get out, again through the revolving door, that still had a very dishevelled doorman, his hat all lopsided, stuck in it.

The police arrived and calmed things down. We went back to the bar but Ray had gone. A Turkish copper, who was obviously in charge, came into the bar and saw one of the England boys. With wide-open arms, and a big smile he said 'my friend'.

Apparently the England boy, had been arrested the previous night for fighting and had spent the night in the cells, before paying our policeman friend a decent bribe to be released.

After a few beers we spotted some taxis and decided to make a run for it. We jumped in them, and headed back to our hotel. We ended up going for a meal in the old part of town, in an upstairs restaurant. The service was incredibly slow.

When the food did eventually come, the chips were stone cold. We ate up, then after a beer, went for a drink in another bar, but the bar was in a really dodgy area, so we went back to the hotel and played cards and drank there.

Thursday

The next day the Saint's boys in the hotel were going home. They got up early and apparently, drank eighteen pints between six of them at the airport, before their 8 o'clock flight to London.

I had a lie in, as now I could use the bed, then I had a shower and a decent breakfast. Not bad for free.

I got into a taxi and made my way across town to Ray and Gary's hotel. I was still too early for them to be up, so I dumped my bag and went and bought a bottle of coke, from a shop, round the corner. When I got back to the hotel, they still were not up, so I got their room number and went and woke them up.

It turned out they got pissed up the night before and had got surrounded by Turks in one particular bar. Paul and the Villa lad, who got arrested the previous night, got locked up again. This time, the police said it was for their own safety.

They were still put in some cells for a while and could here a Turk in the next cell getting a severe beating. It turned out they got some good photos in the end, some of each other wearing police hats and holding their guns. After a couple of hours the cops gave them a lift back to the hotel.

I went downstairs and checked into the hotel. It was quite expensive, but I hadn't spent much yet, so I paid up for the convenience of not having to find a cheaper alternative.

I decided to have something to eat, then we walked to the world famous pudding shop. This was where the American drug smuggler 'Billy Hayes' had been arrested. This was dramatised, when he was on the run, in the film 'Midnight Express'.

It was about 1 o'clock when we arrived and we ended up spending all day in there, drinking Effes lager and eating kebabs. We had Shish to start with, and donner kebabs a couple of hours later, when we were steaming drunk.

Cod was in there at a table next to us. He was a famous Chelsea fan, and he told us many funny stories, to do with following Chelsea.

One such story was on an away trip to a northern town, when he set fire to a toilet on the train which most of the Chelsea fans were travelling on. After the fire brigade had put it out, he went to talk to the firemen.

One fireman was saying, what a twat whoever had set the fire was, as it could have killed all on board. Cod then went off, and set fire to the toilet at the other end of the train.

There were some nice girls in the 'Pudding Shop' but they were mostly hippy types on their way to Pakistan or wherever. There were also some dodgy people, one of whom, was trying to sell us stolen travellers checks, we told him to 'piss off'.

On the wall there was a notice board for the hippy community. This offered cheap digs, or cheap transport to all point east.

At about seven o'clock we went to the bar next door. It had a type of disco in it and we had a great night, as our numbers swelled. Some of the boys who turned up there were Rich, Stuart Hill, plus other Chelsea and West Brom boys.

One song we sang and danced to was 'free Malcolm McDonald', the Arsenal player instead of the correct words of 'free Nelson Mandela'. We were all on the dance floor singing at the top of our voices. Some Australian girls had joined us.

As the conversation was about Mandela after the song, he was called a terrorist, and a 'fucking Kaffa' by some of the boys; the Aussie girls got the hump. Cod ended up getting a slap across his face from one of them. We all laughed.

We did the conga round the bar; the staff were trying to stop us. Someone had offered to pay for a drink, with a torn note, and when it was refused by the bar staff I tore it in half.

I shouldn't have done this, as it had the revered 'Attaturk' on the back of the note. It was against Turkish culture to do anything insulting towards him. The police were called. I mingled into the crowd then left by a side door, only to bump into a group of Irish lads that we had upset earlier, when we were singing the sash and other loyalist songs.

Luckily the bar was then closed and the rest of the lads came out. We got into a 1950's style, American taxi that took eight of us easily. Gary and me decided to get out, as it passed by the red light district.

The red-light district was just a small street leading to two other streets, which were dead ends. It had a police patrolled gate at the open end. Down the streets, on either side were about twenty windows with 'girls' posing in them.

Gary and Me were allowed in by the police, and we had a walk round. There was plenty of Turks looking at the girls, but it was us two English lads the girls were after. They were all shouting for us to come over.

One or two of them weren't too bad, but on the whole they were fat horrible things. We asked how much they were, just to be polite and make conversation, but I wouldn't have gone in if they were paying me.

Their fashion was also awful, they seemed to think that white ankle socks were a turn-on. They gave each other the odd peck on each other's cheek as if that constituted a lesbo show.

There was a black bloke, who was a tourist from the U.S, also in the street and he appeared to be even more popular with the girls than us.

After a while we walked back to our hotel, which also had a panoramic bar. We ended up having a couple of beers in there. The bar had a nightclub attached to it. In the nightclub there appeared to be some fit American girls, but we were too pissed to get in, so we went back to our beer, drank it and then called it a night.

Friday

The next morning we were feeling rough, but got up in time for breakfast at about eleven. Gary had kept Ray awake with his snoring so everyone was knackered. A few of the boys from last night appeared in the lobby and we all went for a walk to the old part of town for some fresh air.

After a while we saw the fish market and went to have a look at the types of fish that had been caught.

We thought about going to the 'Blue Mosque', which is a famous Istanbul landmark, but after a quick drink in the Pudding Shop, I suggested popping over to Asia on the ferry across the Bosporus.

This was decided to be a good idea, so we walked down to the quayside and boarded the next ferry, the fare was very cheap.

We docked at Katikoy in the shadow of the Bosphurus Bridge, and had a walk round the Asian side of Istanbul. This felt like a real 'Midnight Express' area. After a while we returned back to Europe by the next available ferry, and went back into the pudding shop.

I got talking to a really fit Australian girl, I couldn't believe it when she told me that she was in Istanbul to marry a Turk she had met. The boys and me carried on drinking in the hippy café for a couple of hours, then went next door again.

That night they had different bar staff, so luckily nothing was said about the torn note. We settled in for a session. Unfortunately the group of grumpy West Brom fans, from the first night, turned up and soon ruined the atmosphere.

They started taking the piss out of Ray from Orient, and though he was a bit of a mess with his 'zz top' type beard, there was no need. Next they turned on a lad from Blackpool and started throwing food around the bar at various people.

A ginger haired Chelsea fan said something to them, but they gave him a quick response of 'fuck off'. They threw an ashtray and it hit an Aussie girl, who ended up with blood coming out of a head wound.

Gary and me weren't too happy as the arseholes were ruining everyone's night and even they didn't seem to be enjoying it.

Ray from Orient had a word and they started threatening him, then Cod asked them what was up with them, then he wouldn't leave it, and was getting under the West Brom groups skin.

A punch was thrown and all of a sudden, the West Brom lot were fighting their way out of the bar. Everyone wanted a piece of the anti-social pricks, and they got a good slapping outside, and were on their toes back to their hotel.

Me, Gary and Rich decided to go down to the red light district again, but this time the coppers on the gate wouldn't let us in, as they said we were too drunk.

We ended up in 'Disco Two Thousand' at the Sheraton Hotel.

By now, we were on the Raki, a Turkish version of Ouzo. Rich was telling some stories about when he was an active member of the National Front, and the marches they went on in Bristol and London.

Apparently his mum was having tea with the vicar one afternoon at his house, when one of the organisers of a march came round, dressed in a World War Two German 'ss' uniform.

Rich told us that, at one meeting all was calm and a man with a loud speaker was addressing the crowd in a measured polite way. Towards the back of the market place a black bloke walked by. The bloke with the loud speaker couldn't help himself when he saw the black, and shouted 'nigger, kill that nigger'.

Another time they were on their way back from a meeting, when they were lucky enough to come across a coach load of Celtic fans at a motorway services. The Celtic fans, who were just on their way back from a match, didn't know what had hit them as they were battered all around the car park.

Saturday

We were up late. After breakfast we had a walk down to the market. Apparently it was the biggest indoor market in the world. The thing that struck us, was that there were no women on the streets, or in the markets, and all the 'blokes' that you saw, seamed to be holding hands.

The progress up the alleyways was slow because of the throng of people. We ended up buying a couple of t-shirts, after much haggling, and for some reason Ray bought some worry beads, another quirk that the Turks seemed to have.

That afternoon was spent back in the pudding shop, but this time we had an excursion to the Hilton hotel, to have a look at the fit women staying and working there, more than anything although beer was involved.

We ended up in another American car, and no one was sure whether it was a taxi or not, but we paid the driver as he dropped us of back at the Sheraton.

We finished off the night, by pissing it up in the 'Piano Bar' in the Sheraton Hotel.

Sunday

We were up early and off to the airport by 7 a.m. Security was strict and we were searched before we even went into the terminal building. As we were sitting waiting for our flight, a woman opposite had a baby with her who was crying. She did no more than flop her tit out, and started feeding it. In a country where most women are dressed to look like coke bottles, this seemed a bit strange.

The flight was called and we were searched again, as were our bags. We sat at the back of the plane. The West Brom lot were on the other side of the plane, also at the back.

The plane was going down the runway and sounded no more powerful than a knackered old Hoover, but after what seemed a long time, it slowly started climbing, but in a snake like fashion, weaving from side to side.

The stewardesses were quite ugly, and the food they distributed was horrible. It wasn't long until the West Brom lot started chucking it about, at anyone in general, but Ray in particular. He was sitting in the row in front of us.

Other passengers started to complain to the stewardesses, who then came and told the West Brom lot off. It was embarrassing, but it all seemed to be in a days play to the West Brom fans.

Funnily enough they never seemed to enjoy themselves, and seldom smiled; it seemed they just wanted to make sure no one else could have a good time.

As we crossed over the Alps the plane was hit by the worst turbulence I have ever encountered. The plane kept loosing altitude, then slowly climbed in its weaving manner, its engine mounted in the tail sounded pitiful, as it climbed to its original height, then would drop like a stone again.

Alarm bells were ringing, the stewardesses seemed to be in a state of panic and near to tears. The wings were going up and down so much that Stuart, who was next to me, slid the window cover closed. This turbulence went on for about half an hour with only mountains below. One of the West Brom lot completely lost it and started gibbering and shouting 'get us to Munich, let us land at Munich'.

We were gripping onto the armrests and every time the plane dropped it left our stomach behind. Eventually the flight became smooth. until we were approaching Heathrow, and then, for some reason, the pilot put the plane into a steep dive and after a bumpy landing we came to an abrupt halt on the runway.

The doors were opened quickly and on marched some British coppers. The West Brom lot were arrested, they ended up having a big argument with the stewardesses. They were saying that they didn't throw any food. They were like, caught out schoolboys. We had to laugh at them.

They responded by saying they would catch us up, and cut Rays beard off.

I got the tube into London and had a pint, but no one else showed up in the pub we had said we would meet up at. I phoned Caroline, my girlfriend at the time, and arranged to meet her that night. Then I caught the next train home.

Northern Ireland v England

1985

I was travelling with Andy Smart, a lad from Matlock. We had a few beers at the Moon pub then we caught the first train into Derby, then the next train to Crewe.

Crewe were playing Tranmere that night, and we tried to see if we could get in for the last twenty minutes. We did this and watched until the end of the game, then we went down to the pubs, that run along the main road from the station.

In one, we were playing pool and a good-looking black girl started chatting me up. This was very embarrassing in front of my mate, but I tried not to be rude to her, as I declined her various offers.

Andy was about pissed and full of beer, we caught the night train to Stranrear after getting back to the station. I knew quite a lot of the lads already on the train; we sat with Rich from Oldham and the Arsenal lads.

Also on the train along with a load of other England fans was Taffy from West Ham, some Pompey boys and Mick from Southampton.

At Stranraer we boarded the ferry, here Benny and The Tinman joined us, as they had driven to the port. We arrived at Belfast by catching the train from Larne, and then jumped into taxis and told the driver to take us to the Shankill Road.

Passing a funeral cortege, which seemed to add to the atmosphere, we arrived at the 'Orange Cross pub'. Here one of the boys knocked on the door and said that we were all English. This seemed to be the magic password and we were let in.

Quite a lot of Chelsea fans were already in there; they had travelled via Dublin the previous day in a coach. We ended up playing pool with some of them, I lost a fiver to Jerry, but it was on the black ball.

After a while Andy and me got in a taxi to the Europa hotel. We had a drink across the road in 'Robinsons Bar', where we met up with Big Paul, John and Sprake. While we were doing this, some of the Chelsea boys had also got a taxi and were doing the sights of Belfast. They had taken pictures of various murals and cemeteries and then decided to go down the Falls Road.

Half way down the Falls Road. A notorious Catholic and nationalist street, the taxi driver stopped the cab and got out, he shouted at the top of his voice 'English bastards'. The Chelsea boys got out of the taxi and ran. At the end of the Falls was a police station and the boy's legged it to it, meanwhile all the terrace house doors opened and the Catholics ran out, sensing blood.

At the police station, the sentry opened the barricade, and the boys ran in. the police then proceeded to give them a bollocking for upsetting the Catholics. The Chelsea boys pointed out to the cops, that as a British citizen you are aloud to walk down any UK street. The cops wouldn't have it, but did give them a lift in a Land Rover back to the loyalist side of Belfast.

Meanwhile we moved into the Linfield supporters club. This was in the hope of picking up some tickets, and also to read all the 'no surrender' literature plus look at the history of the club.

We hoped we would meet up with some good boys, which we did.

We were all singing 'no surrender to the IRA' and other loyalist songs such as 'do you know where hell is', 'when I was a kid, I had a flute' amongst others.

Some of the Ulster boys, told us they knew of a turnstile operator that would let us in, so we went to the ground with them.

We went to the turnstile and I offered the operator five pounds to get in, but he said 'no, your English, just climb over' which we all did, he was a top boy.

The game ended and the final score was 1 – 0 to England. One of the Ulster boys we had been with asked if I would swap my England shirt for his Northern Ireland one.

As they were good lads, and had looked after us I did. Rob, a lad from Belper saw this and had a go at me for wearing a Northern Ireland shirt. He was a bit pissed off with me, as I was now doing all the England games and he wasn't.

We could see Parrot in the main stand having a toe-to-toe fight with some Irish boys, heaven knows what he had said, or done, to upset them. Then after the game we were kept behind because of a bomb that had been planted at a nearby petrol station.

This was detonated and we were allowed out of the stadium. We were marched by the RUC down another route in to Belfast, as the petrol station was well alight.

After the match we had agreed to stay with the lads we had been drinking with, but unfortunately there was a bit of a fight between the English and some local lads, so we didn't see them again.

We walked to the station to catch a train, but Alf from Southampton, had a coach waiting outside in the car park, so we climbed aboard and headed off to Larne. Again we slept in the waiting room until the early morning ferry took us to Scotland.

We got the ferry to Stranraer and then onto a waiting train to Glasgow. As this filled up with commuters, we made a bit of room, but one England lad just lay across the four seats in our compartment and wouldn't budge, much to the annoyance of the Jocks.

We get some breakfast in Glasgow then the next train to Crewe. At Crewe we had a few beers and some chips then caught the train home.

Romania
1985

Monday

I had decided to travel with Alf from Southampton on a semi official tour. I met him and some other lads I knew at Gatwick airport. When we had checked in, and gone through passport control, we got on the bus that took us to the plane, amongst our group were some Pompey boys and Rich from Oldham. As the bus crossed the tarmac we were all laughing at a plane in the distance.

It was really old and still had propellers; we were making out that that was the one we would be flying on.

. As the bus pulled alongside it we were not laughing anymore. It was like something from the 50's and not the best. I looked at Alf and he looked nervous especially as this was his first ever flight.

When we boarded the plane, I could see that Ken Bailey and members of the press were already seated in the better area of the plane. As the plane took off everyone clapped, as we weren't sure it would make it.

When I went to the toilet, I told the boys the vibrations from the propellers, nearly ended up giving me a hard on, as I was holding my dick having a piss!

The food and beer on the plane were all right, as actually, was the flight. When we arrived at Bucharest the press got off first. Some of them were so pissed up, one of them ended up falling down the steps of the plane, and fell onto the tarmac. As he staggered to get up, we shouted 'you're not the fucking Pope, stop kissing the ground'.

We went through customs and a bus was waiting to take us to the hotel. After a mass check in, Alf and me went to our room. It wasn't too bad compared to what we had been expecting, and it appeared to be furnished in a fairly modern style. We then went downstairs for dinner.

We had been put on a dining table with a very odd couple from Smethwick, a place near Birmingham. He was thin and wore a nineteen fifties type leather jacket, while she was short and fat, wore a shell suit, and had incredibly thick horned rimmed glasses. They were married and appeared to be in their twenties. Both spoke with broad Birmingham accents. Alf happened to be wearing a replica England tracksuit top, and the female from the odd couple, started pouring over it and stroking the badge. The bloke started to get jealous; he had the three lions badge sewn onto an old blue jumper. During the meal, they explained how they loved Bobby Robson, and that they wrote to him every week.

After dinner Alf and me changed up some money at the hotel reception, then with Rich and the Pompey lads headed down into town. We got into a taxi, that was waiting outside the hotel, and asked the driver to take us somewhere good. We ended up at a weird type of nightclub.

We went in and there was a strange floorshow going on. This comprised of local peasants who were dressed in national costume and a band with all odd Eastern European musical instruments.

At about 10 p.m. the show ended and the lights came on. We thought it must be the interval, but we were wrong, the club was closing. It had cost us quite a lot to get in. We left, and outside it was pitch dark, it wasn't just the club that had closed, but by the look of it, the whole of Romania!

We got a taxi back to the hotel and ended up drinking in another lad's room. He had bought some beer earlier from the hotel and was willing to share it. For some reason, he started jumping on his bed and thumping the ceiling, as he got pissed. The manager of the hotel came into the room, and we were told that, we all had to go off to our own rooms.

Tuesday

After breakfast we were hanging around in the lobby area. Another English lad came into the hotel; he had been ripped off on the money exchange just like in Hungary. Again it was a note top and bottom and then newspaper cut to size to make a wad.

We walked into town, with some Norwich fans, but couldn't find any bars. We ended up trying to buy bottles of spirit in their equivalent of a supermarket.

The shops were basically empty but still the locals were queuing. At the market it seemed that the only thing for sale was carrots and other vegetables plus a few scabby apples.

We found a bar opposite a police station but the local beer was awful; but still the bar got crowded. Alf was telling me, how he and his mate were now into trips abroad, particularly to Amsterdam or France, with the sole intention of getting spaced out and stealing designer clothes.

The weather was quite warm by now. Across the road we could see the train station and new that it would have beer for sale. As we went towards the station we had to climb over a rickety old fence, and then we walked across the mainline tracks.

At the station we managed to buy a couple of bottles of wine. We bumped into Rob Jones and some of the Belper lads, they had just arrived, courtesy of the free rail travel they got because they worked on the railway back home.

Another train pulled in half an hour later and Alf hid behind a post. He wanted to surprise Big Paul, Sprake, John Paul and the Hull lads, as they didn't know he was going to this game. They didn't really act that surprised to see him, and it pissed on his fireworks.

It turned out they had a bit of a laugh on the way down to Bucharest. At the border Big Paul had all his tapes and his cassette recorder confiscated. Then the guards came to search the compartment at the next Hungarian/Romania border. The guard left his ladder, which he used to climb up to search the top bunks, in the corridor.

Big Paul decided to open the window and throw the ladder out of the train. The guard, on returning to the corridor for it, couldn't find it anywhere. When he asked the boys if they had seen it, they all acted dumb. He then drew a picture of a ladder on a piece of paper. Big Paul said to him 'ah' and started playing noughts and crosses on the paper.

The guard was raging mad, Sprake ended up laughing so much that he literally pissed himself as he sat there.

John Paul had met a girl somewhere along the journey, and he had ended up screwing her in the train's toilet.

We went and bought some more wine, and then the lads who had just arrived checked into a hotel that was across the main square. There were some bars around this area, so we had more beer, then we went to the Intercontinental Hotel and pissed it up in comfort. During the evening we were joined by Stuart, Benny and The Tinman. They were talking about organising a counter Mayday parade, for the next day, which was the first of May. They said that everybody should march to the central square behind a St Georges Flag.

We were all about pissed, and this seemed to be a fine idea. At the end of the evening Alf and me got into a taxi with a Stockport lad who was also staying at our hotel. We got back to the hotel and got some sleep.

Wednesday

We got up early and had a poor breakfast in the hotel dining area. Then we decided to use the hotel's swimming pool, but the water was freezing cold. As we were getting changed, a cleaning maid came into the changing room and was looking at us, as if she wanted shag.

She probably would have been on the game, but we were still freezing from the swim and got changed so that we could get out and into the sun.

We went and met the boys at their hotel. The press had heard that there was the proposed National Front march, Benny had mentioned, to oppose the Mayday parade. They were getting all excited about the prospect. They were thinking a story like that would help sell their various papers.

Of course this was just lads talk and the march never materialised. We ended up going on the piss all day. One bar was selling decent chicken on a rotifer. We all filled up on chicken served with the usual cold chips, that you always seemed to get in this part of the world.

We weren't given tickets for the match earlier while we were at the hotel, so me and Alf had to go to our hotel to pick them up.

Once back at the hotel we had a couple more beers, and killed some time by talking to a couple of Arsenal lads in the bar, then we were then given the match tickets.

The hotel had laid on transport to the ground. Rich and the boys were already on the coach, which was waiting outside the hotel.

Me and Alf and Kev from Villa got on the coach, as it reached the centre of Bucharest, we saw the rest of the lads in a bar.

We got the coach to stop, but the Rep wouldn't let us get off, and he wouldn't open the door. We went to the back of the coach and opened the fire escape door and jumped off. Before we got off I told the odd couple to 'get stuck in, if any fighting starts'. They looked at me as if

I was from a different planet.

In the bar, we also met up with some more Arsenal lads, who by now were really pissed. We had a couple of beers, but most of the England fans then left for the match meaning that we all got split up.

As Alf and me turned a corner, on our own, some locals jumped us. A couple of punches later and I had got a major nosebleed.

The fight was soon over as the Romanians went off looking for other small groups of English. I managed to stop my nose bleeding and cleaned the blood off me as well as I could. We saw a run down grocery shop across the road and we went and bought a cheap bottle of wine each.

As we approached the ground we ended up drinking the last of our wine and Alf shared his bottle with some soldiers. We got into our section and although the Romanians in the next block were unfriendly they couldn't get to us.

Meanwhile Big Paul, Sprake and the rest were taking their chances in the home end. We saw them enter onto the terrace, but it wasn't long before we saw the Hull lads getting a beating. The Saints lads were helping out for a while, but then all of them were getting another joint beating, before the police arrived to save them.

Big Paul was badly injured and was put into an ambulance, but as usual, he didn't want to go to hospital. As the ambulance stopped at a traffic light he managed to get out of the back door and did a runner. Sprake appeared in our end. He had a badly gashed leg. The cops, who had moved him to our section, kept telling him to sit down, but he couldn't bend his leg and he ended up getting kicked out.

As it happened we were near the official F.A party so towards the end of the game we started a chant of 'we hate Croker', this made him look very uneasy as he looked over.

The bus was waiting outside the stand for us after the match, this meant we could get on without fighting the locals, but for the rest of the England boys it was a daunting walk back into town.

Back at the hotel we had a few beers and a wash before a dinner of sorts was served to us. We were given little pennants and badges as a sign of friendship from the Romanians.

Unfortunately, this was repaid by a food fight, during which an éclair landed on the odd couple's jumper and you could tell he was really pissed off about it.

A chicken landed in the middle of one table splashing gravy everywhere and trifle ended up smeared up the wall. The room was a complete mess and we were asked to pay to clean it up. Some of the richer older English fans gave the hotel people some extra money and everyone seemed happy.

We went and pissed it up in the bar and Alf decided to nick the Romanian flag that was flying on a pole in the hotel garden. This involved much drunken planning.

Thursday

It was an early start; the wake up alarm was at 6 a.m. We got on the bus to the airport. Alf couldn't find his passport and thought he would have to go back to the hotel, but it turned up in his bag when he searched it again.

An older England fan who looked like a bit of a tramp, he was known as 'the professor', had purchased some shoes and a Gabardine Mac while in Bucharest and kept telling us what good value they were.

At the airport, Alf was pleased to get talking to one of Southampton's chief scouts. He talked for a while; the scout then asked Alf if he knew a lad called Fox. The scout told Alf, that apparently that was one fan who Laurie Mcmennemy, the Southampton manager, couldn't stand.

Alf pulled a down in the dumps face, and looked gutted, I smiled, as Alf's last name was Fox!

At the duty free they sold European beer so it was Heineken all round. We got back on the same plane as we had travelled out on, and during the flight home Alf insisted on tape recording an interview with me about the trip. I thought this was silly, but wonder if he still has all those various recordings.

The only real thing of note on the way home was when someone aimed a chicken roll at Ken Bailey, hitting him on the head, and a small chorus of 'sex case, sex case, hang him, hang him, hang him' was started.

We landed at Heathrow, said our goodbyes and headed home.

Finland
17th May 1985

Friday

I finished work, went home and got changed. My friends Spliff and Bernie gave me a lift to the railway station. My train was a bit late, but I arrived in London in plenty of time to meet the boys.

I caught the tube across London to Liverpool Street Station and then went in the 'Apple and Pears' Pub at the station. I was first there and, as I was having a drink outside the bar, a tramp, who was just a youth, asked me for some change.

I told him to 'piss off' and he wanted a fight. I was going to hit him but wasn't sure what I would catch, so I ended up going back into the bar and had another pint.

I then used the side door to go up the road, so as to miss the tramp, to another pub but it was full of businessmen, so I went back to 'Apple & Pears' again. I ordered another beer, then a lad from Essex called Noddy came in.

He suffered from a skin complaint where he was constantly scratching himself. He had to keep covering himself in cream to keep the condition in check. I was talking to him thinking the tramp might have been a safer option.

After a while Big Paul and Sprake came in, then John Paul, Duggie from Hull and some Chelsea boys. We had a few more beers then got the train to Harwich.

We all sat in an end compartment and looked at photos some of the lads had bought with them, mainly of previous trips while we drank cans of beer. At Harwich we had to buy 'port tax' and then we got on the ferry.

A bloke from work happened to be on the ferry. His name was Joe Carter, and afterwards, at work, he always went on about me getting off the ferry in Holland with just a bin liner full of bottles of Smirnoff Blue Label vodka.

On the ferry after we had sat in the bar for a while, we went to the duty free shop, to get our provisions for the trip. Some of the lads nicked their bottles of spirits, but we bought our bottles of mainly vodka but also some gin and whiskey.

The lads asked me where my luggage was, I replied that I was travelling light; I just had the bin liner for my duty free. We all sat in the corner of the bar, had a few more beers, and then went into the ferry's casino

I had a few goes on the roulette, but the sea was a bit rough and every so often the ball jumped into the next number! I didn't end up winning. Jerry, a Chelsea fan asked if we wanted to play cards, but we said no, some Leeds lads who were also travelling to the England match did. With Jerry there was only usually one winner, as he almost supplemented his income by being a professional gambler.

We all sat down for a steam up, some youths on the boat were going playing hockey in Holland. They had some black and Asian players with them, so they got a slagging off from some of the England boys.

As we slowly got more and more pissed one of the Leeds lads started joking about the Bradford City fire, a fire that had recently happened, where a number of Bradford fans died.

A Chelsea fan said he was out of order and smacked him. One of the Leeds lads who was playing cards lost about £160, £60 of it being his mate's, Jerry ended up winning about £300.

Saturday

In the morning we docked. Joe, from work, watched me disembark with a bin liner full of bottles. I got through customs with no bother by holding the bag tightly so that the bottles didn't 'clink' together.

We got on the waiting train, which was going to Hamburg. We had a bit of a sleep on this. As we were going through a town called Osnabruck, I woke up and got talking to sexy pretty German girl. She was wearing a short leather skirt and although she was a bit punky she was still quite nice.

John Paul walked down the train and tried to force his way in to the conversation. I was getting on really well with her, but decided to withdraw from the conversation and left him to it.

We arrived in Hamburg and found the left luggage lockers then dumped our bags. At the station a lot of Chelsea boys were waiting for Jerry. These included Legg, Jim Hopkirk and a few other famous faces. We got some money changed at the weasel, as we called it, which was the German name (wiesel) for a money exchange booth.

We then went onto the underground. About fifty of us all bunked the tube, we hardly ever paid for undergrounds when we were in Germany, or abroad in general, as the tubes were run on more of a trust thing. Often at stations, although there was one at this main station, there were no actual barriers as you entered and left the platforms or stations.

Another scam we were doing, was that we had taken loads of five pence pieces with us. These worked out to be the same size and weight as a Deutschmark, which at the time was worth about fourty pence.

Legg took photos of us all jumping the barrier. We got the train to St Paulie; this was the underground station for The Reeperbahn, which happened to be Hamburg's famous red light district. When we arrived we all split up, Silk and some of the Belper lads decided to come with us. Silk later had a wank in a sex booth, shooting his spunk onto the seat, then one of the other lads went in, and sat in Silk's spunk that was all over the seat.

We went into a bar and ordered beer and food, then, after we had eaten and drank, we just walked away. The bar staff didn't do anything.

We went down the street and at the next bar we had a few games of pool. Manchester United were on the TV, in the F.A Cup Final, but we didn't really bother watching it. We finished our beer and then headed off towards the red light area.

At one 'cabaret bar' we went in to see a show, the bouncer reckoned it was dead good.

As we walked in. through the curtain that draped across the entrance, the Chinese bird that was on the stage got up and started dancing, as we were the only customers inside the place.

As soon as our beers arrived and we had paid, she sat down. We took some photos of the various girls in the club who were walking round; some were either naked or topless. We got told off, by the bouncers, as this was against the rules.

When we left, we told people who were looking to come in, that it was shit and not to bother. As we were saying this, an obviously rich bloke came out; he must have been in a private booth. He was in a business suit, and a gorgeous blonde girl, who had been in the club, was all over him!

We walked down a gated street that was blocked off at both ends. This was where all the girls, who were on the game, sat in various shop windows trying to persuade the tourists looking at them, to come in.

Lots of the girls in the windows were really fit, but some were fat, some thin, and some were ugly. We went down the warren of streets in that area, looking at the various girls of many nationalities, the Thai girls seemed to be very popular.

We carried on walking to the top of the street, where there was another gate that allowed you access, and headed to the Liverpool bar which was ten yards further up the street.

We had yet more drinks then went to a 'topless' bar across the road.

A really fit girl, in a very short mini skirt, outside the bar asked me if I wanted sex. I asked her how much it would be, and the price was the equivalent of twenty pounds. Sprake and the lads had already been to Hamburg, with Southampton when they played in the UEFA cup, and he warned me about getting ripped off.

I decided, as she was so pretty, to go with her. We went up to a room above the shops using the side stairs. She promised she would do everything for thirty deutschmarks.

Once we got in the room, and after I had paid the money, the girl got a Johnny out.

I said 'there was no chance of me getting a 'hard on' with a Johnny on', but she knew what she was doing, put it on me and started to suck me off. Thirty seconds later I had a 'hard on' and she started wanking me off. I felt her tits and fanny, but she wouldn't let me fuck her, and she just wanked me off.

Afterwards I told her she was a fucking slag. When I got back out on the street I was slagging her off to the lads, but they thought it was dead funny that I had got ripped off.

Meanwhile, Noddy had gone off with another girl from the street. When he re-appeared he said that he had had a proper shag and that it was dead good. With his scratchy skin condition, I was not quite sure how he had managed it, but all of a sudden he was short of money!

Then we went round some back street pubs. A really fit girl in one bar kept looking over, but she was already with a bloke so that was a no-goer. I bumped into Stuart Hill; he was quick to tell me that he had already had a proper shag.

Smoke, John and me went to a fish bar I stole a cold chicken from the display cabinet. The Chinese bloke behind the counter, realised what I done and came at me with a meat cleaver. I put it back and did a runner, and for some reason so did Smoke, this meant he lost his money as he had already paid for his chips but hadn't been served yet!

By now there were loads of England lads in the Reeperbahn. Most were nicking magazines from sex shops. Me and Sprake went into a sauna place that looked good on the photos that were posted outside, but it was a private members club. We walked into the swimming pool area, but then got chased out.

We decided to go down to the Eros centre, which Sprake had been saying was really good the last time he was here. It was just an underground car park with private doors going off the main area. The girls in there, and there must have been about fifty of them, just came up to you, and started rubbing you up. Sprake was right, this place was brilliant.

We then went to some more peep shows; luckily we still had loads of five pence pieces left, although we had got rid of a load of them, in various fruit machines and cigarette machines, selling the cigarettes to the Germans at a profit.

After this we went back to a bar that had loads of prostitutes in it, and a bit of a sex show going on, on a small stage. Big Paul said that for five deutschmarks you could take a bird into one of the cubicles that were along one wall.

I decided to have a go, so chose a fit Thai girl, paid the money and went into a cubicle with her. I started sucking her tits and she got my cock out and sucked me off. It turned out all lads were taking it in turns to look through the cubicle door keyhole to see what I was doing!

More beer was then consumed, then we went to some more sex shops. We were all flicking through all the hard-core porn magazines that had pictures of women with animals, Women shitting and pissing, and transvestites doing all manner of things. We ended up stealing a few of these books just because we could.

It was getting quite late and we decided to go into a nightclub. I knocked off a really fit girl, meanwhile all the lads were on the dance floor, dancing stupidly and then doing balancing acts. It was a really good night.

I tried to stay with the girl I was with, and told the lads I would catch them up in Copenhagen, but in the end, I wasn't sure if she would let me stay with her. I left her and bunked the tube back to station. The train was already in, so we all piled on after getting our bags out of the luggage lockers. We managed to get a couple of compartment to ourselves. This meant we could spread out and sleep for the next part of the journey.

For some reason a bloke on the platform was staring at Paul, so he leapt out of the train and slapped him. As the train pulled out, the bloke gobbed at Paul. Paul went to throw his bottle of beer at him, but he couldn't throw it because of all the coppers that were about on the platform.

The next compartments was also empty so as the train left Hamburg we were four to a compartment. The seats pulled right out until they met in the middle so we basically had flat beds. We had lost Noddy in the Reeperbahn; somebody said they had seen him and he was nearly crying because he had lost us!

Further down the carriage were the Leeds lads from the ferry. One lad, who everyone called Daisy, kept going on about the donkey video he had just seen back in Hamburg.

Sunday

I woke up early as the train arrived into Copenhagen. Again we found the left luggage lockers and got rid off our bags for the day. I had a wash in the station toilet, then went and changed some money into Danish Kroner. We walked round for a bit, to kill some time, as it was still early, then crashed out on some benches outside a store that was also a café.

We were all asleep, but it was quite cold and after few hours we woke up and had another walk round the town. We went to a shop and bought a few bottles of elephant beer, which was about eight per cent proof, and walked into the old town.

The bars were now open so we went into one, bought some more beers, and as the sun was now shining and it was nice, went and sat outside.

As the shadow from the building opposite blocked the sun, we moved our seats so we were sitting in the gutter at first, then into the road from the pavement. Busses and other traffic had to go round us, and then we moved again and sat in the central reservation of the road.

The owner came out and told us to give him back his chairs.

Noddy arrived; somehow he had found us, after catching the next train from Hamburg. He was taking photos of road signs and buildings as he thought he was a bit of a professional photographer. He had taken loads of photos, plus he had loads of photos with him from previous trips. When he went back to England he reckoned he had booked himself in for photo shoot of the model Sam Fox.

Noddy was trying to impress the boys, and he kept going on about the local derby in 'toy-town', which would be Trumpton v Camberwick green. He was on about the resulting pitch invasion involving Windy Miller and the firemen.

We took the piss out of him because he supported Newcastle, Luton and Trumpton. The bar owner then came out and started shouting at us again to get out of the road. We all drank up and decide to go to Tivoli gardens, a park and amusement centre near the station.

When we got there, you had to pay to get in and there were doormen at the gates. We joined a queue of school kids and just walked in at end of the group. We were all about six foot tall and the school kids we went in with, were about four feet tall. The gatemen didn't say anything to us. A couple of the lads also sneaked in through an exit gate. Once in we had had a look round, there was the usual fountains and a band playing at a bandstand. We went for a drink and a hamburger in the park cafeteria. All the lads were chatting up the waitresses, as they were typical Scandinavian stunners.

After we had consumed the food and beer, we went on the roller coaster that was in the amusement area. It was quite small but it was still a laugh, and we took photos and sang 'England' as we rode on it.

Afterwards we bumped into the Halifax lads, they said they could hear our England chants from above their heads and wondered where the noise was coming from. We all left late in the afternoon, after another walk round and a look at the various stalls.

We went to the red light district; this was on the other side of the railway station. We looked in the various sex shops and went into a bar for a sex show, it was no good as the girl wasn't interested and was just swaying on stage, though she was naked she looked as though she was drugged up.

We went into another sex shop that had an English girl behind the counter. We got talking to her while a TV behind her, was showing a video. As we were watching it, and talking to her, she screamed and ran round and switched it off. This was because she was in the film being shown!

We went to the bar next door; it was called the 'Spunk Bar'. We had a game of pool and after a while Benny, The Tinman and Stuart came in. Benny got into an argument with a Danish biker, who looked like a Hells Angel. The biker was giving it large, about how he didn't like the Queen.

Benny said 'don't slag off my Queen' and dropped the Dane. A little barmaid rushed round from behind the bar and started hitting Benny. Benny was laughing as the barmaid pushed and shoved him out of the bar.

We stayed in the bar and had a good laugh for the night then went for some food and ended up in an Indian restaurant. Sprake and me just had a curry, while some of the other lads had main meals, starters and side orders.

Smoke ate loads and really filled up, which surprised us as he hardly ever ate. After we had finished we walked back to station, as usual for Scandinavia, there were loads of druggies hanging around it. We stayed clear of them, but we could understand how there had been so much trouble in Copenhagen when England played here back in 1982.

Loads of bikers, Hells Angels types, covered in tattoos and generally of the body builder type size were also hanging around. We got our bags then got on the train that was heading for Stockholm, we managed to get a few compartments and did the same thing with the seats, as the previous night and just crashed out again.

After a while the whole train was put onto a ferry. This was to cross the sea between Denmark and Sweden for about a one-hour crossing. We all went into the restaurant for yet another beer.

Silk was on the ferry and we had a chat. Benny, who was also in the bar switched on his big tape recorder, that he had bought with him. The tape he was at this time playing was 'Hitler's speeches' and 'the swearing in of a soldier'.

Benny spoke the words of Horst Wessel. He had also got a load of Dixieland songs, which were dead funny. We all sat down and had more elephant beer plus we drank some of the gin that we had bought. When the boat docked everyone got back on to the train. It left the ferry and joined the Swedish rail network. We all slept until it arrived in Stockholm.

Monday

We arrived at Stockholm station at about 9 o'clock and again put our bags in the left luggage lockers. Again we had to change some money then went to the ferry terminal to buy tickets for that nights sailing to Finland. Sprake and me were leading the way, while behind us Duggie and John met two punk girls and went off with them. Sprake had originally planned to go by train around the Baltic, but he got his ticket changed for the ferry.

While we were at the terminal all the England boys, who had also gone to get their tickets, robbed the snack bar of cheese cobs, crisps and bars of chocolate then just walked off back into town.

We went to a supermarket and bought some cans of Heineken and cartons of milk. The reason we did this was to disguise the fact we were drinking beer in the street. We poured the milk away, and put the beer in the carton.

This was a good idea, but the coppers on the street still stopped a few English boys and poured their beer away. We sat on some steps next to a market square. A few girls came and sat with us and joined in with the drinking. Then some coppers came and warned us about drinking. After they had left, we drank some more milk and then put beer in the empty cartons and gave it to the girls.

Big Paul was chatting up a girl, when a bird did a shit on her head. We said to her 'in England we think that's lucky', she asked 'why', and we said 'because it didn't shit on us'.

We went back to the supermarket and bought some more beer, then went and sat in a park. In the park there were loads of fit girls generally walking around, plus there was a talent type show, which was being filmed by a television production crew.

Sprake and me had a game of boule and got talking to yet more girls. We sat with them by a fountain and for some surreal reason, a model was having photos taken by the same fountain, so we took some of her as well.

We then went and got our duty free from the left luggage. We went to the bottle shop off licence. Sprake sold the whisky he had bought at the duty free on the ferry and he got a good price straight away, then he sold mine for me. Lots of Swedes were queuing for their ration of hard liquor, and we were like some kind of godsend to them.

I trebled my money on each of the five bottles of Vodka I had left.

After buying a load of food, including salmon, pate, French bread and more beer. We then went and sat in a nearby graveyard and ate it. A bloke walked through the graveyard, we asked him if he wanted to buy our last bottle of gin, he said 'yes' and we made another tidy profit.

We went back to the park; none of the lads had scored with the various girls that they had been talking to. It was time that we went up to the ferry port and boarded the ferry.

When we got there, Legg ran straight on, trying to bunk the ferry. He was followed by some other lads, but they all got stopped and kicked off. The port police took Legg's passport to make sure he behaved and made him buy a ticket.

After he pulled another three passports out of his bag and said 'I'll use this one' and showed it to the boys. We all got on the ferry; it was really smart, more like a liner than a cross channel ferry.

We found our cabins and general bed area and had a lie down. Some of the lads then went for a swim, as the ferry had its own indoor pool, but unfortunately I didn't have a towel so I stayed in my bunk.

As the boat sailed, we went for a walk round and found a kids play area. Duggie played on a bouncy model plane, while we went down the slide into the ballpark below it. We were soon told off by the ferry staff. We then had a penalty shoot-out, on the mini football pitch, but I split my jeans a bit, which was bad news, as I didn't have another pair to change into.

We went down to the boats restaurant and decided to just have the 'smorgasbord'. This was a Scandinavian buffet, with loads of choice as to what to eat. Duggie and Paul reckoned we wouldn't have to pay, so we all piled up our plates with beef, chicken, salad and potatoes. Then we went back for seconds but you could see that the waiter was wary of us.

Big Paul made the first run for it after we had finished, but got caught by the waiter and some other staff. While everyone was watching him and Noddy, who had also done a runner, the rest of us got away.

We went into the bar and got some drinks. The boat was full of teenage Swedish girls most of whom were fit. It seemed to us that Sweden didn't do ugly birds. We got talking to some, but as the night went on decided to go to the nightclub, which was really plush.

Sprake and me filled some half empty coke bottles with Bacardi and drank that to save on the cost of booze at the bar. We sat by some tables near to the dance floor.

Big Paul had got a bottle of beer; he had bought it from the nearby café. When the bouncers tried to get it off him, he took one jump over the barrier and he was onto the dance floor with his beer still in his hand.

He hit the bouncer when he approached him on the dance floor, grabbed his beer and ran for it, we thought this was dead funny, as he was now barred from the club for the rest of the night.

Most of the lads got talking to various girls and I appeared to have scored with a really fit girl. I took her upstairs and was kissing her, and feeling her tits, it looked like I was home and dry. Sprake saw us, he told me the next day everything seemed to be fine, when apparently she just slapped me across the face, and I just waddled off. I don't know what had happened, but I remember she was up for it, so I don't know what I said that upset her.

Back in the nightclub Legg was talking to a black bloke who said he was a Chelsea fan. This didn't impress us much.

At end of the night, we met up with Daisy and the rest of the Leeds lads. We all sang 'God save the Queen' and 'Rule Britannia'. The other lads in the club joined in. One of the Leeds lads was on the dance floor with a fit girl, but he got blown out.

The lights came on and we all wandered out, and headed back to our beds to laugh at Big Paul who had, by then, crashed out.

Tuesday

During the night some Scousers had stolen the equivalent of ten thousand pounds from the boats casino, but mostly in chips! Obviously these were of no use unless you went to a sister casino, however they got caught, and in the morning, before we docked, they were put in the ships brig.

We disembarked once the boat docked at the Finish port of Turku. We all went through customs; Legg was given his passport back. I still had a couple of bottles of Vodka in my black bin bag, that I had bought duty free on this boat, but they weren't that cheap compared to the English prices.

I got through customs all right and then boarded the train for the final leg of the trip to Helsinki. Silk came down to our compartment and had a look through the sex books we had stolen, and that we were passing around. We still had got some hard-core books; he reckoned he could get a good price for them, back at his workplace.

We arrived at Helsinki at about mid-day and left the bags in the left luggage lockers yet again. We went for something to eat and again had to change some more money up. By now every pocket I had, had different countries money in it. After some food we went to the tourist information office.

We found out where youth hostel was, it turned out that it was actually under one of the stands of the stadium, so we got a map and walked to the stadium. On the way we passed a building, which had a load of massive flags on poles outside it, and we considered stealing the British one. We found one of the few pubs in Helsinki. This was called 'Pub 99'.

We had a few beers and I sold another bottle of Vodka, at a good profit, to a pissed up local. I saved one last bottle for myself. We went to the hostel and booked in for the night. Noddy and rest of lads decided we could of bunked in so they didn't pay.

Some of the lads wrote the obligatory postcards, stating how much we hated him and the F.A., to Ted Crocker; I kept one to post later. We went for a walk round, the gates to the stadium were open, but a groundsman wouldn't let us in.

We looked into the ground and England were training on the pitch, so we climbed over the fence to get in and my jeans completely split.

We had a photo call in the ground, and then walked around the pitch. A football was kicked off the pitch by one of the players, so we had a bit of a kick about with it. Les Phillips, one of the FA backroom staff, asked for it back but we ignored him. He tried to make small talk with us, and asked us where we were getting tickets from.

We still didn't give him the ball back; he started pleading with us, so we gave it him back. The next time a ball went out, the England players expected us to kick it back but we just left it.

BobbyRobson, the manager, was telling John Barnes the Jamaican who played on the wing for England, to go down the line to the by-line and to cross the ball to Mark Hately, the England centre forward.

Barnes tried three times, but each time cut in, because the defender wouldn't let him down the line. He ended up just shooting at the goal.

Robson was pulling his hair out, as he kept explaining that he wanted Barnes to get to the line and cross it for Hately.

We were all laughing at Barnes and after his third attempt, Robson said really loudly, so that we could all here, 'brilliant John. I can't teach you how to play. Just keep sticking at it'!

Peter Shilton was coaching the new keeper who was called Gary Bailey, so we went and watched that for a bit. As this was going on and the rest of the players were finishing, the stadium people started videoing what was going on to make sure that the big electronic screen was working.

Pictures of the players and ourselves were coming up on the giant scoreboard and we were all on it as they kept doing replays. All the lads started doing Sieg heils, which again was recorded, and shown on the big screen. Then they kept replaying it, so we all took pictures of the scoreboard, with the England fans on it doing Sieg heils!

All the lads then did a moonie across goalmouth, which also appeared on the big screen! We then left the stadium and headed towards 'Pub 99'. We had a few beers then decide to stage a mock fight in the park opposite.

We split up into North versus South, but Noddy went well over the top. We all got sticks and branches from the trees, but he got one with thorns on it and started whipping people's legs. Everyone had a go at Noddy, and we nicked his camera and stuck it on a rock near the lake.

Noddy went mad in case it fell in. We walked around the lake and over some rocks and found a restaurant. We had some food then some more beer at a bar that was next door. It was still broad daylight at midnight and we headed back to hostel. We ended up just grabbing a mattress each and sleeping on the floor in the corridor.

Noddy put on all his creams on, but was still scratching all night. I moved my mattress further away from him. In the morning we used the hostels communal showers, the first proper wash I had had on this trip.

Wednesday

In the morning as we lay on our mattresses, the boys made up a song for Big Paul. After being on the big screen in the ground the day before, it went:

Paul is a manilow,

He sings on the stage

He is a fucking Jew

He's got the biggest nose that you have ever seen

And he appears on the TV screen.

It was noticed that Sprake had got legs like an ostrich, this was pointed out and Sprake did an ostrich impersonation by running up and down the corridor with his hand for a head and arm as its neck, while singing 'John Paul is a homosexual Jew'.

We went back to the train station and the lads got their things out of their bags I turned my socks inside out, but they were really smelly by now. When I came out of the toilet, the lads had gone ahead to 'Pub 99'. I went to meet them, but they were not there. I ordered a pint, but as it was only half past nine I took it easy.

The boys came in after a short while; they had been to McDonalds for breakfast. I decided to go and have a burger. After the burger I went back to pub and started steaming it up.

Loads of English fans were now arriving, these included Chunny from Brighton, the lads I had travelled with, were laughing at me, because I had smacked Chunny at the last England home game, for nicking my mates stuff in Spain.

Loads of flags were put up on the surrounding fences and trees of the pub. All the lads were now on the piss and singing various England songs. Sprake gave me a whiskey that some Fins, who were also happily drinking in the bar, had bought him. He gave it to me because he didn't like it.

By about 5 o'clock we were well pissed, John and me were chatting to lad I had met in Turkey. We stayed in the bar when most of lads were leaving to go to the match. Me and John decided to have one more drink, but unknown to us; Big Paul had decided to kick the main window of the pub in, and had then fucked off.

John and me were finishing our drinks when the coppers stormed in. A bouncer pointed at me, as he had seen me drinking with Big Paul, and the police slapped a pair of handcuffs on me, and the lad we were talking to who I had met in Turkey. They then told John to come as well, but they had run out of handcuffs for him!

We were all bundled into the back of a police Saab, at that moment the TV cameras happened to be outside the pub, filming the smashed window scene. I didn't realise it but it was all being filmed for the BBC '9 o'clock News'. I didn't even realise I was being filmed for any TV, let alone the BBC news.

I saw a friend called Eddie on the street corner by the bar. He asked me if I was all right, so I smiled at him and said 'yes'.

He asked me 'what should I do'?

I replied to him 'just fuck off to the match' but the edited camera shot showed me, in handcuffs being bundled into a cop car, smiling and saying 'just fuck off' towards the coppers, and that's how the '9 o'clock News' bulletin started.

As the police car went down the street, the handcuffs started to really bite in. they worked on a ratchet idea and once they tightened in one direction they wouldn't go back.

We went past a lad called Chris Whitehouse who happened to be rolling on the floor with a couple of coppers. I knew him from previous trips; apparently he was standing for parliament. He was the prospective Labour delegate for Southsea!

The car sped down road, its siren screaming, to a police station. By now it was about half an hour before kick-off. Later, it stated in the papers that by this time, some of the more 'hoolaganistic'! fans had been locked up.

When we got to the police station, the handcuffs were killing me. We were all told to sit down and the cuffs were taken off. It had taken me by surprise when they were put on, so I couldn't tense my muscles to hold the ratchet off.

We were told to take our shoelaces out of our trainers and empty our pockets. At this moment I realised I still had the postcard to Ted Croker, with a lot of abuse on it.

We put all our belongings in a box and were then lead to a cell, me and John were pushed into a cell and a lad from Villa called Rich Jones was already in there.

We were pushed in and they slammed the door behind us.

It was really warm in the cell, there wasn't a window, there wasn't a clock and the fluorescent light stayed on all the time, so you had no idea of time. In the corner of the cell was a stainless steel bog. There was no bog roll and it had no flush.

After a while another lad was pushed into our cell. He said he had been drinking from a can in the street and had been arrested for that. John told me about the broken window in pub, as he had seen it as we left.

We were given a rough blanket; there were fleas on the floor and the blanket. All we could do was try and sleep, by now there was six of us in our cell, one of whom worked for the police back home, and he was shitting himself in case this cost him his job.

As time went by, we could hear more and more English being thrown into the cells. If you looked out of our peep slot, which was in our steel door, you could see eyes at the other doors. Lads were kicking the doors. I heard some voices that I recognised as Ian and Colin. It was a bit like being rounded up in the great escape.

I asked what the score was, then for the next ten hours just tried to sleep. We had no idea of the time as you couldn't see daylight just the strip light all the time. The lads in my cell started kicking the door, there was a camera in the corner, but we reckoned you could have died in there, and no one would have come.

During the night a lad called Chester could be heard hanging from the bars shouting 'Legg will get me out'. Chunny was arrested for having a knife on him 'it's for bottles'; he kept shouting 'bottles'. Later we all impersonated him on the way home. A Scouse youth walked past our cell in the morning saying 'you're all in for two days'.

Thursday

In the morning after what seemed an eternity, we were told to get out of the cell one at a time and taken down to be given breakfast. This consisted of pea soup, which had thick skin on it, it tasted awful. They also gave us a dead heavy scone, and a cup of milk, which was ok. Then it was back to the cell to eat it.

After about another hour, some coppers came into our cell. We were wondering about John's bag, as we didn't know who had the key for the left luggage. The first two lads were lead out, and didn't come back, then the next two. Then after half an hour they called for John Paul so I was left on my own. After about 15 minutes the police came and got me.

A British Embassy woman was waiting at the counter; I was given all my stuff. The desk sergeant type copper, asked me why I had been locked up. I said 'for no reason'. He replied 'we don't lock people up for no reason'.

The Embassy woman told me 'The Sun' newspaper was after everyone's names, but she had refused to give them to them.

The desk sergeant then said that I was free to go; he said 'make sure all your stuff is in the box'. The postcard was still there, but ten pounds was missing, I decided not to say anything.

I was then released along with John; I tore up the postcard, and put it in a bin. We then headed down to the train station. It turned out that during the night, one lad was released from another cell because he had got a plane to catch. We got to the station and found out that, Stevie hadn't been released in time for his plane, and he was now shitting it, as he couldn't get home.

It turned out that Sprake and Duggie had also been locked up, but they were put in an overspill station, they were allowed to keep their bags, which had beer in them. They also could watch television, so it was as good as a hotel room! We decided to go down to the Embassy to get Stevie a flight. We had been given complaint forms, so we filled them in and sent them off.

At the Embassy Stevie phoned Alf, who was his mate in England, who in turn paid for a one-way ticket back to London. Stevie then rushed off to the airport. We all went back into town and had a drink in a bar near the station that had a rooftop terrace.

We bought some of the local papers and got them translated by the bar staff. In the paper there was a good picture of Duggie and Sprake looking at a police dog. They had got their flags shoved up their jumpers, and it made them look pregnant.

There was also pictures of various fights, one of which was a lad called Eddie who was smacking a Finn, the caption below the picture stated 'fuck you Perkelee' other pictures showed a lot of Finns with blood dripping from their noses.

Apparently the Finns were no mugs and after the match were attacking England fans on the rocks where we had had our mock fight the day before. Big Paul and Noddy were nowhere to be seen and we weren't sure what had happened to them.

It was now too late to get back for the Scotland game, which was to be played at Hampden Park at 3 o'clock on Saturday. Some of the English lads did catch a cheaper flight direct to Stockholm and caught up with where they would have originally been, these include the Chelsea boys 'Punk', Mick T and Jerry.

Apparently Big Paul had been seen, trying to get locked up last night, but they wouldn't arrest him, as all the cells were full and he had spent the night walking the streets.

We finished our drinks and then went for the next train to Turku. When we arrived at Turku, Big Paul was at the station waiting for us. He told us that he eventually stayed with some girl last night. The ship was already in, so we all got on board and found a bed.

As the ship sailed we went on deck to look at all the islands in the sea. It was fantastic scenery, we then went to the restaurant for a smorgasbord and had a load of food, and then went to the bar.

This was a different ship to the one we sailed out on. We sat down and started talking to some girls, but they were a bit too young, possibly only sixteen or seventeen, so we just had few drinks with them, then filled a coke bottle with Bacardi and went into the ships nightclub.

I got talking to a girl but didn't score. The night was spent drinking and chatting to the other lads. Sprake did manage to knock off a girl but then got blown out. At the end of night we went back to our bunks and crashed out.

Friday

We arrived at the port in Stockholm and disembarked the boat. We then headed to the train station. We were all feeling really knackered; the lads dumped their bags in the left luggage.

Colin and Noddy decided to get on the next train heading towards home, so we left them and the rest of us went to 'Albens' supermarket and bought milk cartons and beer and headed to the park.

Again there were some really fit girls in the park, again we sat around a fountain, sunbathed and at one point we had a play fight with Big Paul. Four of us were on top of him, but he just knocked us off him, like we were flies.

The problem with the park was that there were some horrible toilets that we had to use, but at least there were no coppers about, so we stayed there most of the day. There were quite a few drunks in the park anyway, so perhaps the coppers were turning a blind eye.

We kept going back to the supermarket to get more beers. After quite a long time, we went for a walk through the old town and had a beer at a street café.

Then we carried on walking around the harbour area and ended up have a skimming competition, and then a throwing competition, aiming at various things floating in the harbour.

Some weird people were dancing in the street to a radio, then, across the sea, on an island, we saw two naked girls having a lesbian shag. They looked spaced out and when they noticed we had seen them, they ran off into the trees!

We walked past some government buildings and about twenty state limos came past us. Inside some of them were loads of black minister types from some African nation. Duggie stood on the pavement doing Sieg heils at them.

We walked over the Railway Bridge to the station, and the lads got their bags out. The train to Copenhagen pulled in and we ran to find the best part of the train, with the best seats for sleeping; we kept changing our minds and ended up sitting in reserved seats.

The train filled up and we were told to get out of the seats by other passengers. We said to them 'no, the guard told us to sit here'. Then the guard came along and made us move.

We sat in an ordinary open carriage and got talking to a dippy Yank girl. John Paul started reading his passport to her, the bit about let no one hinder us, and after a while she ended up sitting on Big Paul's knee. She told us that she had got a friend in every city. When we asked who her friend was, in various obscure cities, she was confused. Other Yanks on the train were laughing at us, as we took the piss out of her, but she didn't get it. She said she had got pins and needles in her legs from sitting on Paul's knee, so we took the piss out of her, and made out we didn't understand the phrase.

A drunken Swede, along with another youth, got into the carriage at one station and was smoking. Sprake told him to put the cigarette out, and this in turn turned into a bit of an argument. In the end, the drunk pulled a gun out of his coat pocket and Sprake shit himself.

Finally the train was loaded onto the ferry that sailed between Sweden and Denmark and later we arrived at Copenhagen station, by now it was Saturday morning.

Saturday

I wanted to get off the train to go and buy a T-shirt from the spunk bar, but it was too early and meant we would need to hang around for the bar to open. There was a train that was going to Hamburg so we got on it, after about a one-hour wait. This train went straight to Hamburg and was empty so we could all sleep until we got to Hamburg Station.

Duggie had wanted to go to Oslo on the way home, to visit a new country, all the lads, apart from Sprake and me, had agreed, but they then decided not to go and they let him down. He was obviously disappointed, and was quiet all way home. Me and Sprake were ripping the piss out of them all, about this.

They then decided to go to Paris from Hamburg, leaving just me and Sprake in Hamburg. FC Cologne were playing Hamburg so we decided we might go and watch them. We headed off to the Reeperbahn while the other lads went off to Paris.

On the tube to St Paulie, Sprake realised he had left his camera in the left luggage area, so we headed back to the main station. When we arrived it was gone, but we bumped into Big Paul. They had got on the wrong train and had had to come back. They were now going home via Cologne.

Sprake and me went back to the Reeperbahn and went to the pool bar we had been in earlier that week. We had a couple of beers then went into a peep show. There was just a Chinese bird in there, and she said she was not working.

We went down a back street and found a bar where a shot of schnapps was only 1 Deutschmark. We drank beers and schnapps, around us the local Germans were getting pissed and the barman couldn't believe how much we could drink.

He then lowered the price of the beer to one Deutschmark, which was about thirty pence. We watched the Hamburg v Cologne match on TV and during the round up of other German games; we noticed that all the grounds had Union Flags on the fences. We found out the England versus Scotland score, from the game we should have been at. The barman now became slow to serve us, so we carved England in plaster in the toilets and then left to go around the various sex shows.

I decided to phone home, to see if everything was all right. My mum still thought I was locked up, because she had seen me getting nicked on the news; my dad said to me, when I explained I was in Hamburg on the way home, 'you're not in the Reeperbahn are you'!

We went into a sex shop and nicked a load of books, and had to run down the street as the proprietor chased us. We then went back to the Eros Centre, the underground car park that was full of girls. One of the girls was fantastically fit; she had long dark hair and was dressed in a slinky leopard skin dress with killer heels on.

She was feeling my cock and balls as I talked to her, and I decided I would have to go into a cubicle with her.

She was really good, but I had had too much to drink, and even though I was still shagging her she said the time was up. She ended up giving me a blowjob.

We went back down the gated street and had a beer in the Liverpool bar, where we had a bit to eat. Then, as time was getting on we tried a nightclub but it was crap and expensive so we left. We had to get a taxi; the driver put his foot down and got us to the station just in time for the train. Sprake got his bag, and we jumped onto the train, found an empty compartment and slept.

Sunday

We woke up and we were near the Hook of Holland. I decided to throw my socks away as my feet were now cracking up, and the socks were sticking to them. We got some money changed, another currency, this time Dutch Guilders, and paid the port tax, so we could then get onto the boat.

We just sunbathed out on the deck for most of the crossing. I just had one pint and a bit of a snack. As we got to England the clouds were closing in, then there was a massive thunderstorm.

We got straight onto the waiting train at Harwich, which was going to London. Both of us were really knackered. I left Sprake in London at Liverpool St Station and got the tube to St Pancras.

At St Pancras I got the first train going north. On the train home a couple of youths walked up the train, and they stated about the smell in the carriage, which was probably me!

Italy/West Germany/Mexico/USA

v

England in Mexico and the USA

Monday

Me, Spliff and Bernie left Matlock, and Bernie drove us to Golders Green. He was just dropping us off. Spliff reckoned this was best area of London for a beer! We found a nice pub with a beer garden and ended up having about five pints and a bar meal. Then we said 'bye' to Bernie and got the tube and train to Gatwick. Spliff was worried because we were late, and was worrying in case Alf would be worrying! Bernie drove home, and we had a can of lager on the train. When we met Alf he was shitting himself thinking we were going to miss the flight.

We checked in then went to the duty free, and after boarding, took off at about 4 p.m. The plane was full so Alf and me sat together, while Spliff was sat near the back. We had a meal and bought some headphones, then cracked open the duty free and started knocking it back while watching the film. We were seen by the stewardess and she got really stroppy with us, so we didn't drink anymore. When she moved down the plane, she opened an overhead locker and a bag fell on Spliff's head; she was now all apologetic to him.

Spliff was getting pissed at the back with some Yanks; he had used up a full film of photos of the inside of the plane. By the time we arrived in Baltimore we were back on the duty free and we were all pretty pissed.

At Baltimore we passed through customs without any trouble after the usual questions, 'have you got any soil on your shoes? Have you got any soil with you?' Then we got on the connecting flight to Los Angeles. This one was only half full and as it was a DC10 there was plenty of room to spread out.

I was sat near a fit American girl and we got talking, Alf was asleep and Spliff was watching the in-flight film. I seemed to be getting on all right with the girl and she put an arm around me, but I was pissed and ended up falling asleep.

I woke up on the approach to L.A. and after we landed we went and got our bags from the carousel. We decided for now to stick them in a left luggage locker, and as it was about 9 p.m. we just jumped on an airport bus to see where we ended up.

We got on a Marriott bus and the driver gave us free cans of coke. The hotel seemed a long way out, but when we got there we went to the bar. I got talking to a fit girl and she asked me to phone her the next day. After a while we went to a bar down the road. We were minding our drinks when some girls came up and asked us if we really were English. They ended up buying us a drink.

It was getting late so we decided to walk back to the Marriott and jumped on the same shuttle bus back to LAX.

There were some good benches at the airport, so we settled down for the night and apart from the cleaners coming round, we had a good night's sleep.

Tuesday

We woke up fairly early and went and had some breakfast. Then we went to see what flights were going to Mexico. All the flights seemed to be expensive, though there was a two for one deal. By lunchtime we were still at the airport and this seemed a bit crazy as the whole of L.A. was outside the airport doors.

We went and hired a car. The man behind the counter asked me what was my name, so I told him my last name. 'Ok, what's your last name' he said, and Spliff roared with laughter. We got a cheap car, a Dodge Aries, then went back for our bags and eventually we left the airport, and, after a bit of a struggle finding the way, we got into Los Angeles. We parked up and it was not a nice area. There was a Salvation Army hostel across the road and next to it, a queue of people waiting to give blood at a blood bank, as they got paid for it.

A drunk with his foot heavily bandaged, and bleeding, came up to us and asked for money, then Spliff started getting asked a load of questions by a group of blacks near the Greyhound bus station. We decide the bus was not the way to travel to Mexico and then decided to call it a day, and just go up to Santa Monica on the Santa Monica freeway.

We still hadn't sorted any flights to Mexico, and the next thing was to try and find a motel to sleep in that night. The first one we tried wanted $60 for a room, which seemed a bit steep. We decided to go for a drink at an English pub called 'The kings head' to plan what to do.

Spliff had a friend called Jane who had moved to Santa Monica some years ago, and he phoned her from the bar. Amazingly she was in, and invited us round. The address wasn't far away, so we drank up and drove round, parking up outside a nice bungalow.

Spliff rang the bell.

Jane came out, she was pleased to see Spliff and invited us all in. The bungalow was owned by Peter and his wife, friends of Jane, and they were sitting in the lounge.

After all the introductions and a couple of beers from Peter's fridge, they said they didn't mind us sleeping on the lounge floor.

We thought about this and decided to pop back to the pub to work it out. Alf was knackered, he climbed into the hire car and slept, while Spliff, Jane and me got a taxi to the King's Head.

We had a few beers, then Peter and his wife came in and joined us. They seemed like nice people, but a bit loud, and Peter's favourite word was 'horseshit'. We had a game of darts and pissed it up with them, apparently he was a small time actor, but some people in the bar recognised him from a soap he was in.

We decided to crash at Peter's and when we got back, he gave us some sleeping bags, so we could doss down in his front room.

Wednesday

Peter told us where we could sort out some flights to Mexico, so me and Alf went to a local travel agent and did this. We managed to get a two for one flight, as Spliff had decided to stay in LA.

Once we had sorted everything out, we drove back to Santa Monica and parked up on the front. We went into a bit of a dump of a pub, called 'The Dirty Duck', and had a pitcher of week beer.

For dinner we went to the local 'Burger King', then we walked down the front to look at the famous Santa Monica Boulevard.

Later we headed up to the 'Kings Head' and parked outside. Spliff came in and told us that Peter was doing a bar-be-que for us that afternoon. In the bar a really nice looking girl came over and asked if it is all right to talk to me! I said 'yes' and I could see that Spliff was getting jealous.

We got on fine and she asked me how I was getting home. I said 'the car is outside'. She replied 'don't let the cops nick you for drink driving, the niggers in the cell will fuck your sweet white ass'!

She gave me her phone number; I said I would call her when I got back from Mexico. Then it was a very careful drive back to Peters! We used his power shower to freshen up.

Peter had started the bar-b-que; we had burgers and corn on the cob, while playing table tennis in his yard, accompanied by Peter who was constantly bellowing 'horseshit'.

At night we went for a drink in the 'Kings Head'. I was still driving but was careful to keep an eye out for any coppers. We moved on to an Irish bar and met up with some of Jane's friends.

They decided to take us to a nightclub called Bentleys.

Inside there was a soft top Bentley parked in the corner of the dance floor. You could sit and have drinks inside it. The place was full of fit girls, including two at the bar near us. I got talking to them and they said they could tell I was English by the way I was drinking from a beer bottle. It turned out they were from Nottingham and Spliff knew a lot of people they did.

Jane bought us all a drink, and then disappeared with a bloke; we were pissed so got a taxi back to Peter's where he was sat drinking on the porch. Alf and me were knackered and called it a day, but Spliff had a game of table tennis with Peter. Peter kept shouting 'horseshit' every time he lost a point.

Thursday

Spliff dropped us at the airport; we were on an Aeromex flight and had got the last two seats. Spliff was returning the car after we were sure we had got on the flight, he ended up taking the wrong turn and finished up in Long Beach. He eventually found the rental place and dropped the car.

Unfortunately, due to the messing about we had been doing, there was no way we were going to make today's England game in Mexico City, but they were playing three games there in total so it was still worth going.

The flight we were on was to Guadalajara via Le Paz. I was sat next to an American who told me he used to be a pilot. He pointed out the various islands and told me to go to Porta Valletta for the best time in Mexico.

We came into land at La Paz and the plane came in at a really steep angle. The ex-pilot said 'these Mexicans don't have to pass hardly any flying standards'. When we landed, it was really hot in La Paz; we went through customs, and then onto the flight to Guadalajara.

At Guadalajara we had to book a new flight to Mexico City, but this was quite cheap. We had enough time for a beer in the bar then caught the flight. On arrival we were flying over Mexico City for ages, it was massive.

We had decided to go straight to Acapulco, so we jumped into a taxi at the airport. On the way to the bus station there was a big car crash just in front of us. We passed the England players hotel, so decide to go in for a beer. We talked to Bobby Charlton the ex-player and Bert Millichip, the FA Chairman, but the actual players were having a meal so were not about.

After we left we went down the road to the bus station and bought tickets for the bus to Acapulco. While we were waiting to board, Rich, the Pompey boys, Stuart, Jerry, Mark and Cod arrived. They were going to Acapulco as well.

We left at about 12 p.m and the driver was crazy. We were going really fast around tight mountainous roads, but I managed to doze off at the back of the bus.

During the night the bus started to slow down, as there were a load of lighted bins placed on the road. As the bus stopped a bandit got on and started demanding money from the passengers. From nowhere, the army arrived, and there was a lot of shooting outside.

The army came onto the bus and disarmed the bandit and dragged him off. As we pulled off we all just went back to sleep. After one toilet stop we arrived at Acapulco at about 6 in the morning.

Friday

Acapulco appeared to be a bit of a doss hole, especially around the bus station but we bought our return tickets and then headed towards the beach.

We sat down for breakfast at a beachside restaurant, while a couple of the lads went and found a hotel. We finished breakfast and booked into the place they had found. It wasn't bad, apart from the shower, which stunk, and the fact it had a lot of lizards in the room.

We unpacked then decided to catch up on a bit of sleep before we met the boys. We all met up later in a beach bar, Frank told us all about getting locked up with Parrot in Vienna when they went shoplifting on the way to the Romania game.

Cod told us how he jumped in a taxi to get to yesterdays match and didn't realise it was an early kick off, so he had arrived as the match finished. He ended up having a beer with the taxi driver instead.

Cod had been travelling for a while and hadn't heard about what had happened in Heysel a week earlier, where a lot of Juventus fans had died, in the match against Liverpool. He was shocked so many had died.

Cod had been out in the States for a while and had ended up in Las Vegas for a bit. While he was there he went to one of the whorehouse ranches on the outskirts and spent a £1000 on various women, which he had paid for, all on his credit card.

We went for a walk round and stopped and had the odd beer here and there. For some reason Alf had to tell Stuart, who was a staunch loyalist, as most of us were, that he was a Catholic.

I couldn't believe he told him, but Stuart seemed to be all right about it.

There were loads of nice women about, but by about 9 o'clock most of them seemed to have disappeared. A bloke called Chris Whitehouse had wound Stuart up, and they ended up having an argument. Some of the lads went to a nightclub, Jerry and Cod got off with two prostitutes, while me, Alf and the Pompey lads had a few beers then went back to the hotel.

Saturday

The next day after breakfast we all walked round to the famous Quebraga Cliffs to see if anyone was diving off. As we walked I talked to Jerry. He told me how he made a lot of money out of gambling. He told me how he could tell when people had a good or bad hand, and the various ways that he bets on the horses.

Jerry knew all the cockney slang and it was funny talking to him with all the rhymes he used.

It was a long walk and very hot, and as we walked round a headland we saw a villa which had a pool in its front garden. Stuart said he was going for a swim and just jumped in, we all did the same. The owners came out of their villa and were pretty angry with us, they called the police to come and get us out. We were cooled off by now, so we got out before they arrived and carried on walking.

We found a roadside bar, it was a bit of a shack, and went and had a few beers and a laugh about the villa owner. Someone mentioned about the bandit on the bus two nights previously, and we were all on about it for the first time, and how it could have ended badly.

We walked on to the Quebraga Cliffs and went into a restaurant that overlooked them. It was expensive but the views were good, plus there were a few divers practising their dives. It was a long way down, and the sea looked quite rough.

We walked back into town and had to pass through a slum part. A load of kids came out and were trying to sell us souvenirs and the like. We couldn't get rid of them and they followed us for a while. It was by now getting towards dusk and we went for fish and chips at a decent fish restaurant.

On the front we found a strip bar. The girls who were outside, touting for business, tried to drag us in. Some of the lads decided to go back to the hotel, while a few of us carried on drinking in the back streets.

We saw a disco and went up to have a closer look, but the local lads didn't like us, and there was a standoff. We decided it wasn't worth the bother so four of us headed back to the strip joint, the rest back to the hotel.

In the strip joint, one girl was really fit. She seemed to like me and kept coming over. By this time Alf was asleep in his chair, she told me that she finished in half an hour. When she got close, I could see that she was really fit. The area around the strip club was just a bit too dodgy, so I decided to go back to the hotel with the boys.

Sunday

At breakfast Cod couldn't believe I didn't go with the girl, with hindsight, I probably should have. We paid the hotel bill and some of the other lads had decided they were going to stay on in Acapulco and not bother with the next match.

We had a wander to a beach bar, and as we were sat on the sand, a big wave came in and soaked us all. Alf was on about going sea fishing but I didn't want to, as I would probably be sick. I went and bought some t-shirts. They cost about $2 and the woman seller thought she had done really well.

When I got back the lads hadn't gone sea fishing, so I suggested we all have a go at parasailing around the bay. We all ended up having a go, it was quite good; we got some good photos of each other taking off and landing.

A group of local lads offered to play us at football, so we played them and were beating them for a while. It got too hot, and we started to tire and loose, so we had to give up. We spent the day drinking in various bars, including the piano bar at the Acapulco plaza, which had great views of the resort.

Outside another bar was a fountain, so we had a photo of us all in it, but it was a bit too much like being a Scotland fan! We went back to the hotel and got changed then headed for the bus station and caught the midnight bus.

Cod was sat behind me, and started chatting up two girls across the aisle. Jerry had been offered some food by a family, he was sat near, and we think he had eaten all the kid's sandwiches.

As the night progressed Cod kept trying to chat up the girls and was getting more pissed. He was repeating the questions and laughing more, and generally pissing people off who were trying to sleep.

A Mexican told him to keep quiet and he replied 'fuck off, mehico' in a Spanish type accent. He then kept moaning on, for about twenty minutes, saying why should he be quiet. When we arrived in Mexico City Cod was still trying with the girls, and as they get off, he grabbed one. She was not happy about that and Cod then spent the next ten minutes apologising. From nowhere her mate came up to me and kissed me goodbye.

Monday

We jumped onto a tube at a nearby station and went to a hotel Stuart had stayed at. Across the road was a restaurant called 'Jamboun' where we had breakfast and killed some time. I appeared to have the shits; luckily the restaurant toilet was clean.

Cod told me that when it happened to him he just shoved a wad of toilet paper up his arse.

Stuart's breakfast had refry beans all over it; and he moaned to the waiter about it, but the waiter didn't know what he was on about. At about ten we paid the bill and went and checked into the Hotel Callum, which was back across the road.

Alf and me had one room; Stuart was on the next floor up. He went to his room, but walked into the wrong room, which was next to his. There was a threesome going on, on the bed, he just walked out again, and said nothing, until he told us later.

We set out for the match and caught the tube to Tasquena Square. As we travelled Rich was telling us about how he used to be a singer in working men's clubs, up north. He said that he did a lot of Gilbert o' Sullivan songs. Apparently the last time he sung Clare on stage, the audience threw a load of bottles at him.

We found a bar, it was smelly and the only beer it sold was Carta Blanca, which was tasteless. We still stopped, and had two or three beers. We moved on and it turned out, showing on the television in the next bar, which had the BBC world news on, that the National Front was being blamed for most of the trouble at Heysel.

Jerry was angry at how they are always made the scapegoat. We left the bar and made the ground in time for the national anthems. The official gate was 12000 in a stadium that held 108000.

Alf put his flag up, but the police didn't like it, as they didn't know what 'Southampton F.C.' meant. They told him to take it down. Alf was dead grumpy, as he wanted his flag to be seen on Television back home.

At least in the ground, they sold the better, Bohemia beer. A Mexican lad from the section below was shouting and yawping at us, in Spanish, so Mark climbed down and gave him a slap. The police just watched on, as he climbed back up to our section. Jerry was still angry about the National Front getting the blame for everything in Belgium. He saw the 'Daily Mail' reporter Jeff Powell, who often wrote that kind of shit, in the press box.

Jerry ran over, and gave him a kick up his backside.

As we left the ground, lots of the badge sellers were selling football club badges with swastikas and the like on them, which seemed a bit strange.

Cod, Stuart, Alf and me ended up in 'Arthur's steak bar'. Cod was buying everything he could on his credit cards, and getting the money off us, as he was going to ignore the repayment requests even if he decided to go home. At the time, he was unsure of what he was going to do.

Some Mexicans came in and thought we were players from the England squad, as we were wearing England shirts. We ended up signing quite a few autographs. Martin a lad from Chelsea came in to the restaurant and told us that Ken Bates, the Chelsea chairman, wanted to interview Chelsea fans about any National Front activity. This wound Jerry up even more.

We moved on to more bars and ended up in a nightclub. It was £5 to get in but all the drinks were free. What we didn't know, was that you were still supposed to tip the waitress, and after a while, she got really upset. When we realised why, we clubbed together and gave her some money.

I managed to knock off a German girl who was on holiday in Mexico. The rest of the boys were on the dance floor and Cod, with his peculiar way of dancing, was leading the way.

Alf ended up on the tequila and he got absolutely hammered and on the way back to the hotel, in the taxi, he was almost sick over the driver who tried to rip us off, and made out there was sick in the taxi, we told him to 'piss off'.

As we got out of the taxi, two prosses were outside the hotel. Jerry and Cod decided to go with them, Jerry did his in his room, while Cod who he was sharing with, did his on the flat rooftop of the hotel, on an oily tarpaulin he found up there.

We went to our room and I noticed you could actually see the streetlight outside, through a hole in the carpet.

Tuesday

The next day I had a shower, Alf was too ill to get out of bed. I went across the road to 'Jambonnes' and had a breakfast. Martin came in; he told us his hotel had a pool we could use so we headed off there.

We spent the afternoon in the sun by the pool. The hotel opposite Martin's was the 'Camino Real' and when Alf arrived, we went over there for a beer and got talking to Terry Venables, Mike Channon and Bobby Robson, all ex England players. We had photos taken with them, and then the odd couple from Smethwick turned up, they couldn't believe we were talking to Bobby Robson, their hero.

There was a nice older, obviously rich, Mexican woman in the bar and I ended up buying her a drink. I ended up drinking with her, while the lads went to the restaurant. They ended up ordering one soup and ten beers between them, as the food was very expensive.

It started to pour down with rain so we headed back to our hotel. Cod and Frank decided to go to a club, but the rest of us just went back to the hotel and crashed out.

Wednesday

Stuart woke us up in the morning and we went for breakfast. They put refry beans all over his again, and he got really mad. A few months later the earthquake would hit and Stuart said, he hoped the waiter that messed his breakfast up every day had bought it!

Andy and Sheffield Joe arrived, having just flown in from London. We told them the stories of what had been happening. Meanwhile Jerry and Alf started chatting up two not very nice looking Mexican girls, they ended up buying them an ice cream each. For that they both got a shag back at our hotel.

The rest of the boys and me went to Martin's hotel, The Reforma, and lazed by the pool again. A couple of the lads went off to look at the pyramids, which were near to Mexico City, but we just killed the day, and ended up back in Arthur's steak bar at night, where Alf and Jerry eventually re-joined us.

Thursday

We got up on our last day in Mexico and checked out of the hotel, but left our bags in the foyer. We found a decent bar before the game and pissed it up. It was Kerry Dixon's debut and England won 3 –1. After the game a weirdo geezer, offered us a lift back to the centre.

His car was so big 4 of us fitted in the boot, 4 in the back seat and 3 in the front. The trouble was the weight was making the bottom of the car hit the road, and the police tried to stop him.

We thought he was drugged up, as he put his foot down to go past the police, the car was too heavy to out run them, and they stopped him at the next set of traffic lights.

We all got out and carried on by foot, while he had to pay a traffic fine. He shouted at us for some money, but we told him to piss off, and we carried on walking.

We met up, back at the Reforma hotel. Andy had managed to pull a fit Mexican girl. There were a lot of Yanks about in the hotel as they were checking in, apparently they were in some kind of marching band, and one had a bad stomach. Her mate was shouting to anyone who would listen, that 'she has the craps'.

We were all on the way to LA but on different routes. Some were direct; Cod was flying to San Diego, then onwards by bus. Alf and me were flying via Guadalajara.

We went to the airport and dossed down there, for the night, as most of us had early flights. The bar at the airport was expensive, so we didn't have too much to drink.

Friday

In the morning Jerry was off first, then it was our flight, which left at 7 a.m. We got breakfast on the plane, changed at Guadalajara, then had a short flight to Loreto where we went through the customs for leaving Mexico. As we came into land, I said to Alf 'we are going to miss the runway', and we did, as we landed half on the tarmac and half on the grass.

On arrival at Los Angeles, we got straight out of the airport this time, and boarded a bus to Santa Monica. It went via U.C.L.A and seemed to take ages to get to its destination, but by dinner, we were back in the 'Kings Head' pub, eating fish and chips and having a beer.

Spliff came in at about 4 p.m. with a lad he made friends with. He was called Walter. Walter had a VW Sirocco, and, after we had had a beer he gave us all a lift back to Peters. We told Jane and Peter about our trip, and how we had got the shits. They called it Montezuma's revenge.

We each had a shower, then got changed and went out for the night. We tried a different bar, before going to the King's Head and met up with Cod, Stuart and Mark. They had hired a beat up old Ford Mustang, and were staying at a motel on the front.

We were at the bar, when an ex-pat came in saying 'a pint of Bass, a pint of Bass'; he had just driven 150 miles through the desert for this! A few more ex-pats were about and they bought us jugs of beer. We pissed it up all night then me and Alf walked home.

This involved going past a dodgy pool hall, where the locals were hanging about outside. They stared at us, and we just stared back. We were knackered and just wanted some sleep, meanwhile Spliff had gone clubbing with Walter.

Saturday

We woke up and Spliff had gone off to the Magic Mountain theme park. Alf and me were a bit pissed of about this, as we would have gone as well, if he had asked us. We went down to a shopping mall and had dinner. Alf was on about stealing some designer clothes, but I said that I was not sure if it was a good idea out there, as a lot of the shop owners and security guards had guns and big sticks.

We went back to the King's Head. Stuart had knocked off a fit girl. She had a soft top Volkswagen and was chauffeuring him about. The girl I met from before, Kelly, approached me and asked me why I hadn't phoned her. I lied to her, and said 'I had only just got back', but she didn't really buy it.

We went to the beach and met up with all the other lads. Someone bought a ball and a North v South game was arranged on the beach. I actually scored a goal, the South lost and Jerry wasn't happy about it.

Jerry and his crew, had been to Disneyland. They were all taking the piss out of it, by telling everyone to have a nice day! Stuart told us about the girl he was with. He had met her last night, and apparently he had said to her that 'he was too tired to do anything, and would screw her in the morning'.

She replied 'no way, you're going to fuck the ass of me right now'!

After the match, we went to the Dirty Duck pub. We spotted Cod in there singing Chelsea songs with a black bloke. We all took the piss out of him, but because of his money problems, and everything else that was going on in his head, he got a bit emotional and started to blub a bit!

We had some beer with him to cheer him up, and ended up playing darts.

After a while we headed for the King's Head. We walked in and showed our I.D as we always had to, then I sat at the bar. A girl called Joanie was also at the bar and I got talking to her. Alf managed to get talking to a massive Jewish girl, and as he was thin, they looked like a very odd couple.

I ended up kissing Joanie, and then, the Jewish girls mate came up to me, so I had a choice. She wasn't that bad, so I said to Joanie, to help me make up my mind, 'do you want to kidnap me'. She replied 'yes'! She was also with her friend, but at about 10 o'clock we left the bar.

Her mate was not happy as we climbed into Joanie's car. Her mate said that she came out for a drink, not to get laid. We headed off to a place called Springs; although Joanie said she lived in the valley.

On the way, we stopped at a liquor store; I bought a couple of bottles of beer and wine, and some food. After a few more miles, we arrived at the house she was staying at.

The house was Joanie's friends; she got a mattress out and set it up in the front room for us. We drank the beers then her friend went to bed, but, as Joanie and me were on the mattress, she walked through to the kitchen. I'm pretty sure she would have joined in if I had asked her.

It turned out Joanie had just come second in the California Rhythmic Gymnastics. She was a fantastic shag, and could take up incredible positions.

She gave me a blowjob and I said I would give her oral but she said to me 'hey, that would give me an embarrassment stage!' So I lay back, and let her get on with it. She was so hot; I ended up screwing her six times through the night.

Sunday

Joanie said to me that she had to go to work, and that she was sorry that she would never see me again! After kissing her goodbye, I headed towards a bus stop, not really knowing where I was, or where I was going. There were lots of Mexicans about, so I put my money in my sock for safety, and when a bus came along that said Pacific on it, I jumped on.

The bus dropped me near Peter's, and at about ten I arrived back. This was just as Spliff arrived, he had been out all night with some English girl he met, and Alf was not back yet!

It turned out that Alf had borrowed Stuart's girl's soft-top that morning and had been down to Hollywood and to the Chinese cinema with some of the Chelsea boys.

We headed to the Kings Head, Spliff had got Jane to paint a St Georges flag on his cheek, but I didn't take the piss out of him, as we needed to make up a bit.

Dave from Sheffield had just arrived, and all the travelling England fans were in the bar, plus a lot of ex-pats. We pissed it up and sang some songs, but the ex-pats didn't know any of them. We went to the ground in a mixture of lifts, and a taxi, and ended up racing each other down the freeway. The boys in the VW soft top had a St Georges flag blowing in the wind.

We got as near to the Coliseum as the traffic allowed, then paid the taxi, which worked out at $25. We walked to the ground over some railroad tracks and Jane lay down on them like in the old 'talky movies'.

We bought some tickets at the ground, but managed to steal a number of programmes. In the ground we stood away from the ex-pats. We stood behind a goal where Smoke and Colin had turned up, after flying in from London that morning.

After the anthems some of the ex-pats started singing 'flower of Scotland!' You couldn't make it up.

Cod and Mark arrived, it turned out they had been offered a job in LA and were thinking of staying on. Cod's credit card bill was so enormous, he couldn't really go home, as he only worked on the London underground and reckoned his wages wouldn't pay the interest charges.

At half time we walked to the other end of the ground. Jerry walked up to the press box and took a picture of Jeff Powell, just as the press felt they could take pictures of us.

We thought one bloke, who had started hanging around us in the bar, and now in the ground, was asking too many questions, and was a member of the press. It turned out Chris Whitehouse sold him a story later.

After the match we all got split up and I ended up catching the Pacific bus back to Santa Monica, and went into the King's Head.

I was starting to run out of money and the night was spent drinking in various local bars and having the odd game of pool.

Monday

Geoff, Paul and Rich turned up at the King's Head at dinner; they told us that they had been robbed of some money from their room. Smoke and Colin also turned up, and they had done all their money too, they were just waiting for their plane home, they had only been out for the weekend!

Some of the England players, Peter Reid, Peter Shilton and Chris Woods came down to the pub and they ended up buying us a few beers. Peter Reid seemed to be trying just a bit too hard to be liked, and was swearing, and being the big man, but they were all right on the whole.

In the afternoon we all went to the beach, had a swim, kicked a ball about and looked at the fit girls. We went for the occasional drink but everyone was broke.

At night I went back to the Kings Head and got talking to a fit American girl called Rebecca.

It turned out she was part of a band that had, had a 'number 1' record in Germany. At the end of the night, she asked me to phone her the next day. We got back to Peter's quite early, he cracked open a few beers and then started saying 'horseshit'.

Tuesday

In the morning we had a walk down to the beach and just sunbathed and listened to some girl's radio, who was sat near to us. At night there was only about four of us in the pub.

Two nice girls got talking to Spliff and me, but I was doing better than he was again. Spliff decided to try and swap the girls, and started chatting mine up, but she didn't want to know him and she got pissed up and left.

I was now with the other one, her name was Diane. Later Kelly, the girl I met earlier in the week came in, they knew each other and they started talking about me.

Kelly came up to me, and asked if I was leaving the next day. I told her that I thought I would have to, as I had a flight booked. She then asked me to go outside with her and into a park that was around the corner from the bar. She started snogging me. She was really pretty, but had very small tits. I ended up shagging her from behind so I could play with her nipples while she arched her back into me. Afterwards I put her knickers in my shorts' pocket, and we went back into the bar.

Kelly sat opposite me as we drank, and her bare fanny was rubbing against my bare knee. She only had a short dress on and it must have been fairly obvious what she was doing, to anyone who cared to look over. I finished my drink and then we went outside and I screwed her again, this time behind the pub down an alley.

She asked me to stay with her, she told me that she had a big house in L.A. and a flat in New York, plus it was her Porsche outside.

I had to make my mind up, either stay with her, with no money, or fly home the next day. I shit out and told her I was going home. She walked to her car and hitched up her dress and said 'this is what you will be missing'. Then she got in her Porsche and drove off.

I went back into the pub and Spliff said he didn't believe I had shagged her. Luckily I still had her knickers, so I took them out of my pocket, and shoved them in his face.

Walter then turned up and gave us a lift back to Peter's. We had earlier bought Peter a bottle of vodka for letting us stay at his house, and when we got back, we had a drink with him. I then went to sleep but Spliff played table tennis with him, drinking the vodka. All you could hear, was the ball bouncing on the table, and the word 'horseshit' being bellowed out.

Wednesday

We woke up early and I was thinking about phoning Kelly, but then decided, what was the point. Peter gave us a lift to LAX, the airport, and we sat and had breakfast and watched the news on the local TV station. The news included a hi-jacking in Beirut, and a bomb at Munich airport!

We boarded the plane to Baltimore and watched the film and dozed.

At Baltimore we changed planes and after a beer and a sandwich at the airport, plus going through the customs, we cracked open the duty free and got pissed on the way home. The stewardesses were not happy, but they just refused to sell us any more drink, not realising we had our own.

We landed at London and I was so pissed I thought it was still in Baltimore. We said bye to Alf, then Spliff and me got the train home.

Israel v England

1986

Duggie arrived in Matlock and stayed at my house, that night we went up to the 'Moon pub' for a few beers.

Tuesday

We got to the station and just missed our train. We had to wait for an hour and then got the next one. We had to get straight across London; we grabbed a couple of cans of beer at Victoria, then got the first train to Gatwick.

At the airport, we met up with Smoke, Sprake, Dave, Titch and Paul and went and checked in our bags. A bloke there asked us if we would carry his bag through customs, I told him to 'piss off'. The customs people asked us, if he had asked us to carry his bag, and we said 'yes'. They then told us that they were going to arrest him.

We got to the bar and I realised I had left some cans of ale in my bag; I said I hoped that they wouldn't explode with the pressure on the plane. In the bar there was an oversized, about twice as normal, settee. We said it was Big Paul's armchair. We had a few beers, and were just about to order another round, when we heard our names being called out on the tanoy for last boarding. We had to run down the moving walkways to the gate, which was a long way away, finally coming to a skidding stop at the Dan Air check in.

Smoke, Duggie and me sat in a row of three seats, Duggie's seat was broken and would only stay vertically up. When the person in front reclined theirs, it meant he had hardly any room at all.

We started on our duty free, and noted that there were a few other England boys on the flight including Jerry. I mentioned to Smoke that I was going to pack in following England when I got to 109 caps. This was one more than the record appearance at the time, set by Bobby Charlton, and he had a right go at me, saying he would never pack in following England.

People were asking us to be quiet on the plane, and even Dave, who hadn't travelled with us before, complained to Sprake because we were so drunk; Sprake said to him that 'we would be ok'.

I was so pissed that I couldn't really remember going through customs, but we got our bags from the carousel, and checked that the cans were all right.

Like a fool, Duggie had also put his wallet in his bag, and of course this was now missing. His face was a picture as he realised he had no money for the whole trip. He had to go to the police station at the airport, to report the loss, and we waited for an hour for him to re-appear.

Duggie came back, he was well pissed off, but there was nothing that he or the police could do. We went and got a taxi and it took us to a hostel, where we booked in for the night, four to a room. We dumped our bags and went out to some of the local bars. Smoke and me ended up in a disco bar and as it was hot inside, so he took his jacket off and left it on the back of a seat.

We got talking to some Yanks at the bar, and when we went to leave, Smoke's jacket was missing, unfortunately it had his wallet, passport and all his money in the inside pocket as well!

We headed back to the hostel, but on the way we saw a police station. Smoke went in and reported his coat as missing. By now it was past two in the morning, and the curfew on the hostel was 1 a.m.

We left the police station and found a block of flats that looked like the one our hostel was in. We were sure we were correct, even though we couldn't see a sign for the hostel. We went up to the 5th floor and started banging on the door, so that the hostel night porter would let us in.

'What do you want' said an Israeli voice.

'Open the door and let us in' we replied.

'This is not your hotel' the Israeli said. We realised at this point that we were in the wrong block of flats and completely lost.

We went back to the police station and asked if we could sleep there for the night, but the coppers said 'no', had a look at our hostel card and phoned us a taxi.

We arrived at the hostel really late, and again kicked the door, until, eventually, the owner opened it up.

The owner said he wanted some more money from me, for waking him up, so I gave him some; unfortunately I only had a large denomination note. The owner said that he had no change and would give it to me in the morning.

There were some Germans in the next room to us, and they were shushing us, but we just got into our beds and explained to Sprake what had happened and then went to sleep.

Wednesday

The next morning the Germans were up at dawn and making a racket as they prepared their rucksacks for the day. They wanted us to be quiet the previous night, but they didn't give a shit now. We told them to be quiet; one said something back to me, so I got out of bed and hit him. They were a bit quieter after that.

Much later on we got up. Smoke had lost his passport; Duggie had still got a face like a smacked arse. They both went off to the Embassy to report what had happened and as Duggie walked out he said loudly, 'so this is bleeding Palestine, where's Jesus now we need him'.

The rest of us went for a walk down on the sea front. We were singing 'we can play the P.L.O' to the tune 'I can play the piano', as we were walking along. Every so often we would ask one of the locals where things were, and point in a Nazi salute manner, to the things in question.

Sprake and me went to a bar and bumped into a lad we knew from other trips called Lloyd. We had a few drinks and after a while Smoke and Duggie came in and joined us. After a few more drinks we went to the players' hotel, The Holiday Inn, to see if there were any spare tickets available.

The bar staff at the 'Holiday Inn' wouldn't serve us, as it was reserved solely for the England squad and officials, plus residents. Bobby Robson was sat in a corner of the bar, so I said to the barman 'its all right Bobby Robson knows me' and pointed at him. He replied that he didn't know me at all, and I said, 'Bobby, what about the photos we had together in Brazil and Mexico?'

Don Howe, who was with Robson, just shook his head and Robson stormed off. Amazingly Bert millichip, the FA Chairman, came over and was quite polite and explained that it was for security reasons that we were not allowed in. We had a chat for a while then left them to it.

Smoke had to go to the police station, with his filled in forms and photo, to get an official theft form. We jumped into a taxi and went to the local station. When we arrived it was the wrong police station, so we refused to pay the taxi. It wasn't really the taxi driver's fault, but Smoke was adamant that we weren't paying.

It turned out the taxi drivers from the hotel then refused to take any English people anywhere after this, including Bert Millichip and the England officials!

We got into another taxi, dropped Smoke at the right police station and then headed towards the beach area, where we got a pizza and some more beer.

Later we managed to get a minibus taxi to the ground, and we were dropped off at a shopping centre nearby, with about an hour to go until kick off. In a bar, in the centre were some of the boys we knew.

These included Stuart, an Arsenal lad, and a lad we called 'free Joe Pierce' as he had a sheet with that written on it. He was a youth from Birmingham, and he wanted to get the sheet on the fence at the ground so it would be seen on TV,

After a short while Stu from Bexhill and Lloyd also came into the bar. We ordered jugs of ale and pissed it up.

We got into the ground in time for the anthems and loads of the English fans were doing 'sieg heils'. The 'free Joe Pierce NF' sheet was on the fence, but the cops ripped it down. As they did so, they were bombarded by half empty cans, from the England boys.

At half time we walked to another section of the ground and nearly got stuck as we scrambled under a fence. We were seen on TV, whenever the ball came down our end, as this part of the ground was pretty empty.

After the game, some lads who are living on a kibbutz in Israel, offered us a lift into Tel Aviv, they took us to a bar where it turned out, Sprake knew the owners daughter, as they had gone to school together.

We had some free beers, courtesy of the kibbutz lads and the bar owner, then bought some back and ended up playing poker dice for most of the night.

After a while Sprake and I went to another bar and ordered food and beer. We decided to do a runner, and sneakily made our exit. Some other lads, who were in the bar, told us the next day, it was dead obvious what we were doing, but the bar staff just ignored us.

We ran out of the door of the bar, but as we ran there was a pelican crossing right outside the bar, and the man was on red for 'don't walk'. We waited outside the bar, then, when it turned green we ran off across the road. Apparently the barman just watched us and must have thought we were a right couple of wankers.

Somehow we ended up in a bar where there was a kind of fashion show going on. If you clapped loudly, after each girl appeared, we were told you got a free beer. The models were gorgeous, and as each one came down the catwalk, Sprake and me started cheering and yawping. We were given quite a few free beers, and it turned out to be a really good night.

The bar closed and we walked down the street. We came across some scousers who had just been kicked out of a nightclub. They were threatening the bouncers, and one of them picked up a scaffolding plank, from some road works, and hurled it through the nightclub window.

We all ran off but Sprake tripped up, he went full length along the pavement, the scousers carried on running and he ended up with some of their footprints on his back.

I helped him up, and we ran round the corner and out of sight. When we arrived at the hostel, it was locked again and we ended up kicking the door again.

The owner was really pissed off this time, I asked him for my change from the night before. He said he had given it to me. I went to bed and decided to confront him later.

Thursday

In the morning the owner was not about. We packed our bags and left. I told the cleaner, who happened to be in our room, to tell the owner that he was a wanker. We met up with Stu from Bexhill, and walked to the bus station, getting some soft drinks on the way.

There were loads of army blokes at the station and they kept accidentally banging our legs with their guns as they walked past. We formed a queue, but when the bus arrived, it was everyman for himself as everyone tried to get on it.

Stu from Bexhill knew the time of every bus, where they stopped, when the banks opened, in fact loads of useless information and he was doing our heads in by trying to tell us everything.

We arrived in Jerusalem at 14:35 as Stu had predicted. He and Lloyd were doing their own stuff, so we parted company and agreed to see each other later in the year, in Mexico, at the World Cup.

A tout was at the bus station dishing out hotel cards to any tourists passing by. He suggested the King George V hostel was good, so we piled into his minibus, which he had parked up outside the station, to have a look at it.

It wasn't good, in fact it was a glorified doss hole, but we were only staying one night so we signed in and discovered that there were a lot of hippy types in most of the rooms.

Apparently someone was actually living under a plastic sheet on the balcony of our room, the hostel owner said to us 'don't worry about him he's living on the cheap'!

On closer inspection he had slung a hammock across the balcony and was lying in it.

Dave, by now, had the shits, so I gave him a diahorea tablet, which seemed to help him.

We then headed out to have a look around Jerusalem. We headed towards the old city and on the way stopped for a coffee and a roll. After this we went through the old town wall gate and entered into a busy market.

We walked towards the dome of the rock and the local stallholders were shouting 'fish and chips' as they realised we were English. They were trying to make us buy things.

As we walked past the St.George memorial a local Arab youth came running down an alley. He had a knife sticking out of his back and was covered in blood.

We ended up buying some t-shirts, post cards and a plate for Sprake's mum. He usually bought a plate for her, when we went on a trip, and she had them all on her living room wall.

We enjoyed the haggling and did the usual 'Life of Brian bit', where we said to the market stall owner, 'how much, a Shekel for my life story, I'll give you a Denarii', then started going up instead of haggling the price down, and said things like 'you're taking the shirt of my back'.

We finally arrived at the Wailing Wall and the Dome of the Rock. You were not supposed to take photos, but we took a couple without anyone noticing. It was a crazy sight as all these black-suited, ringlet haired blokes, were nodding at the wall. Apparently the orthodox ones, with the Billy goat type side burns, only washed themselves on a Saturday.

We looked at the Mount of Olives, and then walked around the city wall. All the orange trees were loaded with oranges, though we didn't try any of them. By now, even though it was February, it was really nice and warm.

An Arab was leading a camel along the road and we offered him some shekels for a ride. He saw a good deal and took us up and down the road, Sprake first, then Dave who had bought a Lawrence of Arabia tea towel headscarf and looked the part, then me.

As we rode the camel we were all singing the Lawrence of Arabia music.

Afterwards we went to a restaurant and had lunch. It was decided we would have to do another runner, as two of us had had all their money stolen. We were all feeling the pinch, as we were helping out with their costs as well as our own.

As we got up and started to run down the street, the waiter managed to rugby tackle and then grab hold of Tich, so we had to go back and pay for everything.

We wandered back to the hostel, but it was no place to hang around, so went out on the piss where we bumped into some Blackburn lads. We had a good drinking session with them, and luckily for him, Dave's shits appeared to have dried up.

The bar shut and we went back to the hostel. We had all settled down for the night in our communal dormitory, when the bloke sleeping on our balcony, decided to cook himself some food at three in the morning, clattering saucepans about.

Friday

We made a decision to travel to Eilat, rather than going to Jericho. According to the hostel owner, everything in Jerusalem shut by mid-day on a Friday, so we headed for the bus station, and bought tickets from 'The Egg head Bus Company's' counter, and got on the next bus going to Eilat.

On leaving the hostel, Duggie wrote graffiti on the bedroom wall. It read 'Hull City mental mentals' with a swastika under it! He was now singing 'Oh West Hull is wonderful' and wouldn't have it, when

I told him that what he was singing was a version of a Manchester United song.

The bus was going to Eilat via Masada. We had bought some bread and drinks for the trip. We were sat at the back of the coach, and somehow, I managed to lose my camera on the bus, it must have slipped under a seat. The coach climbed up a steep hill out of Jerusalem, then headed down towards the Dead Sea.

At Masada, there were a couple of hotels, along the shore of the Dead Sea. They all had swimming facilities in the sea, the sea being roped off, and the beach was full of sun loungers, also there was showers were on the beach. It would have been nice to have got off, and have a bathe, but Stu from Bexhill wasn't with us, so we didn't know when the next bus was!

The coach climbed up to Masada, then, after picking up some more passengers, turned round and we headed towards Eilat, after passing the cable car station that takes tourists to the archaeological site at the top of the monument.

The bus stopped after another hour or so, for a toilet break. There was a café, and tourist shop at a snake farm, which was by the bus stop. The farm also had ostriches in a field, it was noted again, how Sprake's legs were like an ostriches. We were all laughing at Sprake and he ended up 'talking' to the ostriches.

We got a drink from the bar, then had a game of patonc with larger stones by the grass verge. As we were playing, and looking for decent size stones to throw, Dave spotted a scorpion under a rock, we could have easily have got stung.

When we reached Eilat bus station, there were the usual touts saying which hostel was best. The one we chose took us in a mini bus and we all ended sharing one big room. This hostel was a lot cleaner than the last couple we had used.

There were some fit Danish girls in the next room. We said 'hello' to them, then went out on the piss. We went to a decent restaurant, and had a really good steak. The night was spent going from pub to pub, then back to the hostel.

Saturday

We got up late and made our own breakfast of omelettes and coffee, in the communal kitchen. I went for a shower, and then we headed for the beach. We saw some of the pubs, where we were last night, and got our bearings.

Dave pointed out a particular bar, that he was drinking in last night, and he said that it had a lot of girls in it.

We spent the day sunbathing, going in the sea, and looking at the women, a lot of who were topless. Sprake, Smoke and me decided to go for a walk later in the afternoon, and ended up in a bar where the barmaid was from Henley. When we asked her, her dad apparently did have a yacht and a Porsche!

We had a few drinks and I paid for this on my visa card, as we had also decided to have a small meal. We then walked along the coast to the underwater aquarium via a couple of bars on the way. It was very good and had lots of sharks and turtles.

The aquarium was by the border with Egypt so Sprake and me decided to hop across. Smoke had to wait as he had no passport, we paid £8 for a visa at the border, and once past the customs we were into 'no man's land' between Israel and Egypt.

A jeep appeared, with a girl driving it, and gave us a lift to the Egypt customs about half a mile away and we went through. They asked us how long we were staying in Egypt and we said about half an hour. We had to change some money but there was a bar down the road, so we went and spent it on beer.

The customs weren't too happy when we turned up, to go back to Israel, and asked lots of questions, plus they made us wait while they went for a prayer. We eventually got through and the girl in the jeep gave us a lift to the Israeli customs. She thought it was dead funny what we were doing, but we were quite pleased with our new stamps in our passports. These were quite impressive, with proper postage stamps used.

We met up with Smoke and then got the last of the sun on the beach, with the rest of the boys.

At night we had a rest then went out on the beer. We split up, Sprake, me, Gary and Tich ended up in posh bars showing videos or American wrestling. In one we ordered a meal and did a runner, this time Gary was caught by a waiter, but he managed to struggle free, and then managed to lose the waiter in the shopping complex.

Sprake and me ended up in a nice bar that had a load of women in it. We were having a good time and decided we would stay up to see the dawn over the red sea. Unfortunately the bar shut at 4 a.m and the dawn wasn't till 4:30 so we went back to the hostel and crashed out.

Sunday

We had a long lie in, then made breakfast. We paid the hostel bill, then went and bought bus tickets to Tel Aviv. In the afternoon we went for a drink in the 'Red Lion pub'.

I got talking to a girl called Linda in the bar. She was a nurse from Glasgow.

She asked me to take her down to the beach for sex. I was thinking about it, and it seemed like a good idea, and we talked about it for ages. In the end I said to her that I didn't want to get sand round my dick and it to turn into what looked like a cauliflower.

We decided that as a compromise, we would go back to her room where we had sex before my bus went.

We ended up walking to the bus station afterwards, and were approached by a druggie English bloke, who apparently has stabbed someone, and was on the run. We gave him a wide birth and ignored him as he pestered us for money, I made sure Linda was all right and on her way back to the hotel, and then told him to 'fuck off'. I got on the overnight bus, the lads were already on it with my bag, and then we tried to sleep on the journey to Tel Aviv.

Monday

We woke up as we arrived in Tel Aviv at about 5am. We got our bags then went and sat in a café at the bus station until it warmed up a bit. We then walked to the beach and got our flags out and had a bit of sleep under them until about 9 a.m.

We had been told about a good hostel to stay at in Tel Aviv, while we were in Eilat, so we went and found it. After cramming into a tiny lift, and going up to the top floor we checked in.

The hostel was clean, with really good views over the city. The wife of the bloke who owned the hostel appeared, she was a right flirty tart who definitely wanted it.

We had a coffee then headed for the beach. We took a large St Georges flag which had 'Hull City' written on it to lie on. After a while sunbathing, we decided to have a walk to find a beer, only to come across the Argentine Embassy.

We unfurled the St Georges flag and sang 'Galtierris a wanker', 'what's it like to lose a war' and 'The Falklands are ours'. The Argies appeared at the windows and there was lots of pointing and some shouts from them.

We wandered back to the hostel after a couple of beers, then got changed, we had some food and a few beers in one bar and then ended up at the fashion show bar again. This night we ended up with a 'playboy group of girls' at our table, and again the table making the most noise clapping, got the free booze. We ended up getting a few bottles of wine.

A table of Sailors by the bar, on shore leave from a US Navy ship, took up the challenge, and they won a bottle of wine, so when the next girls came on we really made a noise. It was dead funny; we won the last bottle of wine. The girls were really fit too. At the end of the night we staggered back to the hostel.

Tuesday

On our last day we had a lie in before paying the bill at the hostel. We decided to have a look round the old Muslim quarter of Jaffa. We ended up having shish kebabs for dinner, with loads of salad, which Sprake managed to get for free.

On the bus to the airport we bumped into Jerry, he was with a girl he had met there. For some reason Dave then told us a story about when he went to a Wham concert in Bournemouth with his mate. They were about the only blokes in the place, with a lot of sexually excited teenagers. He reckoned you couldn't fail.

At the check in, and customs, the security was really tight. An Australian lad at the front of the queue was not happy about his bag being emptied; he said 'watch out for those socks, they're loaded'. He was marched away.

Smoke was panicking, as he had now picked up a new passport and flight tickets, but the height in the passport stated he was five foot tall, when he was actually six foot. He was allowed through without too many problems, and we got on the plane.

On the plane an old Jew just wouldn't sit down, and kept messing about in his bag in the overhead bin, even when the plane was taxiing, he stood up again, and he tried to open the overhead bin to get his bag again.

We all shouted at him to sit down, and the stewardess in the end forced him to.

As soon as we touched down in London he was back up looking in the overhead locker as the plane was coming to a stop.

Sprake shouted at him to 'sit down you fucking Yid' a woman who was with him turned and said to us 'He's not a Yid, he is British'. Duggie told her not to be so stupid.

As we got off the plane, we were still wearing our shorts; it was cold and trying to snow. We all did a funny walk into the terminal, and a copper said loudly that we were all bloody stupid.

It was quite late when we eventually got to London, and the last train north had left. Duggie and I had to kill the night by sitting in the Burger King at Kings Cross. Our first train home was at 6 am. I finally arrived home at about 11 o'clock in the morning.

Russia v England
1986

Monday

A lot of the Chelsea boys were arrested by a police operation, a month before the match, so we were struggling to get a Russian Visa, as all fans were under suspicion. We decide to travel with 'Visa Travel', as this was a kind of, official travel agent, and they sorted out all the paperwork.

We were going to stay at a friend's house the night before we flew, but most of the lads we knew, that hadn't been not locked up, didn't want to bring any more attention to themselves.

People like Andy, were saying that they wouldn't even be able to watch game on TV, because he was so sickened that he couldn't go. We decided to sleep at Heathrow as we had an early flight. We all travelled down the night before and managed to get our heads down for three hours sleep or so, in the departure lounge.

Tuesday

We went for breakfast and a beer in the bar. Meanwhile the other lads who had also managed to go to Russia, the same way as us, were now arriving at the airport.

Rich turned up, he remarked about how many Pakistanis were working at the airport. Heathrow had a suggestion box, on how things could be improved, so he filled in loads of the suggestions slips, proposing that they stopped employing so many Pakistanis.

After breakfast we went to the correct terminal and met up with Reg, the leader of the trip, and the rest of the party. He gave us our tickets and group visa. I managed to get the visa photocopied on the way through customs, to keep as a momento. We went and bought our duty free then boarded the Aeroflot plane.

Ken Bailey was in the departure lounge; he said to me 'you're looking well'. All the lads were ripping the piss out of me for that one.

We took off, and on the plane were given a book of do's and don'ts in Moscow, but I still took a photo as we landed.

That was one of the don'ts.

We hit a big bump on landing, then bounced and landed again with a big bang. Outside the plane it was very bleak. It was 7.20 a.m. in Russian time.

We Got off the plane and went through customs. The long queue took ages, but finally our party was through, except a York fan.

'Yorkie' kept making the machine bleep. The customs kept checking his bags; he finally rolled up his trousers to reveal that he had got two metal legs. It was the first time I had seen him, but apparently he had lots of fun doing this wherever he went. The customs and coppers were knocking on his legs, and then they let him through.

Some people in our group had massive suitcases with them, but eventually they all got through, and the 'in-tourist rep' met us and asked us to stand by a pillar.

Some of the travelling party, Ken Bailey and his friends, were going straight to Tbilisi. People were wandering around, not sure of what was happening. Finally we got out of the airport and onto a bus.

We then had to wait as two people were missing. It turned out they had gone for a meal with the reporter Brian Glanville, and the England mascot Ken Bailey.

We were all shouting to get the bus going, as we wanted to see Moscow. We waited for a further half an hour, then got going. As we entered into Moscow city, we passed a monument that was signifying the furthest the Nazis got in World War 2.

Duggie celebrated, as it was a landmark he had wanted to see. Moscow was very grey and drab; there were loads of blocks of flats, muddy roads and dirty melted snow was piled up by the side of the roads. Most of the cars we saw were old-fashioned Lada types, or their Russian equivalents.

After a while we arrived at the 'Hotel Cosmos'. It was opposite the space monument and park. Our rep was called Igor; he introduced himself on the bus, PA, by saying. 'Hello my name is Igor', to which, we at back of bus chanted 'Igor, Igor, Igor'.

He said 'we will all meet under the broken bicycle (a sculpture) in the foyer after we have checked in to the rooms'.

Sprake and me shared a room on the 19th floor. We all said 'fuck Igor' and agreed to meet for dinner in about an hour. I switched the TV on, in the room, and got an electric shock!

As we were so high up we had a good view of Moscow from the room. We each had a quick shower then got the lift downstairs. In the foyer I changed some money and made sure I kept the receipt, as we were told to. It turned out the hotel only took 'hard currency' rather than roubles, so this was a bit of a waste of money.

Apparently the local Russians were not allowed into the hotel. Sprake walked across the foyer and shouted 'bottles'. This was a thing we occasionally shouted. It was after Chunny, the Brighton fan, had been arrested in Helsinki, with a knife on him. We heard him pleading with the coppers that it was for opening bottles, 'BOTTLES' he kept shouting.

We had a beer, then went into the restaurant and had a meal that was not too good at all. The whole of our party sat together; amongst them was Rich, Smoke, Pompey, some older fans and the odd couple.

After dinner me, Sprake, Smoke, and Duggie went out of the hotel and down the escalators into the underground. The boys were asking everyone 'where's this Lenin bloke?' The escalators were really steep and long, and while we rode them, all the locals were looking at us.

Everyone seemed to be wearing jeans. We jumped on a tube train and travelled for a while, then, we got an escalator to the ground level and looked for a bar. As we had just got off at a random stop, finding a bar was a long shot, so we headed back to the hotel.

Sprake worked out the Cyrillic alphabet, but it still took us a long while to reach the hotel.

Lots of the girls on the tube were fit, and one in particular kept staring at me.

At the hotel we drank Heineken in the foyer bar, and then decided to go to the disco that was in the hotel basement. We had to buy tickets to get in. once inside Duggie was soon dancing with a bird, which surprised us. Sprake and me were getting pissed at the bar with the Pompey lads.

Sprake said to me 'do you fancy dancing with those two girls', first Duggie then Sprake dancing, I wasn't sure what was going on. The girls in question were as fit as fuck.

I said to Sprake 'yes if you ask them'

Amazingly, he did, and even more amazingly they said 'yes'. We had a dance with them! I decided to save my embarrassment and did the 'Cod dance', copying his style of dancing from when we where in

Mexico, where he just doesn't really give a fuck.

After the dance we sat down with the girls. They were fantastically fit, and I bought them a drink. The girl I was talking to could speak good English, it turned out she was a Russian prostitute, no wonder she said yes to a dance.

I decided against shagging her, as it was now nearly 4 a.m and we had got to be up at 5 a.m for the flight to Tbilisi. We decided to go up to our room, Dave from Sheffield was with us, and he was completely pissed up.

Along with Dave, was this other lad, who had travelled with his dad. He turned out to be a right arsehole, and Dave threatened him. He kept apologising, so Dave threatened him again, so he fucked off, as did Dave, pissed out of his head.

The next minute Smoke came into our room. He was pissed up, and for some reason launched the table lamp out of the bedroom window. It smashed on the drive nineteen stories below. We switched the light off, so it was less noticeable where the missile had come from; meanwhile Smoke just kept on drinking.

Wednesday

At 5 a.m the alarm went off, we got our stuff together, and went down to the bicycle sculpture in the main reception. The prostitutes we were dancing with, were now sitting in the foyer, and we said we would see them when we came back.

We all had a drink from some cans of Tartan bitter I had packed with me, before I set off from England.

The bus arrived outside the hotel and we all piled on. There was no sign off Dave from Sheffield, and it turned out that he had been arrested for sleeping in the corridor, and he was being held by the local police.

They questioned him for about two hours, then released him, but by then he had missed the plane to Tbilisi. As we left the hotel, we got talking to one of the few Chelsea fans who had managed to make the trip, he was 'Freddie the case', who we had met in Hungary, and his dead fat Chelsea mate.

We arrived at the airport and soon we were boarding the plane. We went through check-in quite easily, as there wasn't any customs formalities. We just walked across the tarmac in ones and twos.

This was a different airport to the one we landed at from London. It was only about half an hour away from the hotel. We sat in the middle of the plane, the seats were broken, the curtains filthy, and it was quite cramped.

We Took off. Then flew over some mountains and then had an uneventful flight to Tbilisi. As we touched down, all the overhead lockers flew open, and any seats without anyone sitting in them tipped forward.

A new guide met us at the airport, and after getting on another coach, we were taken to the hotel, we were to stay at.

At the Hotel Cosmos they had prepacked breakfast, but Sprake had thrown it out of the window, at the same time as Smoke had thrown out our table lamp, so I was quite hungry by now.

We booked into the hotel, it was not quite as good as the Cosmos, but it was still all right. We were told to meet in the dining room. After putting our bags in our room, we met up and the hotel had laid on sheesh kebabs for lunch. They were quite nice, and as a bonus, in this part of the USSR, they produced their own wine, so we had a bottle of wine each with the meal.

After lunch, we were told what time we had to meet to go to the match, as we had a bit of time to kill, we decided to go for a walk. We went to the England players' hotel but nobody was about, but there happened to be a genuine Georgian bar around the corner.

We bumped into Yorkie, the lad with the metal legs, in the bar. He told us how the odd couple had managed to get all the autographs of the Russian team. Apparently they were all neatly organised in a scrapbook alongside a picture of each player.

The bar was full, we went up to the counter and everyone was staring at us. We got a pint of brown, local beer and went and stood by a little table in the corner.

The place stunk of piss, and the beer tasted awful. Rich, who was wearing his garishly stripy shirt and flamengo hat, this really didn't blend in with the black leather coats all the Russians were wearing, said he could drink four pints of the beer, one after the other, for £10.

He set about the task and necked the first two straight down, the third was a bit more of a struggle and on the fourth he drank half, then threw up, to much cheering from us and the Russians.

We then went back to our hotel room and Sprake and me finished the tartan beers, grabbed Sprake's Southampton flag, and met outside the hotel for the bus that took us to the stadium.

As usual we were trying to confuse the rep by asking 'is this the way to the pet show', or 'where is the flower show, no we don't want to go to football'.

At the ground Duggie and Dave went straight in to put their flags up so they would be seen on TV. One youth, who was also on the trip, reckoned he was part of column 88, and was going to put up a banner up. We decided that he was a twat.

There was obviously still no sign of Sheffield Dave, we presumed he must have tried to stay at the hotel in Moscow, and would be watching the match on a TV, in a hotel bar.

Rich and me went looking for a bar with the Pompey lads. We walked around the ground, and ended up back at the bus, which was parked under stadium. There were only soft drinks available at the kiosks, but we did see a Russian selling a box of programmes. An English lad grabbed about half of them, for himself, as they were a small thin programme. We did manage to get a few ourselves, but the lad who bought half the box, wouldn't give any to other England fans, as he was selling them when he got home, what a wanker!

The locals were all looking at us, but Rich swapped some badges with some of them and arranged to meet a youth who had loads of badges later at the hotel.

We went into the ground and saw Duggie and Dave's flags on the other side of the stadium; so we walked around the concourse to meet them. There were a few English, on the other side of the stadium, but no one we knew, or wanted to sit with, as they were all the strange group of older fans who had transferred straight to Tbilisi, at Moscow.

When we met the lads, Sprake had to watch the match by looking through his camera. This was because Dave had a flag with Basingstoke on it, and Sprake was on the sick. He was seen very clearly on TV, and the local paper back home, 'The Basingstoke Times' did a spread on it, about a group of England fans going to Georgia, USSR, not USA, to watch the team.

When Sprake got back to work, his foreman asked him, 'are you feeling better Sprake? Was it Russian flu!'

At one England corner in the first half, Dave shouted at the England

Midfield player, Glen Hoddle, to line the ball up with his nose. This was a reference to the fact that Hoddle played for the Jewish owned side Tottenham.

An egg landed near to us, the youth who threw it, was thrown out by the local police snatch squad. The whole of that part of the crowd then started throwing eggs and concrete at us. The local plod steamed into them.

The crowd was quiet, apart from when Russia was on the attack, which was when they started whistling, which seemed a bit back to front to us.

The USSR got a penalty and Peter Shilton, the England goalkeeper, saved it and we went mad. Now the whole stand was staring at us.

More missiles rained down on us, and the coppers dragged more youths out, and then surrounded us for our own protection.

As usual we got one local, who was trying to better himself, and practise his English, asking us lots of questions. I told him to 'piss off', but he still persisted and asked more questions, for about another five minutes. I just ignored him, and eventually he went away.

Lots of young kids were sitting near us, because they hadn't seen people like us before, and still the rocks came down at us. Then England scored and we went mad again. We sang the National Anthem and The Sash.

At the end of the game we were surrounded by about 500 youths, but the police put a cordon of themselves, in a semi circle, round us and we climbed onto the pitch side. We then walked around the perimeter of the pitch, to where our exit was.

The other England fans were also getting a bit of trouble, but we all got out without any major injuries, and onto the waiting bus. This was still sheltered, by being parked under the stadium.

Loads of local youths gathered around the bus and it looked like they were going to attack it. Someone threw an England hat out of the window and they started fighting for it. There was loads of fighting for the hat, so I dangled a scarf out of the window then pulled it back in at the last minute. There were still loads of little fights going on, and I hadn't help to calm the situation. Someone threw a rock at the window and it cracked. The bus then pulled out of the stadium area under a hail of stones.

We got back to the hotel; the bus wasn't to badly damaged, got changed and went down to the hotel bar. Then a Russian came and presented us with a pennant and a glass of vodka. He was a very nice man!

We went to the bar and had a few beers and as the bar seemed to be quite good, we didn't bother going to England players' hotel.

We sat down and ordered a few bottles of wine. There was a wanker from Southend, who was wearing England shorts, in the bar and he was dancing and showing off.

Sheffield Dave then turned up, he had managed to get his own flight and a taxi to the ground, and he said that he saw the game.

At the end of the night I went to bed knackered, but before that, the youth from earlier outside the ground turned up with badges to swap with Rich.

Dave swapped a Chelsea shirt with the badge seller, because his own dad had got a massive badge collection, mostly Nazi WW2, and the lad had some badges that Dave reckoned were dead rare. We still had a bit of a go at him for swapping his Chelsea shirt though.

Thursday

We got up late for that mornings excursion, so we didn't bother with it. We couldn't get any food, so we had to wait until dinner. Apparently the Southend twat had fallen and injured his leg, at least that should of stopped him dancing again. In the afternoon we went on a trip to a monastery and the old city of Tbilisi. A long bus ride took us past a lake, to the monastery. The rep tried to be our guide, but we just walked in and took some photos. All of us were feeling dodgy.

We went down to the old church in the local village and bought some wine at a stall, and got rid of the roubles we had exchanged earlier. There were lots of gypsies in the church. Duggie ran up, and pretended to kick in a window, and the rector gave him a really dirty look.

It was quite warm so we went for a walk, then after a while, got the bus back to Tbilisi and went for tea, back at the hotel.

After tea we went to the hotel bar, then downstairs to the nightclub. We were all drinking heavily apart from Dave, who only came down for an hour.

Two Finish girls, who were also staying at the hotel, asked Sprake and me for a dance, so we had a slowish one with them, which was quite embarrassing.

All the beer got sold out, so we just drank the wine. The Southend twat was hobbling about, but now he was with a bird.

Duggie said he couldn't stand red wine, but we told him to drink. Freddie's mate then got slagged off for being a Catholic; he got pretty mad about it. Duggie started getting really pissed, as we drank more and more wine, he eventually fell asleep. I went and got my camera, then we put lighted cigarettes in his ear, and up his nose and took photos, as he was still drunkenly asleep. Yorkie was now talking to us, and we were having a great time.

It turned out that Sheffield Dave had also been fined for being drunk in Moscow.

We asked the odd couple, who were still in love with Bobby Robson, if they would have kinky threesome with him. This did not go down well, and they went off to their room in a right huff.

The Southend twat had managed to sell a pair of jeans, but he had run out of money again, so as he had no roubles left. We sold him 5 roubles for a pound.

Duggie then threw up, we took photos of it, and it was dead funny, he was in a right state. Dave came down and took him off to bed. I took some more photos and called Yorkie over for a picture. He was wearing his new York City top, and was dead proud of it.

As he came over, we all shouted 'watch out for the sick', but he didn't hear us, his false leg slipped in the sick on the floor, then for a while he was horizontal, about two foot of the ground, then he landed on his back in the pool of sick.

His shirt was absolutely covered in sick, plus he had some in his hair. We were pissing ourselves; someone shouted 'you should have put your best foot forward'. Yorkie was dead mad. I could hardly breathe, because I was laughing so much. Rich stated 'that it is about the third funniest thing I have ever seen'.

The table was now full of bottles, we took over the disco, a little old lady came from a back room to clean up the sick. On her way back, with a bucket and mop, she fell down a small hole behind the bar, spilling the bucket of sick and water all over her. Again I couldn't breathe for laughing, and I was lying on my back struggling for air. After this merriment, we had a few more shorts, then the bar closed so we all crashed out in our rooms.

Friday

We had to wake up early to go to the airport. Duggie was feeling like shit, and when we got to departures, he ordered a fresh orange, then another. The waitress brought the bill and it was £10. He told her to stuff it.

After the rep intervened, he still had to pay £5. One of the lads, the one who had travelled with his dad, was having a sit down breakfast. He said 'Dad, can I have your sausage' we all thought it was dead funny. We all got on the plane, and Reg told us not to order anything, until we knew the price.

We flew to Moscow and arrived in the early afternoon. We got onto a dilapidated old bus, which had holes in the floor where you could see the road, as we travelled along. We sat at the back and Igor, the rep from before, welcomed us back.

The road was blocked after a crash, so it took a long time to get back to the hotel. We booked into the hotel again, then went for a meal in the restaurant. We ended up in the posh part of the restaurant, so we were told to move, to where our food was already laid out in the 'not posh part', but it was actually a good meal.

Sprake was telling us stories from his schooldays; he still drank with a lot of his schoolmates. One story was about a school bus trip they went on, when they got done by the traffic police for mooning out of back window. After the meal we went for a drink in the bar.

Sprake went and got his flag, then it was back onto the bus for an organised sightseeing trip of Moscow. First stop was the Lenin stadium, where the Olympics had been held. We were singing on the bus and chanting 'Igor, Igor' so he turned the 'mike' on, and said, 'ok, you like the singing, I sing for you'.

He started off with 'little peter rabbit has a fly upon his nose' I thought he was going to make a right cunt of himself, but all the lads joined in and he was made up.

We went past the KGB building; Igor said 'from this building you can see Siberia', which was his idea of a Russian joke.

We went past the Bolshoi ballet, and the biggest hotel in the world. The bus stopped and we went for a walk in Red Square.

We walked past St Basils Cathedral, and watched the changing of the guards. Sprake got his flag out, and we took a photo. The soldiers, from the changing of the guard, came over and grabbed Sprake and the flag. Then Igor joined in, and tried to take the flag off us, but we wouldn't let go. 'What does this Southampton mean?' they kept asking.

We told them Sprake did it for a bet, and they carted Igor off to question him for about an hour. Reg was shitting it, then the duty free bag that the flag had been in, got blown across red square, it came to rest against Lenin's tomb. Then with a final gust and roll, the bag disappeared inside!

We weren't allowed to cross any of the roads until a copper whistled for you to cross, when we did cross, the first time, without the whistle, and the road was about six lanes, we were sent back. We went to the government tourist shop to buy some souvenirs and then went back to the coach.

We were taken to look at the British Embassy, which was by the river, we took some photos but Reg was dead wary. Smoke went to the riverbank, and he slipped over, he nearly ended up in the river. Back on the bus Dave and Duggie were making out they were Mongols, waving out of the rear window to the following traffic.

Back at the hotel we had time for a shower, then it was time for dinner. Everyone was sitting at the same, correct table this time. The odd couple and Freddie the case, had not even bothered leaving the hotel yet.

There was a weird geezer, who was wearing a suit and makeup, who was on the trip; he had just been to the Australian embassy to buy a t-shirt.

Half the group were going home in the morning, the other half in the afternoon. Sheffield Dave was travelling to Carlisle after we arrived home, to watch United and he reckoned he would be there in time for the second half.

After dinner we went to the bar and really pissed it up. We were buying cans of Heineken and got talking to some fit American girls.

It turned out that Duggie knocked off one of them and she was an American Jew. The lads were taking the piss out of me for talking to them, but Duggie seemed to be getting away with it. I went and sat at another table and the Southend lad bought us all a drink.

We managed to build a 'can mountain' out of empties, from the table, which was quite a low coffee table type thing, to the ceiling, which was really quite high. We just managed to wedge the last one in, buy getting on each other's shoulders. Everyone in the hotel was looking and the Yanks burst into applause.

A little Yank tourist had bought a Ukulele. Rich took it off him and started playing the George Formby 'when I'm cleaning windows' song. Unfortunately all the strings broke as he was strumming it.

He gave it back to the little lad, who looked none too pleased. To be fair, he had been on about how good Gilbert o' Sullivan was all trip; perhaps he should have played one of his songs!

We then decided to have a mass scrap, and everyone ended up on Sprake, he then got a chair trapped on his arm, and somehow managed to throw us all off. After this we went back to the downstairs disco.

I met the fit Russian girl, from the last time we were in the club; she said it was £15 to take her upstairs, so I did. Freddie the case, was just coming out of his room as I passed, and he pleaded with me 'after you, mate'.

Sprake had got nowhere to go with his, as he was sharing his room with Dave, and he wouldn't get out of bed.

In the morning, Dave said, if Sprake had asked he would have got out of the room for a bit, so Sprake was well pissed off.

It was a really good shag. I had her up against the wall in the end. When Duggie came back later on, she left; otherwise, I think she would have stayed all night.

I had a chat with Duggie, before going to sleep, and it transpired that he had shagged the Jewish Yank.

Saturday

In the morning we ripped the piss out of Duggie. Everyone was surprised as he was the last person you would imagine to go with a Jew. Most of the lads had now gone; they saw us staggering out of the disco as they were going home. During the day, after breakfast, we had a walk to the space monument. I wanted to go to the Aussie Embassy for a tee shirt, but no one else was interested.

We queued up for the tower, which was by the monument, but you had to buy tickets previously, so we didn't bother, it was dead foggy anyway. The snow clearing machines were out, and basically it was a cold grey day in Moscow.

We walked back to the hotel and the bar. Sprake could have sworn that the colour of the seats had changed from the night before. After messing about in the lifts, for something to do, we got our bags, then we met up in the foyer with the rest of the party and then boarded the bus for the trip to the airport.

We said goodbye to Igor, Reg made a speech thanking everyone for being good company, then we went into the airport. We had to fill out the various forms and the odd couple gave me their roubles. This was because they were scared to go through customs with them, as you were not supposed to take them out of the country.

We went through the customs and to the bar, I just had an orange juice and then we had to hang around. A really strict Russian woman, was bossing loads of Japanese tourists about, as they que'ed for their Air France flight.

We got bossed about later as we waited for our Aeroflot flight. As we left the guards gave us loads of leaflets, that were full of Russian propaganda, about the war, and how good Russia was.

On the plane home we were given orange caviar for lunch, but I didn't like the taste much, as it was like salt water and looked like frogspawn. I looked out of the window and a plane on the right hand side was coming straight at us, it obviously missed, but it still looked close.

As we landed at Heathrow another load of Japanese, who happened to be on our flight, were all at the windows taking photos. It must have looked like a laser show from outside.

At St Pancras the escalator was broken, which meant I just missed the train and the next one was not until six in morning. I decided to catch a train to Nottingham, and from they're got a taxi as far as £8 would take me. I ended up walking the last four miles home.

Canada v England
1986

Friday

We met up in London at the 'Shires' pub at St Pancras. I had already met Dave, on the train to London, and we had a couple of cans of beer. We ordered a round of beers in the bar and a few minutes later Smoke and Sprake walked in. We got some more beers, and I mentioned to Smoke that this month would fly by.

At this point, I realised that I had forgotten my driving license. I checked that I had got my passport, flight tickets and money, which luckily I had. We left the 'Shires' and went for a drink in the 'Cockney Pride'.

On the way Dave left his bag with us, while he went to the toilet. Me and Sprake walked off and forgot to take it with us.

Dave was not very pleased with us, as he had everything for a month in his bag, plus some money. We had a few beers in the 'Pride' then went to 'Lilywhites sports shop'. The England shirts were dead easy to steal, but we didn't bother, because if we got caught, we would miss the flight.

In the end I bought an England hat. We went for one more beer, in another pub, then went down to the tube, but got on a train going in the wrong direction, we had to change at the first station we came to.

The next tube didn't go all the way to Heathrow, so we had to change at Rayners lane. While we were waiting for the next tube, we drank a can of lager at the station, and messed up Sprake's new trainers by tipping beer on them, and then stamping on his feet.

It was getting a bit late by now, but we got to Heathrow and checked in, we went to the duty free and bought bottles of Smirnoff Blue Label, then went to the bar. Soon it was time to get on the 16.05 plane to Seattle.

The plane was really empty. The stewardesses handed out earphones to everyone on board, but I didn't bother, as the film was 'A chorus line'. We had the meal that was handed out, and it was quite good, then we started on our duty free. We had a few beers from the trolley as well. Dave went to sleep in a row of empty seats, while me Sprake and Smoke pissed it up.

We went up to first class area, then into the galley, where we helped ourselves to various spirits. Another passenger tried to tell us not to, but we told him to mind his own business, wary that we were in the wrong, we returned back to cattle class.

The plane flew over Greenland then the Hudson Bay. I had just about finished my bottle of vodka, half an hour before landing.

On the way over we were chatting with the stewardesses but now, coming into land I fell asleep. The stewardess couldn't wake me to make me put my seat belt on for landing, and in the end just said 'oh forget him'. The other lads were laughing about it.

We landed at Seattle and me and Dave went straight through customs, but Sprake and Smoke were taken into a room and questioned as to why they were visiting the USA. They weren't sure if this was football related or just general questioning, so gave vague answers that annoyed the customs officers. After half an hour they were let through.

We walked around the airport and found a car hire desk. We had to use Sprake's licence but I had to pay on my credit card, as he hadn't got one. We decided to get an estate, Sprake was a bit over excited about driving, as he had only just passed his test and didn't have a car at home. He said he would be all right, but as we were really pissed, I wasn't so sure.

We loaded up the car and Sprake had to drive out of the car rental place. It turned out that he now told us this was the first time he had driven since passing his test, and since his big accident, in which he was a passenger. Plus the car was also an automatic, the steering wheel was on the wrong side, and he didn't know how to drive it.

He shit himself, but was all right, I told him how to put it into drive and not to use his 'clutch' foot. He drove out of the parking lot and stopped around the corner. We swapped over and I drove. We must have been stinking of booze, when we hired the car.

As we drove into Seattle we passed load of erotic girlie bars, and strip clubs. We decided to go straight into Seattle and parked up near the sea front. We found a parking place quite easily, right outside a fire station, then went into the nearest bar for a beer.

We got talking to the barman, and asked him where was the best place to go to, that was good that night. He mentioned a Mexican bar at pier 76. He reckoned this was the best place nearby.

We ordered fish and chips and had another beer; the food was red hot but tasted good. After eating, we walked down the main sea front road, past the various piers, until we got to number 76, then up the pier and into the bar.

The Mexican bar wasn't that good, the bouncers stamped your hand on the way in, but it was more like a restaurant.

We had a beer and I bought a t-shirt as a souvenir. We left the bar in search of something with a bit more life.

We walked down to another pier where there was a nightclub, unfortunately the bouncer on the door wouldn't let us in, because he said that we had got trainers on, we had an argument with the bouncer, just for the hell of it.

We went into a quiet bar and a fit girl came over to talk to us, as we were talking to her, we happened to slag off a black bloke who was in the bar. Two white lads overheard us and said; 'you can't say that, you're in Seattle now'!

After the beer, we walked back to the car, as we had still got to drive to Vancouver, which we thought was about 300 miles away. It was decided we would stop at some kind of Rambo town, near the border, to break the journey and give us a chance to get some sleep. On the way back to the car I had a nosebleed, probably because of the air pressure on flight over, probably due to the excessive amount of alcohol I had consumed. I managed to stop it bleeding after a while.

When we got to where we had parked the car it was not there. We walked around the block, but it had definitely gone, this was definitely where we had parked. Not only had we lost the car, but also the car had all our bags in it.

A massive bouncer, who was standing outside a club across the road, said to us, that it had probably been towed, as it was parked outside a fire station. While we were talking to the bouncer, a girl pulled up, handed me her car keys, and told me to park her car. She thought that I was the parking valet!

She was really pretty and I said to her 'ask me nicely and I might' she then said 'please park my car', but I explained to her that we were just visiting, and had lost our car, maybe I wasn't the best person to park her car. She laughed and got the proper valet to park it.

The bouncer asked some cops if they had towed car, they said that they had, so he shouted us a taxi and told the driver to take us to a specific compound.

When we arrived we saw the car and joined a queue at the pay booth. We explained that we were English, and didn't understand the parking rules, but we still had to pay the bill. The parking attendant gave us the parking ticket and we gave him forty dollars. All the Yanks in the queue were saying let them off. The attendant gave us directions to the freeway, we went to the car, and after going round the block once, we found our way. The freeway was deserted. It then started to pour down with rain.

A girl came past us in a Camaro, so we raced her, and beeped our horn at her, but she gave us a sign of the middle finger, and disappeared up the road.

Before we knew it, we were at the border, so we decided to go through, as there was no queue at that time of night. We got our passports stamped and were asked how long we were staying in Canada, then we were on the way to Vancouver. We stopped at the first service station that we saw and tried to get some sleep.

Saturday

We woke up and the clock in the car said it was 8.16. The match was due to kick off at 11 a.m so we wondered if we had enough time to make it. I started driving as fast as I could, it was still dark, but we didn't know what time it got light around here. We looked at the clock again and it still said 8.16. It still said the same time, because it wasn't the clock at all, but the radio frequency that the radio was tuned into! We parked up as soon as we could and went back to sleep. When daylight came I drove to Vancouver.

As we were travelling along empty roads, Sprake had a go at driving, but he shit himself when two lorries came up behind us, all he could see in his mirror was two massive trucks, and he kept having a wobble as he was steering.

I took over as we got near Vancouver. I drove to the airport because Sprake had found out, that the hotel at the airport, was where the England players were staying. We parked up and went into the hotel but there was no English about. We used the toilets for a wash, then drove into Vancouver.

We drove up to the football ground and parked the car, a security man walked past with a 'Morsons England V Canada Security' t-shirt on. I asked him if I could have one, and he just gave me his. All the lads seemed to be a bit jealous of it.

A little kid in the car park said to his dad 'gee, they have driven all the way from Washington State', this was because of the Washington licence plate on the car.

We got the flags out of our bags and went to see if we could buy a ticket, but they were not for sale yet.

We decided to go and get some breakfast. We went into a diner nearby and had a really good breakfast. We had to order the eggs sunny side up, the bacon how we wanted it, the type of coffee we wanted, but it was worth the wait.

A local Sunday park baseball team came in, and sat in booths nearby. They noticed that we were from England and we had a chat, they told us about some decent bars to go to. We had loads of water with the breakfast, as we were so dehydrated, then went back to the car park. I was going to put 'no surrender' on my flag in orange letters, but the other lads laughed at me, so I didn't bother.

We sat in the woods in a picnic area by the car park. There were loads of squirrels about, and by now it was quite warm. I got four cans of 'Tartan' bitter out of the boot; I had hidden these away, and gave one each to the lads. By now it was nearly 11 a.m.

We went and bought some tickets, and a programme, then walked to the ground. On the way we bumped into Duggie, Freddie the case, Andy and a Fulham kid.

We all went into the ground together, we got quite a few looks from the locals, but they probably thought we were ex-pats.

We found an unoccupied area of the stadium, behind a goal, and put our flags up. A royal navy ship had docked in Vancouver harbour, earlier that week, and there were about 200 Navy lads in the ground, but we kept separate from them.

They were all cheering when John Barnes name was read out over the tannoy as the announcer was telling us the teams. This was something not many England fans of the day would ever do! We slagged off Ted Croker, the FA chairman, when he walked past us.

Before the game there was a marching band on the pitch, then the singer Bryan Adams sang the national anthems; Sprake then got talking to one of his backing band.

Near the end of the game, Frank, The Tinman and Benny walked in. I went and sat with them, they told me that they had been out in the States for a while.

Benny and The Tinman had specially packed a white shirt each, in the hope of getting a job, here and there, as waiters! They had managed to get some dodgy air passes from a corrupt travel agent they knew in the UK, and instead of getting hotels, most nights they were just getting an overnight flight somewhere, and then sleeping on the plane.

They had actually had gone to watch England in an unofficial warm up game against the US Air Force, somewhere in the Nevada desert. After the game they were on a road in the desert, when the England coach passed by, they stood clapping the team as the coach passed them in the middle of nowhere.

They had also ended up going to a 'KKK' meeting while they were in Washington State. They were introduced to the assembled clan as 'our Arian brothers from England'.

At the end of the match, all the Navy lot ran onto the pitch, in doing so they left the Ensign flag, probably from their ship, up on the rear fence. Duggie's Hull City flag was next to it, so, as we took his down, we also took the Ensign.

I asked Sprake to pick the flag up and put it in his bag, but he reckoned he saw it first, so he wouldn't give it to me. He did give it to me later, and I ended up carrying it around Mexico for a month.

We left the ground and The Tinman came with us. He gave us directions to where Benny's hire car was parked, outside a bar. I said to him that he looked smart in his white shirt, and he said 'it's my new image'.

We got in the car, and The Tinman managed to direct us to the right place. We parked up and headed for the bar.

We were straight on the piss. We were in a Canadian Royal Legion bar, and an old boy at the bar told me to take my England hat off, before I came in, because there was a picture of the Queen on the wall. We got talking to the old boys in the bar and had loads of beer. Benny was in his element, as he was a massive Loyalist and was spouting off, the old boys were loving it.

At about 6 p.m. we moved on to another old soldiers bar, that the lads had told us about. On the drive up to the bar, we went past a car crash. I must have been miles over the drink drive limit at the time, and there was loads of coppers about, re-directing the traffic.

Benny had donned a jacket, and was wearing glasses; he looked like he was about fifty years old. We parked up behind the bar, went in and had a few beers. The Tinman was nicking beers as usual, he was arguing with Benny about whose round it was, and ended up cheating at a shove h'appeny game thing, when they played for money.

We went and played pool for a bit, but me and Sprake were 'bolloxed', so we decided to leave. The lads were asking 'why', we said because we wanted too, we left, but we were sure the lads would be stabbing us in the back, and calling us lightweights.

We went into China town, and just had a glass of orange, in a country and western type bar, then went back to the car on a local bus.

A really fit girl started talking to us on the bus, but we were falling asleep. We got to the car and kipped down, me in the back, Sprake in the front.

A few hours later Dave and Smoke came back. They both got in the back as well. It was a bit cramped but we were so pissed that we all slept.

It turned out that they all went for a burger, after the pub, and Duggie had said, 'I'll have whatever Benny's having'!

Sunday

In the morning we woke up and went for breakfast at a fast food place. We then decide to go to Expo 86. This was an exhibition and amusement park set up in Vancouver. We drove down to the car park. Smoke was not feeling very well.

As we were driving towards the Expo exhibition we saw a massive watch. It was part of the Expo display, and was about twenty foot high. We said that it was Big Paul's watch.

As we approached the Expo, it seemed that there were some big dippers and other rides plus other things to do, so we paid the entrance fee and went in. we ended up walking the wrong way round the first exhibit.

We then we tried to catch the monorail but there was a half-hour queue for it, so we didn't bother with that. We changed up some money and got talking to fit shop girl, I bought some postcards.

We went through the Australia exhibition, but it was just a load of televisions showing adverts, saying how good Australia was. We started to wander around, but an Australian girl told us that we had to go on the organised tour, and that it took about half an hour, so we all walked out.

We went through to the Thailand section but it was shit, then into the exhibition for Germany. At least they had a Bier Keller, but it was really expensive so we just had one beer.

We got talking to the barmaid but she wasn't German. Next to the German exhibition hall was the British Expo. We walked around but saw a British Rail train, so we went straight past; as we turned the corner we found the 'Elephant and Castle' bar.

We ordered some beers, and were chatting with the barman about how bad the Watneys Red Barrel, which they were selling was. At that moment a Canadian came in and ordered some pints of it, because he had drunk it in London. He reckoned it was the best, and what everybody drank in England.

The barman wasn't English and Sprake remarked how the pub was nothing like an English pub, as there was no graffiti, torn seats, drunks and druggies. While he was at it, he had another go at how bad the Watneys Red Barrel was.

We all went outside and sat in the beer garden area, when Andy, Joe and Duggie turned up. They had been going up to people asking 'where is the Eiffel tower' then saying 'I told you we got on the wrong plane, and it's the wrong country'. Some of the Canadians were buying it!

Smoke had to go back to the car, as he was really unwell. Andy and Joe left for their plane home; before he went he was on about the magnet, where we all meet up in an unspecified shit bar, working in Monterrey, as it had here in Vancouver. We stayed in the bar all day.

A bloke started playing the piano and we gave him some stick as he was playing rubbish songs. He shouted back at us 'sing England' but it never really got going.

We got talking to some fit Australian girls, they had been everywhere in the world, or at least seemed to have been, but they were out of our league.

After about seven hours, we had a wander around the fair. We went for a ride on the parachute gondola thing, Freddie reckoned that it was dead good, but in fairness it was crap.

We then went on the Pirates ship. It went right over, after going back and forth in bigger and bigger arcs, each one leaving your belly behind at the top. Sprake thought he was falling out. We were waving at the other lads at other end of the ship, as we all sat on the opposite back rows.

Next we went onto the roller coaster, which was quite good, but a very short ride. Freddie had bought a three-day pass; we didn't know what he was going to do for three days. As the Expo was closing, we went back to the car and woke Smoke up. We headed towards where Freddie was staying, he was sleeping in a Canadian family's house, we stopped to have a drink in a bar on the way.

I parked up outside the house Freddie was staying at, Sprake and Smoke went in with Freddie. Dave and me slept in the car, me in the front this time.

Duggie was catching a greyhound bus that night; he was going to Albuquerque and had been shouting 'Albuquerque' all day in a kind of Deep South, Wild West voice. He reckoned there was a big balloon festival on when he arrived there.

Monday

We woke up and the lady of the house came out to the car, which was parked on the street outside. She asked if we wanted to use her bathroom, and if we wanted a breakfast. It was nice to clean my teeth for the first time in a few days. Then she presented us with cereal, orange, coffee and toast. Afterwards I went out to the car and tidied my bag.

Freddie was making polite conversation and asking about trips to Grouse Mountain and Stanley Park. We decided to head off to Stanley Park.

We left the car and caught a bus, then walked the rest of the way. There were no pubs at the park, just hotels, we asked a local where we could go for a drink and something to eat, and he said 'try by the water's edge'.

We went to the water's edge, and found a bar; it was empty apart from one girl and the barmaid. We asked them 'where is good in Vancouver', they said they would take us somewhere when their shift finished.

When the shift was over, we went and got in the girl's car, she leant over the seat to show off her bum. Sprake wanted to have a feel. The other girl's parents had just won $1 000 000 on the lottery, and out of that, she had got a brand new car.

They drove us to 'Orange No 5 bar'. They parked up and we went in. It was a strip bar with a shower, in the middle of the stage.

The girls, who were the strippers, came down some re-tractable stairs from a room above, and then the stairs went back up. The first girl was really fit. We were sitting at the back of the room, we ordered some beers, and watched the stripper, she was a fantastic dancer.

The girls who gave us the lift stayed for one drink and then went.

Between the acts there was a massive TV set to watch, it was showing sport & motor racing. Me, Freddie and Sprake got a seat nearer the stage but the other two stayed, talking football and watching TV in the original seats. They were not interested in the girls on stage.

After a while me, Sprake and Freddie manoeuvred ourselves right to the front. Each time some seats became vacant, we moved forward. At one point there was six girls on stage wearing basques, stockings and high heels. We all clapped loudly when they stripped. They then went into the shower and soaped themselves down.

The next girl was really great; she crawled across the stage staring at me. I looked back, and she came over to me. Freddie and Sprake were jealous of the attention I was getting, then she reversed up to me and put some cream down her bum cheeks from a bottle that was on the stage. Next she wrapped her legs around my head so her fanny lips were inches from my mouth.

She then turned round and put her tits in my face. This girl was about the prettiest stripper I had ever seen, and I have seen a lot! She was really fit. I felt her tits and she grabbed my hand and bit it quite hard, while giving me the come-on with her eyes. She then went in the shower and showered down, while all the time looking at me.

Next to me was a bloke, a Canadian local, he said 'she wants it, fuck her, it will cost you about $100'. Then a massive black bouncer came over and said 'don't touch the girls' to me.

The Canadian bloke next to me, replied 'hey, she touched him, she wants it' He had an argument with the bouncer, and next, the bouncer just picked him up and threw him down the stairs, then proceeded to beat him up.

I stared at the bouncer, but he didn't touch me.

The girl then came back on stage and kept looking at me. She was really fit but, after the black bouncer's show I wasn't sure what to do, and decided to stay with lads and not pursue her. Possibly the second mistake I had made as far as women were concerned in twelve hours, considering that we had let the lottery winners daughter, who bought us here, go as well.

At about midnight, the two others were still talking about football. Me, Sprake and Freddie decided to go to another strip bar.

We went and sat straight at the front. The girls were not as good, but still fit. I got talking to a fit whore in the crowd, but a businessman type, in a suit, hit on her and she went off with him.

Sprake tried to pull a stripper by the stage curtain but she ran off. We decided to leave and outside the bar, there was loads of prosses out on street. The street kept clearing of whores, when the cops drove through.

There were quite a few convincing trannies down one alley, Sprake got talking to them, we were laughing at him. In end the Trannies ran off, in a girly type way, tottering in their high heels.

We asked two girls how much, Freddie did the same to two more, and this time, their boyfriends came out of a fast food pizza place behind us, the girls weren't even hookers. There looked like there was going to be trouble with their boyfriends, and we had a standoff, but in the end it all calmed down.

We went for a pizza. I thought we had got away without paying and left the shop sharpish, but the geezer who owned it, ran after us, we made out that we didn't realise we hadn't paid. I said I thought Sprake had paid, he said he thought I had paid, so we went back and paid. The whole place was also full of hippies.

We had one more walk around block, but to get a girl you really needed a car. Freddie went off with a girl, and she wanked him off for $15. She was dead scared, when afterwards; he reached in his pocket to pay his money.

We called him a fool, as he had already sampled the goods and didn't need to pay at all. We ripped the piss out of him. We jumped into a taxi, which took us back to the house. The others were already in the car so I sneaked into the house and got into a spare bed. In the morning Sprake grassed me up to the owner!

Tuesday

We woke up, had a shower and went for breakfast. It wasn't that good, but there was lots of it. The woman who owned the house asked me for some money, after Sprake had told on me, so I paid.

We got into the car, and drove into Vancouver, Freddie came with us.

We went into a bar but it turned out to be full of queers. Then we thought it was a normal bar, because a fit woman came in, but she turned out to be a transvestite. We drank up and went to a t-shirt shop.

I bought a Vancouver t-shirt. Then we went to another bar and ended up going for a Chinese meal. It took ages to get served, me and Sprake were shouting at the staff, but finally we got fish and chips, sauce and bread.

We walked past the big stadium; this was one of the first to have a retractable roof. After dropping Freddie off, as he was flying home the next day, we headed for Seattle. We were soon at the border, and were just waived through; we didn't even get an entry stamp.

It was fantastic countryside in Washington State, miles upon miles of trees and lakes, as we drove down to Seattle. Sprake had another drive but the lorries were still freaking him out, mind, they were massive and travelled at fast speeds.

We turned off the freeway to look for an Indian reservation, which was signposted. We had to go along a road for a number of miles to reach it. We got gas, food and beer at a store on the way.

The bloke serving us at the store was amazed that we were from England. The reservation turned out to be too far, so we turned around and found the freeway. We went down the freeway and saw a lake so then turned off.

We went down a small road and parked at the lake, made some sandwiches and drank the beer. There were some fantastic views at this point.

We had the usual skimming stones across the lake contest, then just sat for about an hour, then drove to Seattle.

As we got near to Seattle the traffic got heavier, as it was rush hour, we were not sure where we were going and ended up 'down town'. I had to go for a piss and nearly get locked in Lorry Park, where I was hiding behind a fence, as I was relieving myself.

We got on the ring road, filled up with gas again, and asked for directions to the airport. After another hour, we got to somewhere we actually recognised, the strip bars leading to the airport.

We found the car rental place and drove in, dropped the car and retrieved our bags. The bloke at the rental agency didn't notice the dent in the bumper, from where it was towed, and off course we didn't mention it.

We went to the airport, which was just down the road and put our bags in a locker. Today was Smoke's birthday, so we went back down the road for some beers. Sprake finished off his duty free Bacardi, at the airport. We then went into one of the girly bars and had a load of beer that was served to us in jugs.

We left after a few hours, and then went into a real drinking saloon. There was a black bloke playing pool who thought he was really cool, but he missed his shot every time. Next-door was a Denny's restaurant, so we went in and had a big burger and chips.

Afterwards we went into a bar down the road. We went to a room upstairs I was really knackered and couldn't keep my eyes open. Smoke was trying to take a photo off me, asleep at the bar, but he didn't manage it. We had two drinks, then went back to the airport and crashed out on the floor.

WORLD CUP 1986

Wednesday

We woke up in time for the flight to Houston. We were booked on Continental Airlines and boarded the plane. After take-off the pilot said 'as it is such a nice day I will just fly round such and such mountain'. The airhostesses were really friendly. We had breakfast then flew right over the USA. Looking out of the window, there seemed to be just loads of fields.

I managed to get some sleep then we landed at Houston. The pilot came over the tannoy and said 'thank you for flying Continental Airlines' customer service seemed to be king. At the airport we went to the information desk and asked if there were any cheap youth hostels or hotels for us to stay at in Houston.

The woman in the kiosk said that the 'Texas State Hotel' was $8 a night so we decided to go there. We got into a taxi outside the airport and it cost us $25 to go 'down town'. It was a long way, and for a number of miles we were just going down a freeway, but finally we saw Houston on the horizon.

When we got to the grey old tenement building that was the 'Texas State hotel' the taxi driver, who was a black woman, told us that the place across the road, which used to be a diner, was blown up last week. Police suspected the owner.

As we got out at the hotel, rather than the usual 'have a nice day' she said 'watch your asses round here boys'!

We looked at each other, then went into the lobby and asked at the reception if we could have a room. The receptionist asked us if we wanted it for the hour, day or week. We decided to just book for one night, got the key and then went into the old lift, which had an old Negro woman lift operator, to the correct floor.

It was dead hot in the hotel, and when we got in room it was no cooler. In the room were two iron bunk beds. It was a horrible room, but we crashed out anyway and slept for a while.

In the afternoon we went out, after finishing the Budweiser that we had in our bags that was rapidly becoming too warm to drink. We went into a shopping mall nearby solely because it had cool air conditioning. We had a meal in a big restaurant, the meal was pretty good and the restaurant was licensed.

We then went for walk round, and ended up at a bar at the back of the mall. It was a really smart bar and on the TV, Houston was playing Boston at basketball, in their 'World series finals'.

There was a fit woman in the bar and I got talking to her, I asked her 'where is good to go' she replied 'get out to 'Dirtys', but you will need a car'. She then said don't hang around Houston at night!

We stayed in the bar for the rest of the afternoon. The barman gave us a map and told us where to, and where not to go, large areas of the map seemed to be areas not to go, 'especially don't go down Telephone Road' he said.

We then had another meal at a buffet bar. This was quite cheap, then we went to the Greyhound Bus station and bought tickets for the bus to Monterrey.

Next, we went back to the hotel. We had renamed it, as not 'The Texas State hotel' but 'The What a State Hotel'. The lobby was full of hookers taking the 1 hour option with their clients.

There was what appeared to be a poolroom, but we didn't bother having a look at it, instead we went for a wash, then out for the night.

We started off by going to the pool hall next-door, which happened to be down some stairs in the basement. It was dead dark, and once our eyes got accustomed to the light, we found out that it was full of blacks.

One black bloke came up to us and asked if we wanted to buy a camera, a watch, cocaine? When we said 'no', he replied 'say hell, you boys must be from out of town'.

I took a photo and the whole place stopped. We decided to leave, as there was a pretty bad atmosphere in there. We walked round the block but it was like a ghost town. We eventually ended up at a decent bar called 'Warrens'.

As we walked in, it was fairly empty and the owner, who was behind the bar said 'hi my name is José'. We couldn't quite work out where the Warrens bit came from.

We got talking to him and it turned out a while ago, he had bought a London taxi and had it imported to Houston to use for his bar. He was pissed off because someone had stolen the meter on the ship, or as we thought more likely, at the London docks to be put into a dodgy cab.

We kept talking to him, even though he was quite boring, in the hope that he would offer to put us up, but he didn't, even when we explained how dire the hotel we were staying at was.

The bar was laid out just like the one in the TV sitcom 'Cheers'. All the locals who came in were going on about the local blacks, and what a shit area we were in. Not one customer had a good word to say about any blacks. We went back to the hotel at closing time and more blacks asked us if we wanted any cocaine, and again, when we said no, they invariably said 'are you boys from out of town'.

Dave and Smoke decided to go for meal, Sprake and me went to the room, put the key on a hook below the wall mirror and hit the sack.

Thursday

The next day it was red-hot. There was no air conditioning in the hotel and I was sweating like a pig. I jumped off the top bunk but it was dead high and it hurt the soles of my feet as I landed on the hard tiled floor.

I got into the shower and tried to cool off. It was getting late in the morning, so amazingly, and it was probably a first for the hotel, we decided to book in for another night! We went down to the reception and paid.

We went back to the mall for something to eat, but before that, we all went back to the room for our sunglasses. We couldn't find the room key, and a bloke in the corridor helped us by opening the door. We weren't sure if he was part of the hotel staff or not. When we went in, we saw the key, still on the hook below the mirror.

We had just slept in the worst hotel in America, with enough money in the room to keep the four of us travelling for the next four weeks, without locking the door!

In the mall, we walked round for a bit, then got a late breakfast.

After breakfast we went to a travel agent and asked about which was the cheapest way to the airport, as we had arranged to meet Gary today, and his flight was arriving later that afternoon.

They told us that there was a bus from the Sheraton. We walked down to the Sheraton and for something to do; we went for a ride in the external lifts. They were really fast and you got a decent view of Houston as they got higher. It was good to get back into some air conditioning.

There was a piano bar in the foyer and we had a civilised drink in there. We found out where and when the buses were going from. On the first floor there was a swimming pool, we sat by it, and thought about going for swim, but as we had no trunks, we thought that perhaps our underpants wouldn't fit in with the posh surroundings.

We sat for about an hour just drinking cokes, and decided Sprake and me would go up to the airport to meet Gary. The other two were to meet us in the bar we were in yesterday, in the mall, at about 5 p.m.

Sprake and me went down to the bus leaving point, bought two tickets, then sat and waited.

A small bus arrived and took us to the airport. At the airport there were one or two Scotland fans wandering around, looking lost, but we ignored them. Also there was the odd England fan here and there, we went and had a coffee at the bar, then, when we had drunk that, just water because it was so hot.

We just had to wait for the incoming British Caledonian flight from London. For some reason there appeared to be a number of fit girls hanging around, but we didn't bother with them, apart from just looking.

Once the plane had landed, it appeared that everyone had got off; about the last person to come out of the customs area was Gary. He was wobbling all over the place, was the last off the plane apparently, and was heavily pissed up, a bit like the first time I had ever met him, when he collapsed in the street in Oslo.

I took his bag of him, it was really heavy. We told him about the hotel, but he was so pissed, I don't think it registered how bad it was. Then we got a taxi back to downtown, it was $6 each this time.

We went past all the usual strip joints that seemed to be part of the landscape around American airports. After dropping Gary's bag at the hotel, we went to meet the other lads at the mall.

The bar was quite full this time, all the locals were watching the various TVs and cheering on the Houston Astros. Sprake shouted out 'Boston' and the barmaid soaked him with the water, from a soda dispenser, from behind the bar.

We helped ourselves to food from the free buffet, that the bar had laid on. Smoke was already on his third helping. We had a few beers and a waitress, who was particularly fit, kept walking round and we got talking to her.

I ended up buying another t-shirt, as she said that she got a commission for everyone she sold. The bar closed at about 8 p.m., as did the whole of Houston by the look of it, so we went back to the hotel, and booked Gary in, he had to pay $3 for the pleasure of sleeping on the floor of our room.

Once we had done that, we went out again and headed towards 'Warrens'. After a quiet beer we decided to go to 'Dirtys', the bar, the girl had told us about. We got into a taxi as it passed along the street, by Warrens.

The black taxi driver took us miles, but couldn't find 'Dirtys'. The meter in the cab was up to $24 and Smoke started slagging the driver off. I told him to calm down, as he was getting dead mad.

In the end he dropped us at a bar we passed called 'Shiros' and we paid him, after a lot of argument, $12. The bar appeared, by the graffiti and general demeanour of the place, to be a 'KKK' stronghold.

It was empty, so we had a few beers, and a game of darts on the typical American electronic dartboard.

We got talking to the barmaid, Gary fancied her, the rest of us started talking to a customer who had come in, and had introduced himself as 'Red'. We asked 'Red' where Dirtys was and he said he would take us there.

He took ages to drink up, and when he was drinking he kept putting bullets on the table. Apparently this meant, for every bullet, he had bought us a drink. He then gave me a t-shirt from the bar.

Dave ended up getting on with Red like a house on fire, and was talking to him about the 'KKK', and Thatcher allowing the Yanks to bomb Libya from British bases. As the conversation went on, for what seemed like hours, each drink was toasted with 'down with Gaddaffi' it seemed to go on all night.

Eventually, Red had finished his liquor, and we all piled into the back of his pick-up, which was parked outside the bar. He drove us to 'Dirtys'. On the way I lost the back of my camera, as it was windy in the open pick up, but I couldn't get off or tell Red to stop.

We got to 'Dirtys' but it had just closed. Coppers were their clearing the bar, fit girls in cars were leaving by the bucket load, the coppers told us to get back in the pick up and go. It looked like there had been a proper bar room brawl.

Red took us to another bar, but it was a bit dead, and we ended up just sitting and slagging off the IRA. After a drink or two, Red ran us back to Warrens, which was really good of him.

Some younger blokes were in Warrens. More or less straight away Gary fell asleep and they all laughed at him. Jose said 'hey you can't sleep there'. Apparently it was against the law to sleep in a bar in Houston. Before we knew it both Dave and Smoke had fallen asleep! At end of night we woke them all up. Gary was dead difficult to wake up, and he started fighting with us in his drunken, sleepy manner. It was the first time the lads had met him, but they were all right about it. We got his legs and carried him for a while down the street, then decided to leave him. Eventually we thought better of leaving him, and managed to get him back to the hotel, and we all crashed out.

Friday

We woke up and went across the road for breakfast, next to the bombed out building. Today I wanted to go on the cyclone, supposedly the biggest roller coaster in world. We checked out of the hotel and got a bus down to Telephone road, exactly where we were told not to go. We went there as it was near to the airport, as we needed to check up on potential flights home.

While we were there we saw a car hire place and decided to hire a big CF Dodge Van, which was about the size of a large Transit van in England. The girl behind the counter, who checked us in for the van, was fantastic. She said she was going to Dallas for the weekend, when we asked her what she was doing that night. Sprake asked her to stay in Houston.

We loaded up the van with the bags and drove off. Sprake started off driving and turned round the corner, meaning to park up, but carried on and ended up on the freeway. He wouldn't turn left, and daren't stop so we switched while the van was moving and I pulled across some lanes and managed to get off the freeway, before we had left Houston completely.

We decided to head to Astroworld, for the roller-coaster but when we got there it was shut, so we went to the Astrodome, which was next door to the amusement park, instead. I parked up the van and we found out that the time of the next tour was in about an hour. We paid for the ticket then went into the shop and bought some postcards and had our dinner in the onsite café. It happened to be a cheeseburger again.

I took some general photos, then the tour started. We didn't win the lucky prize, which was associated with your ticket number. The lads were ripping the piss out of the guide. They showed us the scoreboard and what happened for home runs for the Astros. It was like a firework display, but for when the visitors were to get a home run, it just said home run and fizzled out.

We went down onto the pitch and they demonstrated how the pitch and stands moved for football games and Baseball games. A pitcher then came out to practice and we watched him for a bit, without really having a clue what he was doing. We were taken on a guided tour around the executive boxes, then to a film show. The Houston people called the stadium the eighth wonder of world.

Apparently when it was first built, it used to have a real cloud, that had formed inside, and it used to rain every so often inside, before a humidifier was fitted.

Afterwards, we drove up to Richmond, an area of Houston, found a mall and parked up, then went into a bar. It was a white only bar, by the looks of it, and was full of rednecks and KKK types. I had a go at the shuttle board, a large pub game that is a cross between curling and shove happeny. On my first go, I got the marker to overhang the edge, which scored ten points. Apparently you only have to get to thirty-one points to win the game.

I said quite loudly that the game was too easy, and walked to the bar. A bloke, who saw my shot, bought us all a beer, by putting bullets on our table. All the lads were laughing at me, but I didn't bother having another go.

All the yanks were drinking from bottles that they had supplied, as it was a 'set-up' bar. We were told, at a set up bar you just paid $1 for a glass and brought your own liquor. I went and got a bottle from the van and we stayed for quite a while. We were later told that the 'Richmond Arms' was a good local pub so at about 6 o'clock we drove up to it. It was only up the road so we parked up and finished the Bacardi we had been drinking in the previous bar.

The Richmond Arms was an English style pub, but not a plastic one, and when we were in it, if not for the Yank customers, you could have been in England. We got talking to two girls in the pub, one of who was English.

Sprake and me ended up outside with them, but we slagged Houston off, and the English girl got shitty about it. We went back in to the bar, but we were steaming drunk by now. I then managed to knock off a really fit waitress called Cathy; I was kissing her, after her shift had finished, as we were playing darts.

She told me she was going to a party and gave me the address. She then threatened that she would come down Mexico and beat me up, if we didn't go to it.

We stayed in the pub for a while, bought yet another T-shirt and got talking to some other fit women, who were in the bar and seemed to want to talk to British people. When the bar shut we all got in the van to find where the party was. The van was constantly on full beam; to dip the lights, it had a foot switch, which I didn't know about, so I couldn't dip the main beam.

At one point I was right behind a cop car!

In the end we couldn't find the address of the house where the party was, so I just turned into someone's drive and parked up for the night.

It was so hot we had to leave the van doors open, we did manage to go to sleep, but apparently I kicked Dave in the head during the night, in my sleep.

Saturday

We woke up early at about six and were feeling rough. A light went on, across the road and a bloke who lived there, invited us in for breakfast. Gary and Dave went, the rest of us slept on. I woke up again at about nine, when a car pulled onto the drive that we had parked on.

A nice girl in a silk dress got out of the car. We asked her if she minded that we had parked on her drive, but she was very good about it, so we asked her if we could use her shower. She obviously didn't want us in her house, which was understandable considering the state we were in, plus the safety issues that she must have been concerned with.

We drove around the block and found a breakfast place. I then left my money in there, leaving it in a bag, on the seat in the diner. I went back in and luckily it was still there.

We drove back to the car hire place and after getting a bit lost, filled the van up with gas and dropped it off. The bloke behind the counter was friendly and he offered to give us lift to the airport. It was pissing down with rain and he told us that as Houston is very low, it often floods.

We had a good wash at the airport using the toilets. Then we got a taxi to a local bar, which again happened to be on Telephone Road. A black woman in the first bar seemed to be really weird and spaced out. She asked us to come in to the bar, then she said she wanted to have sex with us, we said no, and went down the road to the next bar.

At the next bar, the woman owner here didn't want to serve us, so we went from one extreme to another. Apparently she had had trouble with England fans the previous night, as they had been standing on the tables, swearing and singing.

We said we wouldn't do that, so she let us in and we played pool and had some beers. We met a local called Rex. He told us that a man can leave his bottle all day in this bar and no one would touch it.

As we got drinking the owner gave me a cowboy hat to make me look like a Yank. A girl who was working behind the bar, and who was a bit fat, said that she wanted to marry me.

She got a certificate of marriage from somewhere behind the bar and I went along with it. When she filled out the names, I was a bit worried as you never know the local laws and I didn't want to end up married to her for real.

After we had both signed the form she took me into a back room and sucked me off to consummate it!

Meanwhile, Sprake was getting chatted up by some sixty-year-old women. They asked him to go to their house, but he declined their offer. I went back into the bar and carried on drinking and playing pool. My 'new wife' carried on serving.

Sprake and Smoke went to meet Alf, who was arriving that afternoon, at the airport. Gary and me played pool, a bloke who had come into the bar, gave us some baseball caps; mine had the Southern Cross on it with 'ass kicking' written across the flag.

I beat another yank at pool, for a couple of dollars, he was something to do with the bar and afterwards he took us out to the backyard to look at his racecar.

It was like a 'Dukes of Hazard, General Lee' car, and he said, when you race on the oval tracks 'you just put your foot down and turn left'. He had lots of trophies from his wins in the bar. He reckoned he had a few cans of beers in the car to drink when he was racing.

Sprake came back with Alf, who was knackered, but not in as bad a state as Gary had been in. He had a few beers, but we were steaming by now, and we stayed in the bar watching the TV. It was showing horse racing, then after that boxing, as it was set to a Sports channel. In the boxing two blacks were fighting. All the locals in the bar were saying that it was really good to see two blacks hitting shit out of each other.

Towards the end of the evening we got a taxi down telephone road, to the bus station. I changed my shirt, but got told off by a security guard, as you were not supposed to be bear chested in the bus station.

Smoke got a bottle of spirit out of a liquor store. We drank it then went into a coffee shop to kill a bit of time. We had a bit to eat, then went and sat on some spiky grass outside. Our bus turned up, but the security guard wouldn't let us get on. Sprake got into an argument with him and slagged him off. As he had got a gun, Smoke told him to calm down.

Alf went into the bus station and there was a bus to the border at Laredo. He bought a ticket; we could use our original tickets for this bus, so we went to an upstairs bar and bought food and more beer for the journey.

There were a few other England fans in the bus station and we all seemed to be in the same kind of state. We were all tired, but as soon as the bus to Laredo, via San Antonio, came into the station we made sure we got straight on to it.

Sunday

Today was my birthday. I just got my head down the best as I could, and slept on the bus. We arrived at San Antonio at about 3 a.m. We then waited half an hour for the change of bus. We got on the next bus and slept to Laredo eventually arriving at seven-thirty a.m.

We hung around bus-station; it was full of Mexicans even though we were still in the USA. We walked to a MacDonald's for breakfast.

I had got the shits, but Smoke was in the only bog. I had to wait and just managed to get to the toilet in time, before I filled my pants.

We had breakfast then went for a walk. A Manchester youth tagged along with us and proceeded to tell Gary his life story.

Gary kept going on about the local girls. Most of them appeared to be hookers, to me, but he had only been out two days and hadn't sampled the delights of Vancouver.

We walked to the border and decided to go across. Steve the Manchester lad had not got his passport, as he had left it in the left luggage at the bus station.

He decided to go back for it, and asked if he could meet us later. About seven of us were going across the bridge at the border, but two decided against it and turned back.

We walked across the bridge, over the Rio Grande then after going through customs, up the Main Street and into Mexico.

We went into a restaurant and had a proper breakfast, then wandered around looking at some of the shops, which seemed to be mostly tattoo parlours or motorbike repair places.

After a while we went back across border, this time we got a stamp going into the USA. The queue was quite long and it killed some time, we went back to the bus station and Steve, the Manchester Lad, had not returned yet. As he had got the key for Sprake's luggage locker, it was dead funny, as the bus was due to leave soon, and Sprake was starting to flap.

Sprake was getting dead mad; he thought he would miss the bus. In the end Steve turned up just in time, for some reason he was wearing red shoes and green trousers!

We got on the next bus and travelled to Monterrey via Nuevo Laredo. I sat next to Sprake, Alf got his tape recorder out, when he turned around he said 'hey you can't sit next to Sprake'. He was acting like a baby, and said this like a big girlie, so we all ripped the piss out of him.

We travelled for a while then hit a big traffic jam. It turned out the coach in front had crashed. We walked up to see what was happening. A group of Danes in a car were in the traffic jam and we had a chat with them. The bus was a mess but there didn't appear to be any major casualties.

When we arrived in Nuevo Laredo it was pissing down. We just sat on bus all day Sprake said 'it's not much of a birthday for you'. 'Oo oo' Frog, was also on our bus, he had a spot of bother getting through customs because of his hooligan past.

We passed another crash on the other side of the road, this time the driver had gone through the windscreen and appeared to have lost his legs; he was just lying there on the grass by the side of his wrecked car.

We arrived in Monterrey at about 8 p.m. it was getting dark. Monterrey was dead smelly and dirty, particularly around the bus station. We got our bags and got off the bus.

We walked down the road and bumped into some English lads. We asked them where the hotels were, and where we could change some money. They pointed us in the right direction and we tried a few hotels down street. There was a really smelly food stall on the corner and it made me retch.

We tried a couple of hotels but they were full, then at a corner hotel they had rooms. Gary booked into another hotel with his mate, who had arrived earlier. We went and had a look at the room in the hotel, I thought it looked all right, but the lads were not so sure when they saw it.

This was probably because I knew what to expect from travelling around Mexico the year before. A lad who was on the bus called Shane, a West Ham fan, had got talking to us. He also booked into the hotel with us and was now sharing our large room.

We dumped our bags and went for some beers. Someone told us about a bar around the corner, but we couldn't find it. We ended up going into the 'Papillion bar', Duggie was in there and he now appeared to be 'the main man' with a few England fans hanging around with him.

We had some Carta Blanca beer; it worked out at about ten pence a bottle, but it still tasted awful. We moved down to a bar near the market. Duggie and Sprake started dancing in a 'Madness' type way to the music being played.

Duggie said to Sprake 'keep dancing because 'oo oo' Frog is watching us'! At the end of night we went back to hotel and crashed out. Smoke went for a meal on the way back and saw 'Oo Oo' Frog. He told us the next day that Frog was walking like a bulldog, because his arse was so sore from sweating on the bus.

Monday

It turned out that Duggie and his little entourage were also staying in our hotel. The local busses started up at 4 a.m. across the road, at the busy bus station. This woke Sprake up. The noise was unbelievable, as each driver seemed to enjoy revving their engines, and plumes of black diesel smoke poured out of each exhaust.

The windows of the hotel were shaking. We re-awoke at about nine, but Sprake had got a right bag on. Alf went for a shower and took about an hour, which as five of us were sharing a large room, was not good. Finally he came out and the rest of us had the chance of a shit and a wash.

We went for a walk and changed up some money, then went to a good hotel for breakfast. The service was really slow, but the breakfast was quite nice. We met Stuart Hill and Mark in the hotel's restaurant and arranged to meet them later.

We then went back to our hotel and booked it for another night. It was good value at only £2 a night.

Later we met Stuart and Mark in the 'Papillion bar', and watched a match on TV. The toilets in the bar were terrible. There was just a trough, no water and no sit down toilet; they absolutely stank, as it was probably seeing more custom than it ever had.

To add to the shitness of the bar, a group of Liverpool geezers were in there, they didn't appear to be overly friendly to any other England fans.

Stuart told us about a better 'pool' bar and we decided to go there that night. While we were drinking in this new bar, the Papillon bar put its beer up from 10 pence to 12 pence a bottle. This made our minds up and we said we would give it a wide birth from now on.

The owner by this time had bought loads of crates of beer; so many that you could hardly get past them, to get into the bar. No doubt he would make his money from other fans, but not from us.

A shoeshine man came in and I had my trainers cleaned, it cost me pennies but they didn't look much better afterwards. Then Steve, the Manchester lad we met in Houston came in. He told us that his hotel was really good; he said he could 'lay out all his clothes on hangers in the wardrobe'!

When the match finished on TV, we decided to go to the Technicologico ground where England would be playing two games to get some tickets. Stuart took us to the correct bus stop and we all jumped on the next bus.

A busker got on the bus, he had a guitar and we all joined along in a singsong even though we didn't know the words, it was dead funny. After half hour we got to the ground and went to ticket office. We bought tickets, but only for that ground. At the same time, I bought a horrible tasteless ice-lolly and hoped afterwards, that it wasn't going to cause me problems.

We decided to go to the Universatarias ground, where the other game was to be held to buy tickets for that game. We got on another bus to the centre of town and then another one to the ground. For some reason there was loads of schoolgirls hanging around the stadium and Gary and Alf chatted up a car full!

We bought tickets, but they only had the expensive ones left. A scouser had, apparently, just been nicked for stealing a load of tickets for the Poland game. There weren't any taxis outside the stadium, so we had to jump on another bus, but it was going away from town so we got off.

We went into a shop and I bought some wine and lemonade, most of the lads just bought beer, but I was struggling with the taste of it. We bought a football and had a bit of a kick about. Alf was showing off, doing keepie ups, but then he slipped over and we were all laughing at him.

We had a look at the local bullfight arena then decided to walk back to the bus station area.

We went to Papillion's bar and the beer was now 20 pence. I had to have a slice of lime with mine to make it drinkable. We watched the afternoon game; Stuart was talking to the Liverpool youths.

We then went across to the poolroom bar. We got a table and played against the Liverpool lads. Next we played against the Mexicans for money, it was only a pound a frame, but it nearly came to blows, especially when a lad called Sharky lost to a Mexican.

We decided to ignore the Liverpool lot and went down towards the market. We went into a disco and all locals were staring at us, so we had to stick together.

We had some beers, a few whores were hanging around, but they weren't anything special. We left the disco and went into the centre of Monterrey, and to some better bars. The night was spent drinking.

Finally we headed back towards our hotel.

On the way we went into a bar that was showing blue films, there was lots of English fans in this bar.

Two Mexican dwarfs at the bar started arguing with each other, then one punched the other and a fight started. There was blood all over their faces. All the England lads were cheering and supporting one dwarf or the other.

We had another beer and watched the aftermath of the fight then walked back towards the hotel.

There was a whorehouse across the street from the hotel, one of the girls there called us over. Alf and Sprake went across. They were talking to the girl for a while so I went across. She invited us all in but wouldn't give us a price. Alf then asked her if she was a prostitute, me and Sprake looked at each other, as if to say, what the hell do you think she is!

She went into another room and woke up her daughter who was about sixteen and very pretty. Then she got another daughter, out of another room. She appeared to be younger and only looked about fifteen and was wearing her nightdress. She made them sit on the settee.

Then she said 'ah, there are three of you' so she disappeared again, and then brought out a little girl of about fourteen! She was wiping the sleep out of her eyes.

We told her to 'piss off' and that she was sick. Her family went back to bed. She offered us a beer but we refused and left, as we were not interested. She never did name a price.

We went across the street to the hotel and Sprake got some food from a street vendor. Alf reckoned he was tired and was going back to hotel. The bars were closed by now but as we walked into the hotel, we turned around and saw Alf scurry across street to the whorehouse.

During the week we often saw the 'madam' in her house, from our hotel room window, she was always looking and waving at us, the sick bitch.

Tuesday

Sprake woke up with a bag on, as the busses were rumbling out of the station. He moved into the other room, which was probably quieter, and you could use the toilet in the morning, because Alf wasn't in there. He moved in with with Harry, Gary, who had now rejoined us, and Shane. Gary had still not acclimatised himself, and he was coming in at six or seven every morning then sleeping all day.

At about nine I woke up, Alf spent an hour in the bathroom, I could hear all his tops being removed to various deodorants and after shaves banging and clanging. Me and Smoke thought it was crazy.

Smoke was bosting for a shit, he kept banging on the door, but Alf wouldn't come out. Dave was now hanging about with Duggie and his group more than us.

We got up and went for breakfast at the 'Fastoff Hotel'. I had to go the long way round the block to avoid the smelly food corner, which was still making me retch every time I passed it.

We noticed that the 'Papillion bar's' owner was ordering loads more beer. This might have been a mistake as we wouldn't be drinking there, and the Liverpool lads had, according to the other boys we met, glassed someone there last night.

We saw Benny and The Tinman in the Fastoff restaurant. As loads of people had been doing runners, it had now got bouncers on door locking people in! You needed a pass to get out, proving that you had paid! I managed to get a spare pass and gave it to The Tinman.

He told me they had been having a good time in the states, and had been hanging out with the KKK. They told us they had been to an Aryan meeting; somehow 'The Times' in England had got wind of it. Their reporter had produced a half page write up on them, and what they had been doing at the meeting.

While in the States they had also gate crashed some Jewish garden party, but the Jews were all armed and it didn't go to plan and they had to leave at gunpoint. They also went to the 'Emperor of the Universe' meeting and made the mistake of letting the Stars and Stripes flag touch the floor. Again they were introduced as 'our Aryan brothers from England' and had to make a speech.

They were not too sure when they got their Union Flag out, about what the Yanks would say about the writing on it, but as it was 'our' flag they just got on with it. They ended up at a 'KKK' dinner dance. Frank said that he was thinking of staying out in the states.

After breakfast we went back to the hotel to get the flags. Then went to the 'Papillion bar'. Loads of lads were having a big football match in the street outside it. We had a few drinks, but the Carta

Blanca tasted really horrible by now. I tried the Bohemia beer instead, which tasted better, but was more expensive.

We decide to catch a taxi to ground. We got in one with Mark and his missus, Tracey, who were on their honeymoon. It was cheap enough in the taxi and we were soon near the ground.

Tracey had found the toilet facilities in the 'Papillon Bar' particularly bad as there was only a men's toilet, and that just had a trough for a urinal and a hole in the floor for a dump.

There were loads of England fans on the street outside the ground. TV cameras were there filming the scenes, which all seemed to be friendly with a party atmosphere. We went down a side road and had a few beers and a pizza.

'Oo oo' Frog was in the bar, since the last time we had seen him, he had been run over. Apparently he just looked the wrong way and stepped out. Plus he had still got his sore arse. He said to the bar in general, as he was re-telling the story of him being run over, that 'the bloke just drove off'. Frog thought he could off at least given him a hand up out of the gutter.

Frog was with his Chelsea mates Dirty, Benny and Dave and was a much larger than life figure, who had many stories of various escapades. One of these, was where he was at home, watching the Vietnam films, 'Full Metal Jacket', 'Hamburger Hill' and 'Acopolyps Now' one after another.

He had them on dead loud and the Pakistani who lived in the flat below, knocked on his door to complain. When he opened the door he was in such a violent mood, from the films, he just threw the Pakistani out of the first floor window. Luckily he landed in a Rhododendron bush in the front garden and, the window was open.

We walked to the ground and everyone seemed to be in a good mood, we had to meet Shane outside the ground as we had his ticket, but we couldn't find him. Once we went into ground, they were selling beer on tap so we pissed it up.

We met John Paul and Dave Dougan. Dave asked us 'why on the Southampton bus, does everyone call John, the homosexual Jew'! We told him it was from the Finland trip. I Saw Silk, Dave and Steve in the ground they were all having a good time. We also saw the Orient lads; they had a far right flag with them. This later appeared on Television, too much tutting from the left wing B.B.C. journalists.

Some lad, wearing a pair of yellow tights, jumped into the moat that went around the pitch, it kept the spectators from the players. He threw his camera to a press bloke and asked him to take a photo, then the coppers fished him out and told everyone to get off the wall that was overlooking the moat.

Loads of flags had been put up on the fencing around the ground. There was the massive Hemel Chelsea, and nearby a very small one which had Tootham Villa on it. This was Gary's local Sunday team.

Duggie had got in the ground early to get his Hull City flag in a prominent position.

It was a crap game and England lost 1-0. All the lads were moaning about the standard and the result.

Meanwhile the Mexicans were doing the Mexican wave in the stadium, we didn't bother. We came out of the ground and just jumped in the back off any random pick-up truck that was going back into town. Everyone seemed to be doing this; we got one with some Norwegian lads who were following England!

They told me that 'Bills Bar' in Oslo had burnt down! We went for a drink in the centre of town; loads of the local girls wanted our autographs.

We drank in the 'Hotel Monterrey'. There was loads of England fans in there. They had got foreign beer in the bar, so I ordered some drinks and got talking to a really fit girl. All the lads were on about her afterwards.

We went to the next bar down the road, it was called 'Sambourns', and we watched the evening match. The service was really slow and it got too full, so we moved on to a horrible bar in the pool hall.

We had few games of pool, then the lads started singing, they were singing loads of protestant songs. The Tinman was stealing beer and fags. Frank had taken off all his KKK stuff that he was wearing earlier.

Then everyone did the conga around the bar and out down the street. It was pouring down with rain, but it was still dead good. Everyone was dancing about. The local coppers came up to Sprake, because he had a Mexican's beer in his hand.

He said it was just given to him, and pleaded not to be nicked. They took him away, but a Mexican then told the coppers that it was a mistake, and they made Sprake walk off in a different direction.

Smoke got dead mad at the coppers, but I calmed him down. We got into a taxi and went back to the hotel and ripped the piss out of Sprake, when he arrived back.

Wednesday

The busses woke us up, but we managed to get back to sleep as we were getting used to it by now. We decided to stay in Monterrey until the next match.

We got up late and went for breakfast. We met the odd couple at breakfast and a few others from the Russian trip. I realised that I had lost about £20 at the bar after the match the day before, so I was well pissed off. I told The Tinman and he just said 'it's bad isn't it'.

Colin was staying at the 'Fastoff' we had a chat then headed off down town. Colin was sharing with an old bloke so he was happy to come with us. We got the bus and went to the pool hall. Gary was still asleep in bed; I had not really seen much of him yet.

Alf had got an early morning flight to Acapulco on his own.

We were all feeling a bit tired. There was a youth in the pool hall who had been locked up. He was showing off about it. We got some beers and sat and watched the Scotland game. They lost and we cheered, but some of the other lads in the bar wanted them to win and an argument started.

We moved on to a snooker hall and had a game. There were Halifax NF badges all over the place. We played doubles, me and Col versus Southampton. Smoke kept drinking my drink and it was really pissing me off. As the afternoon went on, the place filled up, so we moved again. We went to the upstairs patio bar at the 'Hotel Monterrey'.

We had some beers and watched the locals cruising up and down the street in their custom cars. We waved to the girls in the cars. Gary came down and met us and we went for a walk. We met two fit girls who said that their house had its own swimming pool. We arranged to meet them at about six the next evening.

We went into a smart pub with a big TV, but it had really slow service. They wanted us to sit down to be served every time. We had an argument with the waiter and told him to just serve us. Eventually the drinks came but we all walked out.

We went back to the pool hall and had a big piss up. Me and Sprake went round the corner to a MacDonald's type thing. Andy Parsons came in, and ordered some food. He then told the girls behind the counter that he wanted to fuck them. They wrote a letter back to him, telling him that he was a very naughty boy!

Smoke, Sprake and me went to a posh hotel. We went up in the lift to the bar at the top for the view. Jeff Powell, the Daily Mail reporter, was staring at us, but we ignored him.

We talked to the Moroccan press as we sat and had a beer.

One bloke in the bar was staring at us so we told him to 'fuck off'. His mates apologised and said he was drunk, but he kept staring so we told him to 'fuck off' again. When we left, some girls told us not to go near the bus station, as it was very dangerous!

We got on a bus, back towards the hotel and went in the 'Papillion Bar'. I bought a newspaper from a street kid. We were called hooligans in the press. There were a few photos, but not of us, basically it was just the Liverpool lot causing trouble outside the ground, and the one fan that had got glassed by them.

Apparently the Liverpool lot had all got blades with them and he was lucky only to have got glassed.

In 'Papillon' we bumped into Sprakes's mate Dave Dougan. When we met him we just said 'hello Dave', he was pissed of, as he had expected outstretched arms and a hug, as we were thousands of miles from home! We had a drink with him and then we went to the blue film place, then onto a disco bar.

Stuart Hill was in there. We stayed a while, there were quite a few prostitutes about and the bar was good, but then I noticed Chunny from Brighton was in there. I avoided him because he was such a twat.

On the way out a Mexican called us over asked if we wanted women. Sprake said that he did, so he went off with one that the Mexican called over. Another girl had just finished with another punter, so Dave Dougan went off with her. I waited for them to finish.

As I was about to choose one, the Mexican took me down to the bar, and showed me a real fit one, but she had loads of blokes hanging around her.

I was looking after the boy's money belts, so I turned it down; I went back upstairs and waited. Sprake took ages, Dave Dougan was out first then Sprake, I decide against going in, as I didn't want to lose the rest of the lads.

Dave told us that his bird was on the shitter when he went into the room. The toilet door was open and she wiped her arse and didn't wash her hands. He said that she stunk of shit, while he was shagging her.

Sprake said that his one was quite nice.

We met Stuart and Smoke and walked down the road. Stuart went into his hotel just as an ugly bird was staring at us. Smoke said he was going for some food, but I saw him double back and go for ugly bird.

Sprake and me went back to hotel. As we walked past we saw Duggie and Dave in the 'Papillion bar', so we popped in. Duggie was pissed up; he said that he was in love with a Mexican girl and that he was going to marry her. I just said 'all right Duggie, sure you are'.

Thursday

We woke up late, had a shower without Alf holding us up, and then went to the 'Fastoff Hotel' for breakfast. Again I had to go the long way round to avoid the smell from the street vendor.

We met Dave Dougan and he was already moaning about having itchy balls from the woman last night. The service in the restaurant was as slow as usual, then we went and changed some more money.

They had even got fit girls in the bank. We then went into town by bus. As we walked around town we saw Mark and Tracey, they had been down to Porta Valletta and said it had rained a lot, but it was a good place and they got cheap flights.

Gary had been going on about going there, so we decided we would go down after the next match.

We heard that there was a football match being arranged, so headed that way through a really smelly fish market. The match itself was England fans v Mexico fans and ended up in a 2-2 draw. I scored the first goal.

The press appeared and took our names. They said a report of the match and photos would be in the local paper. I split my shorts while I was playing, but they were still just about wearable.

Nearby was an open-air pool, we went and dived in, we bathed for a bit and I beat a lad from Doncaster in a swimming race.

The guards then came and told us to get out, as some of the lads had stolen drinks and ice cream from the snack bar. I got accused and said 'where have I put them'? As I was only wearing shorts, I then told the guard to 'bollocks'.

We headed back into town. Loads of girls were asking us for our autographs again. I went and bought some new shorts, they were quite cheap, then we went to the 'Hotel Monterrey' for some beers.

After that we had a meal at 'Sambournes' and were sitting down when Brian Glanville, the reporter from 'The Times' came across to me; I told him about the rumours we had heard, that a Scot had been killed in Mexico City. Glanville told me about the last time he was in Mexico when he was covering the student riots of 1968.

We went to the pool bar and had more beers. Gary appeared, and after more beers we went to the FIFA place and Gary ended up chatting up miss Nuevo Leon. He made a bit of a fool of himself when we left, by asking her to come with us, but she was not interested.

We went around the various pubs all night then jumped on a bus, that went up to the bus station. Gary and me had a few beers in 'Papillion', then the blue film bar, then headed down to the red light district.

The first bar we went in, we had some beers and got talking to two whores. We asked for a blowjob and it was £3. They wanted us to go back to our hotel with them, but we were sharing with the lads, so it was not on. We offered £5 for them to do it in the street, but they wanted us to go to their apartment, so we moved on to next bar.

We had a few beers and by now it was about 4 a.m. We went into an upstairs lounge that seemed to be full of fit girls. I was chatting to one of them at the bar, when Gary shouted 'let's get out' and pushed me out down the stairs. I had just got to the point where I was playing with girl's tits, so I was none too pleased.

It turned out he had been talking to a tranny, and that was why he wanted to get out. Down the stairs, after he explained what had happened in the lobby, the girl I had been talking to followed us. She started playing with my cock and wanted a jump, she was trying to kiss me but I held back as Gary was still angry.

Gary went back upstairs leaving me with the fit girl. We were kissing and in a quiet corner. I just managed to get my dick in her, when Gary started a fight upstairs with the tranny.

I had to go and help him. I managed to get him out as he was really pissed. My girl wanted me to come back. I said I would see her tomorrow and gave her some pesos, then Gary picked up a bottle and threw it through the front window and then he fucked off.

I had to leg it, but luckily no one chased after me. It was about 6 in the morning by now; I walked past the smelly food corner and threw up. When I got back in the room, I was bouncing off the wardrobes and tables and woke everyone up.

Friday

I woke up. Alf was back. We went for breakfast in the 'Fastoff Hotel'. Then we went to the bus station and bought tickets for the destination of Brownsville. In Texas, where we had decided to go between the next two matches. We went back to the hotel for our flags and went to the 'Papillion bar'.

I was fed up of Carta Blanca by now and was looking forward to a Budweiser. We had an argument over the bill as we left the bar, I threw some money at the owner and it sorted him out.

Dave had upset some England lads with his anti-IRA statements, he asked me if I would help to beat them up. I said 'yes, but I could do without any trouble really'.

Approximately ten England fans seemed to be locked up each night, then released the next day, but with my bad guts I didn't really want to be one of them.

Silk had been locked up, his Stoke mates delivered Kentucky fried chicken for him in the jail and he seemed to quite enjoy himself. The Mexicans were dead jealous of his food. During the night the guard asked him if he would like a whore, Silk said 'yes', then the guard said 'do you like little boys' and put his arm round him. Silk told him to 'fuck off'.

We went into town and into the pool bar drinking the Bohemia beer. Jim Hopkirk, the owner of the massive, Chelsea Hemel flag, had got his legs really badly burnt. We had hardly been out in the sun yet.

We saw Andy and Sheffield United Joe. They had been down to Acapulco and while they were there had freed a lion that was in a cage on display inside a bar. They said that, as it was a lion, it must be English. It was in a cage, behind the bar, they said it was just a cub really, so they undid the door and it ran off down the street with the owner chasing after it!

They said that there were quite a few Scots in Acapulco, but they appeared to be scared off the English. We had a few more beers then went up to the ground.

I felt like shit after last night, it was not such a good atmosphere this time.

Duggie, Dave and John Paul were staying in Monterrey after the game, as they were all in love! Even Dave had pulled.

I nearly got run over, on way to ground, I was looking the wrong way as I crossed a road and the Mexicans drove on the wrong side of the road. The game ended as 0-0 draw. I bought a t-shirt as a souvenir and had some beers in the ground.

The England fans were singing what a load of rubbish. Ray Wilkins was sent off and the captain Bryan Robson got injured. Alf shouted at Chris Waddle to do something during the match, and he actually started running.

The B.B.C got the police to remove a West Ham United N.F. flag. Duggie's flag was in its usual prominent position.

After the game, we jumped in the back of a pick-up into town again. The drivers didn't seem bothered. It started raining again, as it seemed to have done at some point every day of the holiday.

We went into 'Sambourns' and had dinner.

Later in the pool hall I was talking to Benny and The Tinman, they didn't realise that Wilkins was sent off and Robson was off injured. Tinman said 'it's not a bad result then'!

Benny told me that he didn't attack the Moroccan bus, but he did attack the Portuguese one. The Tinman and Benny started singing proddy songs and we all joined in. Some of the scousers in the bar and Alf didn't join in.

We played pool and pissed it up till about 11 p.m. The Tinman was nicking fags and beer again, usually off Stuart Hill. They had decided not to bother with the next England v Poland game and were off to U.S.A for six months, working as waiters. This was why The Tinman had bought his white shirt. I said to them that it looked like we were out anyway.

We grabbed a taxi to the bus station. We had earlier dumped our bags in Colin's room. Sprake bought a sports bag so he was travelling light, Smoke didn't have a bag and was travelling too light, he stunk later on!

We got on the bus, after having a few beers in the 'Fastoff hotel' while watching the England match highlights again. We managed to get some sleep on the bus. Lots of lads were going in all directions at the bus station. On our trip it was me, Sprake, Gary, Smoke, Alf, Col and Shane.

We arrived at Brownsville at about 6 a.m. the next morning.

Saturday

Once we got off the bus we walked along to the customs. The Yank guard looked at my passport and said 'hey, you've been all over'. Once through customs we got on another bus that was heading to the coast.

We decided to hire a car, as the bus was first, heading for the airport. While we were at the airport we checked-up on flights to Houston for when we got knocked out. By this time it was already really warm, up in Texas.

We had breakfast at the airport, as we looked around there seemed to be only one man doing all the jobs, he was loading cases and checking people in.

We used the courtesy phone to see if we could book in any hotels over on South Padre Island but the cheapest was $110 a night. The Welcome Inn in Brownsville was $65. Sprake said that he wanted a decent nights sleep, after the busses had woken him so many times, so we booked in.

The courtesy van came and collected us. Smoke looked a right state as his shorts were splitting, I felt a bit embarrassed of him, when we were checking into the hotel. We got adjoining twin rooms, but each twin had two double beds.

We had a shower, then went and lazed by the pool and used the Jacuzzi that was alongside it. We all piled into it at one point and took some photos. The hotel gardens were very nice with palm trees and a little stream running through it.

I was sitting down wind of Smoke, on the sun loungers, the smell was really quite unpleasant, so I suggested that we should go for a swim. I was hopeful that he wouldn't stink as bad when we got out.

Colin jumped in the pool, as we were all messing about, after a while a woman who was sunbathing with her family by the pool, shouted 'he's drowning'.

We didn't realise it was Colin who was drowning, because his curly hair had gone dead long. Sprake went over and pushed this body to the edge. A bloke pulled him out and started pumping water out of him. He couldn't swim and didn't realise their would be a deep end!

Smoke and me had to smile, as Colin was brought back from the dead by all and sundry around the pool. Later on, when we developed the photos we had taken, we saw in the background of our happy shots, Colin in various stages of recovery.

Later that day we said that, should he of drowned, it would have put a bit of a damper on the day!

Colin was dead quiet for rest of the day. We spent it by the pool but he didn't go back in! Then we went and watched TV in the various rooms.

Smoke went to our adjoining room and finished his Budweiser. Every day they're appeared to be a good film on the television, today's was 'Cool hand Luke' but we watched sport instead. The US commentator was saying things about the 'soccer game' at the World Cup that was on, like. 'It's a set up on the 6-yard line', he called the goalkeeper a stopper.

I had got the shits pretty bad and the 'Arrets' didn't seem to be working. At night we went for a look round Brownsville but there was not much to see.

We asked a woman if it was worth popping to New Orleans she just went 'oh, oh, oh,' for about a minute. We decided we might go, and would also like to see Baton Rouge for the 'KKK' headquarters if we got knocked out of the cup.

The local paper that we read, in a bar, was slagging off the Mexicans, Mexican whores and the jalopy cars they drove, and the fact they were all coming over the border.

I went for chicken and chips but still needed the toilet on a regular basis.

We decided to go back to the hotel bar. Smoke had no trousers with him, so he was not allowed into the adjoining club. Me, Sprake, Alf and Gary went in. There was a fit singer doing a cabaret show.

In the club we met up with some Blackburn lads, we had met before, when we were watching England in Paris. They told us about one of their mates, that we also knew, who had been jailed in England for life. We had a few beers, but it was quite expensive in the club.

We went back to the room and by now Smoke had drunk a couple of bottles of wine he had bought. He was now pissed out of his face and not making any sense. We ordered some cheese sandwiches from room service, and watched a shit roller-skating film, a bit like roller world. Then we all crashed out.

Sunday

Alf got up early and went and hired a van. He really wanted to. We were on about booking into the hotel for another night, but in end decide on the van and travelling to the resort of South Padre Island. Sprake and Smoke went for breakfast; Gary and me watched a film. Then I went for breakfast, it was massive but cost $4.

I went for a quick swim at the hotel pool and then bumped into Silk, Rob Jones and Dennis. They were on about being locked up again; apparently it was only for a couple of hours this time. I told them that we were going to move onto South Padre Island, and would see them back in Mexico.

The lads from Blackburn asked if they could tag along, we said 'yes'. Alf arrived with the van; he was like a kid with a new toy. Today was a bit cloudy, but still warm. We paid for the room, and packed our bags into the van. Alf had a 'bag on' about paying on his Visa card for the hotel, so I paid for it, and got the money from the lads.

Alf was a bit of a dodgy driver, but at least it wasn't me who was going to get done for drunk driving this time!

We went through Brownsville and over a causeway bridge to South Padre. It was now hot, so we were looking for place to stop, so we could get out of the van. Alf had the reactions of a snail. When we saw any places to park, on the front, he kept missing them.

We saw a pizza place and told him to stop, fifty yards later he did. We went into the pizza place but I didn't want food so we just had a wine spritzer. After Colin had finished his food, we used his plate and went to the help yourself salad bar. Smoke had a big pizza as usual, but this place was expensive.

We walked over to a supermarket and bought some beers. We got eight cans of Budweiser each, plus cheese and bread in the brown paper bag that they put your groceries in, in the States.

We sat in sun until the lads who had ordered food in the pizza place came out, they also bought some beers, then we went onto the beach.

We managed to park the van near the beach after Alf had made a detour onto the beach itself and nearly got it stuck. He really was a terrible driver. We dumped the beers in the shade. There were some other England fans on the beach by the looks of the flags and the various groups of lads that were sunbathing on them. We spent the day in the sea, drinking and sunbathing.

It was unbelievably hot. Me, Sprake and Gary went for a walk down the beach. A nice blonde was on her own, and she looked over, so I went and had a chat. She said her name was Trisha and she was originally from Colorado. I gave her one of my beers and drank mine with her. She was really fit. She told me which restaurant she was working in, and I told her, I might go there for a drink.

She said that she sunbathed every day. I went for a swim with her, then she had to go to work. I went back to the lads and crashed out.

They had been chatting to some of the local girls, but, by now it was the end of the day, and the sun was going down. We went back to the van and drove up the road, passing a pub so we told Alf to stop, but he was too late to turn down a side road. He wouldn't spin it round, and went down another road, that went down towards beach. I said 'don't go down there' but he did, then I said 'don't go on beach' but he did, I then said 'don't go on the soft sand' but he did and got the van stuck.

I asked Sprake if I should drive but Alf reckoned I was getting shitty, so I left him to it. We got towed off but it cost Alf $5. I drove it off the beach to get the speed up and to keep it going over the softer sand.

The Blackburn lads were trying to book a 'condo' so we said 'see you in a bit to them'.

We went and bought some t-shirts then just sat about. The Blackburn lads came back they had managed to get a condo for $50 so we went and parked the van outside it.

They said some of us could sleep in the condo. I went and had a shower; I was red as a lobster from the sunburn. I then went to the restaurant to meet Trish, but it wasn't open yet.

Smoke and me went to a Kentucky fried chicken. Some local youths were in there but they were scared of us for some reason. We went to a liquor store and bought a couple of bottles of wine, which we drank on the way to another bar.

We were in the bar and it soon started filling up. The girls from the beach were there, so Gary went and had a word with them. We were all pissed up by now, and started dancing and having a good laugh. Some other England fans were in there too.

Near the end of the night I went for a beer but was refused, as they said I was too pissed. I threatened the barman but he still wouldn't serve me. The bouncer came over and escorted me out.

On the way back to the condo Smoke and Sprake tried to steal a flag. Smoke said that we didn't do anything these days, so I threw a bottle at a car, like Big Paul had in Paris. The car screeched round it and nearly ran some lads over.

We were really pissed and when we got to the condo we just crashed out on the floor. Alf and Shaun slept in the van. It pissed down with rain through the night, but it didn't wake them, as they were so drunk.

Monday

By ten-thirty the lads were awake and out of the condo. Gary arrived back late, as usual. He had stayed with the girls in their condo. He kept going on about it, but he reckoned he didn't screw them, although he slept with one of them!

We went for breakfast, then drove to other end of the island. Already it was baking hot. When we got to the other end of the island there wasn't much there, except a riding stable and a go-kart place.

We went back towards the centre, but it was too hot for town, and we were getting a bit fed up, so we decided to go to the water slides we had seen the day earlier.

We went in, but I wasn't feeling too good. Sprake was on the beer already. I just sunbathed for a while, then, when I felt a bit better I had a go on the slides. At end of the slide by the plunge pool, was a bar with a nice girl working there.

She said 'hello', when I ended up in the pool and we had a chat. Not only was she working behind the bar, but she was also the lifeguard, she stripped to just a bikini and jumped in the pool.

I had a go down the slide, headfirst and backwards but got told off. We sat on the balcony sunbathing. Alf had driven the Blackburn lads back to Brownsville, he was like a big kid with the van, on the way back, he had run out of petrol and had to run to a garage to get a can full of 'gas'.

When the slide place shut we said 'bye' to girl and headed to the bar we were in the night before. I was a bit wary about the barman and bouncer, but they didn't give me any trouble. We had a few cheaper draught beers.

We put some records on the jukebox, then three fit girls came into the bar. I got talking to them with the lads and it turned out they were all Irish Americans, and their church sent money to Noraid.

I walked away and Alf looked at me as if I was doing something wrong, as he was a catholic and a plastic Celtic fan.

I went and talked to Shane and Smoke while the rest carried on talking to the girls. We pissed it up until about 7 p.m. then Alf drove us back to Brownsville, he then returned the van. We had a couple of beers at the greyhound station and also in the old part of town. We found a sex shop and had a look round at the magazines and the fetish displays to kill some time.

After buying our bus tickets to Monterrey, we had some time before it left, so we went to the local 'Burger King' for a slap up meal. We finished the meal and then got onto the bus. I sat at the front with Shane.

The bus driver was crazy, he was overtaking everything. We had hardly any legroom and I couldn't get comfortable, this was going to be a long journey. There were a few other England fans on board. As we were talking to them about previous trips, Brazil v England in 1984 came up.

Sprake hated the fact that I was one of the few England fans to make the trip, and told everyone that I went on a dead cheap flight.

There was a dog sat in the middle of the road, the driver didn't slow at, all but just swerved around it. Gary did his 'Murray Walker' impersonation, in a high-pitched voice saying 'and it is an overtaking manoeuvre'. Alf then said 'it's used up one of its lives'. Gary replied, still sounding like Murray Walker 'you are right, and I am wrong it's a cat'.

We stopped at a café and bought some bottles of Bohemia beer. Lots of the local people were looking at us; it was like a scene from the 'Magnificent Seven' or a spaghetti western. We had stopped at one of those dodgy places you could easily have disappeared, if you were on your own. There were loads of cockroaches in the café, so we gave them some food. I threw an empty bottle I had finished drinking from. It flew yards and then, landed straight into a waste bin. We got back onto the bus; I did manage to get some sleep. We arrived in Monterrey the following morning.

Tuesday

We were now the bus making all the noise at the Bus station, at five in the morning. We got off the bus and went to the 'Fastoff Hotel' for breakfast. I was still feeling drunk and I had still got the shits. I went and got my bag from Colin's hotel and we walked into town.

We decided we were going to stay at the 'Hotel Monterrey' so we went and booked in. It was a Best Western hotel, so had a much better level of comfort than the corner hotel we had been staying at.

Two of us booked in, then the rest of us sneaked in. It was only for one night. Sprake and me went and bought bus tickets for Guadalajara, and then onwards to Porta Valletta. We had decided to go down there whether England won or lost. I changed some money up; the exchange rate was getting better every time.

We went back to hotel and had a drink in the bar. We got our flags, and headed up to the ground. We met Mark and Tracey, Mark was working out all the different permutations, of who we might play, but Sprake and me were not that bothered as we planned to go to Porta Valletta for a few days, then possibly New Orleans on the way home.

We got into ground and went to the bar that was behind one of the stands.

I met up with Gerry, Eddie and the rest of north London lads in the bar, then Dave, Duggie and Harry came in.

Apparently Dave was now the stud of Monterrey; well at least he was according to Duggie.

Stuart Hill came in and told us that Chris from Manchester was marrying a Mexican next Sunday, and Frank was going to be his best man! We had a few beers in the bar with Dave, while Sprake and Gary went and put their flags up.

I was wearing my Canada v England security t-shirt, and lots of the lads were looking at it. It seemed a long while ago now, but it was nice to wear, as hardly anyone else had made the trip to Canada.

Just before kick-off we went to get in the England end, but the stewards wouldn't let us, so about forty of us, including the Halifax lads, stood down the side. Sprake and Gary were at the bottom of the terracing by the fence, helping a lad called Trevor to put his flag up.

England won 3-0, we kept going for beers during the match and I had an argument with Smoke over whose round it was. Money was starting to become a bit of an issue and Smoke was notoriously tight.

We were told that Benny and The Tinman had been arrested after the last game for kicking in a window. They were both fined £100; The Tinman only had £250 when he started four weeks ago! Benny was interviewed by a British cop, from Scotland Yard, while he was being held in jail.

At end of the game, which England won, all the lads were doing the conga behind the goal. We managed to get into the end with them. The papers that night were now saying that the 'English are wonderful', after blaming us for everything from the weather, to funny noises on the telephone lines, in the days before.

Silk was interviewed on the local TV after the match.

After the game we got out of the ground and met up with Sprake and Gary. It started raining again, so we jumped on a bus that was going back to Monterrey.

We went to the hotel and dumped our flags, then had a drink from the room's mini bar. After a few shorts we went down to the pool bar. Lots of lads had gathered there, and we had some celebratory beers.

Andy Parsons asked me to come down to watch Chelsea more; this was witnessed by Sprake and the other lads. He invited me down to the 'Hand and Flower' pub in Chelsea for first game of the season. I said I would be there, and he said he would buy me a beer. I was now in with some of the top Chelsea boys.

We noticed that there were a few Spanish fans out and about now, as they were playing in Monterrey the next day.

Me and Sprake went for something to eat and bumped into Manalo, the famous Spain and Valencia fan, who followed his club and country, most places they played, always with a painted drum.

Sprake slagged him off for what the Spanish did to us, in the Spain 82 World Cup, where he reckoned Manalo was behind some attacks on England Fans. He went to hit him. I couldn't believe that he was behind any violence, but Manalo ran off down the street anyway.

We saw him being interviewed on TV later, and I wondered if he was saying he had been threatened and chased down the street by England fans.

We went back to the pool bar, by now it was pouring with rain, and massive traffic jams were forming on the street outside. All the English went outside in the downpour and started jumping in massive puddles, dancing about in the street and doing congas up and down the road.

The Spanish who were watching tried to do something similar but their effort was shit. The coppers then cleared all of us off the road.

We drank all night, then went back to the hotel. Stuart Hill was ripping the piss out of me, because I was actually staying in a nice hotel.

We had the last beer out of the mini bar. The lads were having a go, now that I had been accepted into the inner sanctum of the Chelsea fans, especially Shane, as he was West Ham.

Wednesday

We woke up early and had breakfast. We wanted to get out of the room early, before any cleaners came in, as there was five of us in the room. We had time for a shower, as Alf had finally finished 'preening' himself in it. It took a while to work out how to use the shower, as the controls were not actually in the shower room.

We checked out of the hotel, but they said we could leave our bags for the day. The receptionist must have thought the two of us had a lot of luggage. The bill for the mini bar was dead expensive, it turned out that Smoke had hit it hard, without us knowing what was originally in it.

We went for a walk; there were lots of Spanish about today. Most of the English were leaving; we did a bit of food shopping, then went to the pool bar. We had two games then went for a walk in the park. There were loads of fit girls about in the park; they surrounded us, asking for our autographs.

Sprake did a 'noughts and crosses' grid, in one book that was offered to him, by a fit Mexican girl. The girl then wanted to play him. We started walking away, but they all followed us, so we ran to the nearest bar, it was like the old 'St Bruno' advert that was on the television in the seventies.

Alf left early to go to Acapulco with Duggie, Harry, Dave and John Paul.

Me, Sprake, Gary, Shane and Smoke were all going to Porta Valletta. We went back to the hotel and had a drink and some food. Duggie was in the corridor, with a girl that he had been hanging around with in Monterrey, saying a soppy goodbye. I got the bags; they were getting heavier now and were full of smelly clothes. We would have to go to a launderette soon.

We headed to the bus station for the last time. We tried to get a taxi but most said that there were too many of us, then one stopped. Our cowboy hats got squashed when the taxi driver shut the boot.

At the bus station, I bought a bottle of orange; we got on the bus and sat at the back. The bus was heading for Guadalajara. It was an overnight journey, so we sat for a bit, then spread out onto the empty seats and got our heads down.

I was sat next to the onboard toilet, when a fat Mexican woman used it, it stunk for ages.

At one point the bus was sideways, as the driver was skidding on gravel at a hairpin. The driver was fighting with the wheel to keep us on the road. It was really hot on the bus; we had the windows open, meanwhile the driver was driving with his foot hanging out of his window!

Thursday

We woke up on the bus and snoozed for a while. It was difficult to get comfortable and again I was glad that I had got a pillow in my towel. Sprake woke up and shouted 'ok I'm awake now, so you lot can be'. It was amazing to me how he never cleaned his teeth! After a few hours going through some really steep cliff roads, we were getting near to the city of Guadalajara.

We passed through some slums on the edge of city, went past the football ground and the bus eventually stopped at the bus station. We went into the bus station building, and bought some orange juice and found out the time of the next bus to Porta Valletta.

Someone shouted at us and we looked up, Sheffield United Joe was on the balcony above us, so we went and had a chat with him.

It was soon time for the next bus, so we got on, after we had made sure it was going to Porta Valletta. Some Aussies that we had seem in the ground the day before, they had a kangaroo flag, also got on the bus. We had a chat with them during the journey. It was about an eight-hour journey, but at least the bus wasn't very full, so we could spread out.

It wasn't too long until we came across the first road crash; it was a lorry that had smashed into a cliff. We noticed that lots of the hairpin, and normal corners had crosses and shrines to those that had died, placed on them.

On one corner there was about twenty crosses, Sprake reckoned a mini full of Pakistanis, must have crashed.

I took a photo of the crash and after about half an hour, we got moving again, after the wreck had been towed away. The bus driver was having a laugh about the crash with us.

On one bus that Mark had been on, he had told us, it hit a cow and the cow staggered off shaking its head. He said the driver was laughing to himself for hours.

We arrived at a small village at dinnertime and the bus stopped. We looked at some of the food on offer but it was really smelly. Instead we went to the local bar and had a few beers. We watched a bit of the Germany versus Scotland game, which was being played that afternoon.

We had a bit of a wander down the street then went back to the bus. We finished our drinks we had bought, on the bus, then got bit more shut eye. Finally we arrived at Porta Valletta at about four in the afternoon. After the journey we decided there and then, that we would catch a plane back to Mexico City.

We got off the bus and found out which way we wanted to go. The Aussies went in the opposite direction! We headed down towards the sea and found a hotel on the front. It had got rooms available, so we booked a double condo. It was only£3 a night, very cheap, but good and clean.

We booked in for two nights and went and dumped our bags and had a lie down. I later got changed; I hardly had any clean clothes left, so I put on a Falklands Islands t-shirt. At about seven we headed out on the piss. We went towards the centre of town along the beach, but a stream, which also appeared to be a sewer, was in the way, so we cut in land and got a beer at a local bar.

We moved on and had some beer and a meal in an upstairs bar. Then went down the main street going from bar to bar. We went into a video bar, then one where you could get a pitcher, which held six bottles of beer.

Some Scots and Northern Ireland fans were in the bar. We ignored the Scots but got talking to the Irish. They were a bit cagey at first, when we told them that we drank in 'Robinsons Bar' in Belfast. When we mentioned that we also drank in the 'Berlin Bar' and 'The Orange Cross' they started talking to us.

One of the lads gave me his Ulster flag and told me how good Porta Valletta was. He said that he had pulled a girl every night, mostly rich

Yanks, who were staying at the Intercontinental Hotel.

We left the bar at about eleven and tried another one up the road, then came back, but by now the original one was full and the bouncers wouldn't let us in. We started to argue with a black bouncer but he wouldn't budge. We slagged him off, then he got a bit of a slap, along with his mates who came to his assistance. We sang 'England aggro' as we ended up giving them a kicking. Everyone inside the bar was looking out, watching the fight, especially the Scots and the Irish; they knew we were here now.

We moved on to another bar, Smoke and Shane went for food, Gary wandered off, me and Sprake ended up in a queer bar. We didn't realise it was until we had ordered a beer, but it wasn't too bad and we just stayed near the bar and didn't go to the toilet! We finished our beers, then staggered back to the condo and crashed out.

Friday

We woke up late, and went for swim in the condo pool. As I was swimming Gary came back from the previous night. He had been to a disco. Already there were some fit girls sunbathing around the pool. I dried off and went and got some breakfast. Gary went straight to bed, he was still pissed.

We got our dirty clothes, and took them to the launderette, that happened to be just around the block. Then we went to the beach and sunbathed. It was true what we had been told and it appeared to be a beautiful resort.

We ended up having a small game of football against some of the locals. I tackled a Mexican, probably a bit too hard, but after rolling around for a bit he got up and seemed to be able to play on with only a minor limp.

After the game we sat on the beach and got our breath back. As we sat, we saw pelicans diving for fish and then a hump back whale swam across the bay.

At dinnertime we went for a walk and ended up at the 'Apartment Bar' to watch the afternoon World Cup game. The barman liked us as we were English and kept saying 'beat Argentina'. On the way to the bar we saw a couple of Scots and said to them 'have you missed your plane, you've not booked for 4 weeks have you'? And laughed at them.

Gary came and joined us and we went to the video bar, where there was always music playing. Smoke and Shane wandered off for food; we stayed and pissed it up all afternoon. At about four we walked back towards the hotel and had a burger at another bar.

On the way back we were singing 'Jerusalem'. Women were giggling and some Yanks who were on a jeep safari looked at us dead funny.

We bumped into a fit girl who was selling cruises around the bay. It turned out she was going out with a bloke from Cambridge. He came over and he turned out be a right wanker, who was just touring around. We asked 'how much is it to go and watch the diving' she looked at us blank, and we said 'it's famous for it in Acapulco'.

She thought it was dead funny when we said 'this is Acapulco isn't it; shit I thought we got on the wrong bus'. The Cambridge youth came over again and said, 'no, you're in Porta Valletta'.

We picked up the laundry; one of Sprake's shirts had run. It was nice to be putting on clean clothes again, especially the socks and pants.

After we had got changed, and had had a wash, we headed off back into town. We had a beer on the way at various bars. We called into the 'Apartment Bar' again, the barman said 'my friends' and bought us all a tequila sunrise, but first gave us all just a shot of Tequila, with the salt around the rim of the glass. Smoke had two.

Gary who had already had a Tequila sunrise in a disco bar, told us that it tasted nice, and it did.

Two Yanks then came in and they got exactly the same treatment. The sun was dead hot through the open door.

Sprake was moaning about Smoke and Shane always following us. We all went to the upstairs bar for food, and ended up having hamburger and chips again, Smoke had a pizza again.

Gary arrived later on and finished our meals. As we left the waiter complained to us because we hadn't left him a tip, we told him to bollocks, in the end I offered him a small amount, and he just threw it at me. We all left and the waiter had a right mood on.

We went to the video bar and met up with some Liverpool fans. We pissed it up all night, Smoke and Shane went back to the hotel first, me, Gary and Sprake ended up in a long thin bar that was showing videos.

I got talking to an American girl called Page; she was quite pissed up but dead funny. She was slurring her words and was with her friend, another Yank girl, and she thought that we were taking the piss out of her, but really we weren't.

Then a Mexican bloke just grabbed her, and started snogging her. Her mate asked us for help, so we said to Page 'are you ok' but she said 'yes', so there was not a lot we could do. We still hung around to make sure that she was safe.

I had an arm wrestle with a big Yank and lost, which was a rare occurrence. It looked like Page was going to go off with Mexican, so we left. We were annoyed because she was far too fit for one of them.

Sprake and Gary decided to go to a disco, I went back to the condo. They got into a taxi and said the name of the disco. I watched it pull off and it went 50 yards round a corner, which a minute later I was walking round. The driver charged them 500 pesos. When I got back I noticed that there were loads of lizards in the hotel room, but they didn't bother me, I just hit the sack and went to sleep.

Saturday

I was up late for breakfast. It happened to be the day of the Argentina qualifying match and we agreed to watch it in the Apartment bar. Gary took his flag after the owner asked him to.

We walked along the beach, over the bridge, which went over stream or sewer, and on the way we called into a travel agent and asked how much it was to fly to Mexico City. They told us it was £33. As my money was running out I said I would buy Sprake's and mine on my Visa card and he could give me the cash.

We went and watched the match and got free drinks again. We sat in the sun to watch the game, which the Argies won, so this meant if we beat Paraguay we played them. After a few drinks, and being bombarded by loads of flies, we got talking to a Yank who owned the apartments. He couldn't understand our accents at all, so we all took the piss out of him.

Afterwards we went up to the Video Bar. We had a drink, then Shane and Smoke went for a walk. We went and bought yet another t-shirt, then sat on the beach. We just went for a drink every so often. Gary and Sprake stayed in the bar getting pissed. When I went in for a beer we bumped into Page again. She wasn't pissed now, but seemed to be all right after the other night, and when we questioned her, she wasn't fussed about going with the Mexican.

In the next bar we ended up drinking in, there were lots of fit older American women. They kept offering us food, but we didn't want any, as we had eaten. While we were in the bar, we watched another whale swim across the bay followed by a load of pelicans.

Smoke and Shane came into the bar. They had been on a walk to the 'Holiday Inn' and reckoned that it was dead good.

We went back to our hotel and got just soft drinks out of the fridge, I had a bit of a lie down then sorted out my clothes, before we went out to the usual bars. We had quite a good piss up.

At the end of night Shane and Smoke again went for something to eat. Me, Sprake and Gary went back to the long bar for more beer, then went to where Smoke and Shane were eating. It was a right doss hole.

There were two Irish American girls in there, and Sprake and me started talking to them. They told us that Smoke and Shane had ignored them, when they found out they were catholics. The boys gave us some stick for talking to them but I asked them if they were Noraid supporters and they said 'no'; so I decided to keep talking to them. Sprake and me arranged to meet them at about four the next afternoon in the Apartment Bar.

We left the restaurant and Gary, Sprake and me went to a disco that was up a really steep hill. Gary said he knew the way, as he had been there before, but we got lost and had to get into a taxi to get there. We had earlier been given free tickets to the disco, we only had two, but we managed to all get in by passing one back.

A really fit girl was outside the disco. She was pissed out of her head, those Yanks just couldn't drink. We were just wearing shorts and t-shirts, but the disco was a posers place. We sat at the back of the club, all the girls were roughing up their hair in the eighties style, they were wearing really flimsy dresses, and the lads mostly looked like something out of Miami vice.

All the Mexican lads were hanging around the rich Yank women, we didn't get a look in, plus the drinks were dead expensive.

A few of the Irish lads were in there and they seem to have scored. Then the club had an indoor firework display, it was far too posy for us, so we went back to the condo.

Sunday

I woke up late. Gary decided that as he was next to the pacific, he was going to have a seafood breakfast; the rest of us had the normal American breakfast. There were some other English fans about, so at dinner we went for a drink with them.

Mexico were playing that afternoon, so all the locals were in the bars watching the match on TV.

At about 4 p.m. Sprake and me went to the 'Apartment bar' to meet Julie and her mate, the girls we had met the last night, but for the first time while we were there, the bar was closed.

We went to another bar for a beer, then at ten to four went back to the bar. It was still closed but the owner, who happened to be in the bar, said we could watch his TV and use his glasses, after we explained we were meeting some girls there.

There was an off licence around the corner, so we went and bought a bottle of champagne and some beers, then sat in the empty bar and waited. There was no sign off the girls.

We drank all the beer and went back to the shop and bought a load more beers and a couple more bottles of champagne. At least I could use my credit card for this.

We drank all this, and were starting to get pissed. At about seven the girls walked by in swimming costumes, with sarongs covering themselves.

It turned out they had met some Yanks who had the use of a speedboat and had gone off with them for the day!

They thought it was funny how we were still in the empty bar, surrounded by bottles. The girls went to the off licence and bought some more wine and beer. When they came back we sat around and talked.

I was talking to the blonde and mentioned how everyone loved the Queen. This started to wind her up, but I said 'I'm not going to argue I'm right, and your wrong'.

Smoke and Shane walked by and shouted obscenities at us. After a while we left, and went to the video bar. I was still with the blonde, but had started talking to Julie a bit as well. In the video bar Sprake and me decided to swap over girls.

I kissed Julie and Sprake kissed the blonde. We had a couple of beers, then went to the next bar; all the lads were in this bar along with the Irish lot. As we sat down they all threw ice at us. Sprake picked up an ashtray and threw it at them. The Irish lads looked at him as if he was mad.

We had another beer but the service was slow and we had already had a number of arguments during the week, with various waiters, so we left. The blonde, who was with Sprake, then collapsed and crawled on her hands and knees to a taxi, to take her to her hotel.

I told Sprake to go with her, but he didn't and just went back into the bar with the rest of the lads.

Julie and me went to the 'Bucket Bar' and bumped into Page again. She was with another bloke I said 'hi'.

Julie was on about going to a disco but she only had a swimming costume and sarong on. We had a kiss and a cuddle, then we decided to walk back to the old part of town where the hotels were.

On the way we went into the 'Long bar', Gary and Sprake were there. Julie gave Sprake her room number, and told him to sleep there for the night! Things seemed to be heading in the right direction. Paul bunged some more ice at me so I threw nuts, popcorn, and ice over him. Then we all grabbed bar stools and were mucking about. The barman asked us for no trouble.

Julie and me walked past her hotel. It had a floodlit pool and we went for a swim. Some Irish lads, who were staying at that hotel, were in the shallow end, learning to swim. We went into the deep end, Julie stayed at the side while I swam couple of widths, showing off a bit. Then I started kissing and feeling her. She felt my hard-on then I slipped it up her in the pool.

We were making a few waves in the pool as I was shagging her slowly. One of the Irish lads said 'is he fucking her'. We decided to go to bed, and when she went to her room to get a towel, Sprake was there. We went back to my room, in my condo, and I dried her off, then I fucked her twice. At one point as we were screwing, standing up, she was stepping on the back of my calves and arching her back. She had a really nice body and after we had finished we went to sleep.

Monday

I woke up next to Julie. She was just as good looking in the morning. I started playing with her tits and kissing her. All of a sudden the door to the bedroom was kicked in. I covered Julie over with a sheet. Gary burst into the room; he had broken the lock and was pissed out of his head. Apparently he had been in a whore bar till about 8 o'clock.

Julie made an excuse and said she had got to go to a meeting about a trip. She rushed off back to her hotel. As she left, I said I might go on a jungle trip with them, she said to let her know if I wanted to, I said I would.

She went to her hotel and, when she arrived, Sprake was getting on all right with the blonde girl. He was kissing her and trying to get it up when Julie came in, so Gary fucked it up for both of us.

Gary was shit faced in his bed so I slept on for a while. Sprake came back, and I got up at about ten. I went and sat by the pool, it was so hot that sweat was pouring out of me. I went for a swim then Smoke came down to the pool.

We went for a walk down the beach and took a few photos. At about midday we went and sorted the room and got the boys out. I went to the girl's hotel, as Julie had lent me some money, but she was not there.

At about three we got a taxi to the airport. Sprake got one first, but it was too small for all of us. I pissed him off by hailing a big taxi and then saying 'if you want a job doing, do it yourself, just leave it to me'.

The taxi driver took us through the town on the way to the airport. There were donkeys everywhere. At the airport we had a beer, and checked onto our flight.

We went through to the departure lounge and had another beer. Again there seemed to be an awful lot of fit girls about.

We walked across the tarmac and boarded the plane. It started to taxi, without any safety messages and got up to what seemed about forty miles per hour, then just swung round onto the runway, and without stopping went faster and we took off. Gary was shitting himself; we flew out over sea, which gave us a good view of Porta Valletta.

We got a meal of shrimp and a cup of coffee on the plane. Soon we were flying over the sprawl of Mexico City. The lads were well impressed with the size of it, spread out below the plane, as we looked out of the window.

After landing we walked down a corridor to the arrivals hall. There were loads of different fans about, especially Brazilians waiting to go through customs.

We went for a taxi, but it was a stupid system where you had to buy a ticket first. We had an argument with the bloke in charge of the taxi rank. In the end we needed two taxis, we didn't let the porters carry our bags and they got shitty because they were losing a tip.

We told the taxi drivers to go to the Reforma Square. We lost the other taxi on the way but it turned up a few minutes later. I got my bearings, but popped into a hotel to check that I was going the right way. The receptionist in the hotel marked the map I had, and I lead the lads to the Hotel Calvin.

It was a long walk and the boys were starting to moan. Sprake said to me 'don't worry about it, it's good you know where you are going'. Gary's bag was really heavy and he was struggling with it.

It happened he not only had his clothes in it, but it was also full of books on his medical stuff, as he had got nursing exams coming up, plus books on Mexico, which turned out to be quite useful.

After a while I recognised a big square and a traffic island with fountains on it. We turned the corner and the big hotel, that we used for breakfast the year before, was still standing but really badly damaged from the earthquake that had struck in the last year.

I couldn't believe it was that badly damaged, but when I looked down the street only the Calvin Hotel was standing, plus the supermarket that was next door.

We went down to the hotel and booked in. Sprake said 'ask the receptionist if she remembers you', she didn't. We got a big room, which had four beds, two doubles and two singles.

We dumped our bags. The toilet door, off our bedroom, wouldn't shut as the whole building was on a tilt from the earthquake. When I remembered that you could see the road through the floor last year, I just couldn't believe it was still standing.

The lads seem to be quite impressed with the hotel, and we crashed out for a while before we went in search of some Paraguay tickets. We had a wander around, but couldn't find any in any of the usual places like travel agents and banks.

We decided to try again the next day, then, amazingly we bumped into Harry in a city of 20 million people, again the magnet effect. He was on his own, apparently a couple of days ago, Duggie and John had just jumped into a taxi leaving him, and he had no idea where they had gone. Now he wasn't talking to them.

It turned out that Dave had also been abandoned, and had wandered around Mexico City for two days, before he found them again.

Me, Sprake and Harry went for a drink. I had a bad belly from the shrimps on the plane. I went back to the hotel, but got lost and bumped into Stuart Hill who was in search of a beer. I told Stuart I wasn't feeling too good, and carried on looking for the hotel.

I ended up in some subways but they all looked the same, so I stopped a few taxis, but either the drivers didn't know where the hotel was, or they wanted too much money.

By now I was badly constipated, somehow I ended up on the Reforma Road that lead to the square, and I knew my way from there, and walked back to the hotel.

I felt freezing cold so curled up in bed; Smoke and Shane were still in the room. Then I went to the toilet and ended up, puking my guts up. I was backwards and forwards all night from the bed to the toilet.

In the morning, Harry and Sprake told me that they had a great night and were dancing on the tables in the bar. All the Mexican girls were singing 'aria aria van van dooba', as they swivelled their hips in time, wearing their little Ra Ra skirts. Apparently all the girls were pointing at them as they danced, plus a load of Brazilian girls were dancing, and giving it the hip movements, nearby. They had got back at about four in the morning pissed up.

Tuesday

Today I felt much better thankfully; I didn't think any shrimp could have been left in me. Alf arrived from Acapulco, Sprake was supposed to have met him at the airport, so Alf was a bit pissed off about Sprake not turning up.

He brought some 'gear' with him that he had bought. It was basically cocaine, that he had acquired in Acapulco, but he didn't give me any.

We got ready for the game. Alf went to the bank to get some more money, so I lead the lads to the ground, as I knew where to change on the Mexican underground. Then where to get the bus from at Tasquena square. The lads were impressed and Sprake remarked that it had saved a lot of time.

There was a bit of queuing for the bus to the Azteca Stadium. While we were in the queue we were told that lots of the English fans had been nicking from the supermarkets around Tasquena.

We arrived at the Azteca and had a look at what the badge sellers had got for sale. I wanted to go for a beer, but the lads wanted to try and get a ticket first. We tried at the stadium, but had no joy, so went for a beer anyway; unfortunately this meant that I was back on the Carta Blanca.

There was a Black London tout outside the stadium, so we kept away from him, but tried some of the other touts, who were cheaper, and managed to get tickets at a very good price. We saw Mark Dartford and Tracey outside the stadium as we drank the last of our beer. It was a 12 o'clock kick off, with nearly ninety thousand inside the ground.

There was no individual programmes. I checked at a number of kiosks, so we went into the ground. We were high up at the back of the stand. A few rows in front of us were some Scottish lads, one of whom had an Argentina shirt on!

I went and slagged him off, but when I swung for him he ducked out of the way and made himself scarce. I saw Joe Pearson, one of the Arsenal lads that I knew, and he was completely out of his head.

From our seats at the back of the stand we could see out of the stadium. I looked outside and Jim Hopkirk and Vince were running up and down the road with a massive Chelsea Hemel flag. They later ended up in the next section to us and we tried to get through to them, but the stewards wouldn't let us.

England won the game 3-0. At the end of game the Mexican press took a lot of photos of us. All the England fans joined up together and mostly we were singing anti-Argentina songs.

Bobby Robson, the manager, was being interviewed at pitch side below, he looked up at us; he was shaking his head, in that usual scornful way of his.

We left the ground and started walking up the dual carriageway, but we couldn't get a lift. We went in a café but it was really smelly, so in the end jumped on the next bus that was going to Tasquenna, the bus was dead cheap.

We then got onto the next tube and got back to the hotel. Stuart Hill had moved into our hotel, while Gary and Alf said that they were pissed off with Mexico City and were off to Acapulco. They left that night, Gary seemed to have a bit of a bag on with me, and I must admit I hadn't seen that much of him on this trip.

That left Sprake, Smoke, Shane, Stuart, Harry, Duggie, Dave, John and me as the only England fans we knew of, who were staying in the city. We headed down to the bars and went into a steak place and had some food. Afterwards we headed down the pedestrianized road, and really pissed it up in the 'Piccadilly bar'.

Memories of the year before came back and I took the boys into the bar where the song Guadalajara was always playing, but it wasn't being played anymore. We drank until about one-thirty. Then we worked our way back down, bar to bar, to the Reforma. One barman where we used to drink remembered us.

Stuart saw the state of the hotel that we used to have breakfast in. It was totalled, the ground floor was just a pile of rubble, and he was really happy as the earthquake hit at breakfast time, and he hated the headwaiter, who kept putting refry beans over his food.

Dave bunked into our room, by now with the comings and goings the owner hadn't got a clue what was going on.

Wednesday

I woke up and Sprake had already got a drink of orange from the shop next door. I had some of it, as I had a thirst from the night before, then went for a shower. We spent the day wandering around and went back up to the ground in search of tickets but there was none about.

At dinner we went to the Arthur's steak bar and had a few beers. The barman didn't understand what Bacardi and coke was, and after about five attempts at ordering a glass of it, I ended up shouting 'Bacardi and Coke' at him. He then went 'ah, Bacardi and coke'. When I re-ordered the same drink the next time, I had the same problem. I reported him to the manager, the thick bastard.

Stuart Hill came in and as usual was saying what a shit hole everywhere was. 'It's a fuckin carzy' was his opinion of Mexico City. We watched the France versus Brazil game; there were some silly Yanks at the next table. At the penalty shoot-out, after the game ended in a draw, they said 'hey, that's what that spot's for'! Plus they wanted the French to win.

They were dead loud, the oldest Yank introduced himself and his family to the Mexican owner, this obviously wound us up, and we said to him 'sit down and shut up'. Stuart said, dead loud, so everyone could hear 'beat those Brazilian ethnics, they're just like the American mongrels, full of ethnics'. Also, annoyingly, there was a businessman on his mobile phone, which in those days not many people had, he was talking for ages making out that he was dead important and speaking loudly.

We moved on and went down to the 'Piccadilly Bar' for the Mexico v Germany game.

As usual, whole Mexican families appeared to be eating together while watching the football. All the English in the pub wanted Germany to win, and when a big cheer went up, after another draw and another penalty shoot-out and the Germans had eventually won, the Mexicans got a bit upset and wound up with us.

We said afterwards, if that happened in England, and a load of Mexicans had cheered when we lost, they would have all have got smashed up.

Some Geordies came into the pub with a youth from Yeovil, who was wearing an Argentina shirt, you couldn't make it up. Everyone was looking at him and we were slagging him off. As he walked past, I told him that he was a wanker, he just walked on by.

That night in the garden part of the city, some of the English lads were involved in fights with the locals. Lots of Mexicans were driving around with flags hanging out of their cars, even though they had lost and were eliminated from the cup. There seemed to be about twenty people sitting in, and on, each Volkswagen Beetle that went past.

We went on the piss with Stuart and the Manchester City lads. While we were out we bumped into some West Ham lads and got talking to one of their famous fans, he seemed all right, but he didn't ever seem to smile.

We were in the 'Guadalajara Bar', when a busker came in. he was playing a guitar so we all danced and sang along, but when he wanted some money we told him to 'piss off'. Out on the streets, in general there were lots of street beggars, usually women holding babies while sat under blankets. I didn't often give them money; if I did they would all come for it, and give you more hassle than if you hadn't given anything in the first place.

We went to a disco on the corner but it was shit, as it was a bit too smart for us. We went back to another bar, and a local ran in and shouted 'Argentina'. I threw my glass at him and it smashed on his head.

Sprake said 'that was a great shot'! Stuart said 'leave it' and the barman came over and said that I was crazy and he wanted me out. We drank up and left.

A girl who was selling roses gave one to one of the lads, so we said 'thank you'. Then she wanted some money.

We said to her 'no, you gave it to us' in the end she got a copper to help her, so we threw it back at her. Sprake had already asked her 'what would I do with a rose, why would I want one'.

It was pouring with rain as we walked back to the hotel; lots of Mexicans were out in the street partying. There was some Argentineans about as well, Shane had a word with one in the Intercontinental Hotel but nothing came of it.

Some other Argies were hanging about round a fountain but nothing was said to them, then we passed the posh part of the Reforma, this was where the Germans seemed to be staying, as there were a few German flags hanging out of hotel windows.

We had spoken, during the night, to some lads who had done an all-inclusive tour for the World Cup. They were not happy with their accommodation, they should have seen ours.

As we walked back a load of coppers were sheltering under the canopies of various shops. They went quiet as me and Sprake approached, then they all charged at us. We shit it, as they got close, then they all started laughing and patting us on the back.

Meanwhile there had been some English arrested in town, plus the Mexicans were, by now, shooting guns in the air and apparently one or two of the locals had been shot.

We got back to the 'Hotel Calvin' and a big party was in full swing in the street. Lots of people were dancing on cars roofs and bonnets, heaven knows what it would have been like if they had won.

Thursday

We woke up late and then told the rest of the lads about the coppers the night before. Later Sprake and me tried to buy some Argie tickets. After some confusion in the bank over what exactly we wanted, in the end we managed to get a couple for a good price. The price of tickets was rocketing, and the rest of the lads were panicking about getting them, so we had done well.

Today I decided that I had got to go back home, after the Argy game, come what may. If we won, I decided that I would fly back for the final.

I went to a travel agent and booked a flight to Laredo for the Sunday afternoon after the game. It took a lot of sorting, and while I was in the shop I was bosting for a shit. When it was all done, I dived into a local Denny's restaurant. Unfortunately there was a big queue for toilet. In the end I just manage to hold it, and get in a cubicle in time, before I filled my pants.

Later back at the hotel I Left the room and locked ourselves out, I could have shimmied along the balcony from the next room, but it was quite high above the pavement. Luckily the manager was about and he came and let me back in. Stuart was in the next room, and he told me about last year, when he could see a couple having sex from his room, in the opposite hotel.

We went for dinner at Denny's. The service was really slow as usual. By now I had to use my visa card more and more. The waitress asked me for a tip, but I said 'no, it was slow service'. Smoke as usual always ordered soup as a starter, which meant we had to wait even longer for our main meal.

We walked down the Reforma and met Mark. He told us about the bus to Acapulco he and Tracey had just been on. It broke down as the gearbox wouldn't work, and the driver just left them for five hours, until the next bus came along.

We decided to go on a tour of the pyramids the next day, so we went and sorted this out at a travel agent. Later we called into fast food burger place, but it was so slow for the food as usual. We got the chips, but then had to wait for the burger, so ended up throwing the chips at the server.

A lad called Lloyd; who we had met in Israel, when we happened to be complaining about service in a fast food place there, walked in and saw us arguing again. He seemed to think we were moaning about nothing. When he ordered his food the girl behind the counter went and started cleaning the tables half way through serving him!

Duggie was in one of the bars. He was wearing really loud shorts. He told us that he was staying in the U.S.A. after the world cup and not bothering about going home.

We went for some drinks around the 'Piccadilly Bar', then by about five in the afternoon it was pissing down again.

This was starting to get Sprake down, so we got a taxi back to the hotel and bought drinks from the supermarket and got pissed in the room.

On every corner there seemed to be old women under tarpaulins cooking horrible smelly food. Once the rain had finally stopped we went back out, but it was so cold that I had to wear jeans and a jumper. For some reason we really pissed it up on cheap beers in the Piccadilly and Guadalajara bars.

A little Scouser in one bar, tried to pick an argument with me as we were talking about various teams back in England. I told him that Liverpool didn't follow England to normal games anyway. Next his big mate joined in and had a go at me for not going to club matches.

There was a few Spanish about and at one point; in one of the streets between bars there was a certain amount of pushing and shoving between the Spanish and us. The coppers just looked on, but didn't do anything.

At the end of the night we went to a club. It was about £5 to get in, but this included some free drinks. The club was a bit small. There were one or two girls by the bar who we got talking to.

Some Scots were inside, so we gave a loud rendition of 'God save the Queen' and they reared up. A Rangers fan, who was also in the bar, came over and joined in with us, on our side.

I punched one of the Scots and laid him out, but was then pulled off him by the Rangers lad, it all calmed down as the rest of the Scots left.

Stuart and Sprake were working out in great detail; how they could steal the bog attendants tip money. It was dead funny listening to them planning this crime of the century.

Stuart knocked off one of the two available girls. She was a local and we were ripping the piss out of him by saying 'how's your catholic girlfriend'. She turned round and in the only English she had learnt, she said 'I am a protestant'. Stuart was dead pleased; he must have been teaching her to say that, as soon as he had met her.

We went back to the hotel. At about six o'clock the next morning some girls called at our room for Harry. They were all giggling and they couldn't speak English. When they came into the room, Harry spent hours reading the English/Spanish dictionary they had bought with them. I turned over and went back to sleep.

Friday

I woke up and had a shower at about ten in the morning. Harry had disappeared with his Mexican girls. I went back to the bank to check if they had got our tickets that we had ordered the day before. The girl who served us was dead fit and was wearing killer heels.

We paid for the tickets. Unfortunately we couldn't get Gary one here, but managed to buy one for him from a Mexican youth in the street later. At long last, I also managed to buy a World Cup programme.

We went back to the hotel and got Shane, Harry, who was now back and Smoke for the trip. Harry couldn't get rid of the remaining girl he was still with, and she tagged along. Eventually she got the message that he wasn't too keen on her, and she cleared off.

Stuart had been screwing his girl all night so was now knackered, and had decided that he was staying at the hotel. On the way to the pick-up point we passed lots of little old women still cooking away on the various street corners.

I went and bought a bottle of coke, it cost about 12p and you got some money back on the bottle, if you took it back! We got to the tour place a bit too early so went for something to eat at yet another 'Burger King'.

We got on the bus at about two; one or two other tourists were on it, some Brazilians at the front and some Yanks near the back.

On the way to the pyramids the guide told us about the Catholic Cathedral in Mexico City. Apparently it had the biggest unsupported roof in the world. It has been built on the spot of two shrines, where a peasant had seen a vision of the Virgin Mary years ago in an apparition. The disciples and sinners visiting the cathedral walked on their knees for about the last half a mile.

When the bus stopped at it we got off, but we wouldn't go in. Harry did, as he was a Catholic. He tried to get us to go in, but we were saying to him 'where's this vision then?'

We then asked who was that figurine; it was a statue of the Pope. All the nuns appeared to be selling rosary beads and trinkets. We asked the tour guide how much longer we were going to be, as we weren't told that this was part of the trip.

We were on about picking the pilgrims up, of their knees, just when they nearly got to the church, 'here let me help you', then they would have to do it all over again.

The guide was getting pissed off with us, and said 'everyone to the bus'. We sang 'no Pope of Rome' and 'fuck the IRA'. Harry only joined in a bit. We got on the bus, still having a go at the Catholics, and the guide had got a right 'bag on' with us.

The Brazilians were not on the bus, but it still left with their bags on it. The Yanks were talking to us about all the earthquake damage. Finally we were on the road to the pyramids, going past shantytowns and we arrived as it started to piss down.

The guide said 'we'll wait for rain to stop' and we all said, 'if you hadn't pissed about at the church, we'd have been ok'.

Me and Smoke decided to walk in the rain, Sprake followed and we went up the moon pyramid and the rain stopped. The usual hawkers were trying to sell us stuff, the guide was saying how beautiful the paintings they had produced were, but we couldn't see it.

Then someone tried to sell Sprake a statue, 'what would I do with that' he said, then he said it was dead good, and got the hawkers hopes up, then he said he didn't want it!

We went up the sun pyramid and liberated it, claiming it for Queen and country. The air was really thin at the top and I was knackered.

We wandered back, it was raining again. I bought some onyx jewellery as a present for Julie, for when I arrived home, and a chess set for myself, as it was quite cheap.

The bus then took us to a factory where all the items were made and the guide tried to sell us some more stuff.

We didn't buy anything but at least they give us free Tequila as we went round.

We got dropped off near the hotel and it was pissing down again, Sprake refused to get wet again, so we had to get a taxi.

We got changed out of our wet clothes, then had a game of chess. After that, we went out to the usual bars on the piss. Local kids came up to us with hands out saying 'money, money' but we were used to it by now, and just ignored them or said something to them for a laugh like 'have you got a goat or a sister'.

Saturday

I slept in late, as it was my last full day. I sorted out my bag and paid the hotel bill. I was just about out of money now, but the day and night was still spent eating and drinking.

Sunday

We met Gary and Alf and sorted out the money for their tickets. In one bar I met Silk and Rob Jones. Rob was moaning about the lack of fit women in Mexico City, he reckoned that he had fallen in love with a girl in Monterey, and had asked her to marry him. She had said no, and he was really cut up about it!

All the lads were on about where they were going if we got knocked out, most were saying they were off to Acapulco, but Shane was going to Belize and then the States. We got taxis to the Azteca Stadium, and met up with Chris from Manchester in a bar. He told us that he was marrying a Mexican and had met the mamma and papa. Apparently they were dead pleased, especially when he told them how much he earnt in England. He was now waiting for his birth certificate to be sent over to Monterrey. His mate was sending it, as his mum didn't know that he was planning on getting married.

Chris couldn't speak Spanish, and the girl couldn't speak English, but she reckoned that she could get a U.S passport. Stuart Hill had a bit of a go at him, but he said that he couldn't say too much as Chris was a bit emotional.

Frank said that he had never seen him so happy, and he was a changed man. Some weeks later he bought her home. When he arrived home, in England, he was arrested on suspicion of stealing from the place he used to work at.

He had only been back in the country for two hours, so Frank had to go and look after the Mexican girl, as she knew no one else.

Lots of Argies were in cars, approaching the stadium. We were all staring at them, a busload went by and we all gave them the two fingers.

We stopped at a bar and bought the bars last cans of bohemia. Sprake and the boys wanted to get in the ground, so I stayed and had a drink with Frank and Gary. Gerry and Eddie, two friends of mine came into the bar and we had another quick drink.

Frank had a go at Stuart for wearing a blue tracksuit; he said he looked like he was supporting the Argies. Stuart replied that he never wore colours.

Some Argies walked by and shouted 'Malvinas Argentinas'. We retaliated by singing 'the Falklands are ours' but nothing came of it. We went into ground and were in the other end this time, opposite to where we had sat when we played Paraguay. The ground was packed.

We saw Duggie in the concourse before we went into our seats. He was now speaking with an American accent. West ham fans were in the section below us and as the game started they had a ruck with a load of Argies.

In another corner of the stadium the Argies set fire to a Union Jack. I met up with Sprake and two fit English girls. An Argie behind us said something, and Stuart swung a punch at him, but the Argie shit out.

A fight started in the stand behind us but some coppers moved in to break it up. While the coppers were about, the Argie behind us decided to hit Stuart, but it didn't hurt him and at half time Stuart smashed him in the face. During half time about 400 Argies attacked a group of 20 English on one of the concourses. There were lots of punch-ups around the stadium; the score at the time was 0-0.

In the second half the Argies went 2-0 up, it was sickening, most of the English fans were quiet. The team made a good fight back, but couldn't get level and we were out.

At full time we were chanting 'Robson out' and a bloke in the stand said to me 'you're joking', I told him to 'fuck off'. Smoke said that he might come home with me, as he would qualify for his redundancy, if he got home in time.

We started to leave the ground. All the England fans in our area gathered together on the walkway. We now had the numbers, and the Argies, who had been picking on twos and threes, now, shit themselves.

We ran the Argies; they threw glasses back at us. Smoke ran past me, straight into the Argies, one of whom had put an empty pint glass down his tracksuit bottoms, presumably to use as ammunition later. Gerry, following Smoke into battle, kicked the Argie in the balls, and blood spurted out of his belly.

England fans then grouped up outside the stadium. About 5000

Argies were looking out from the walkways around the stadium, but they didn't dare come down.

I saw Benny and he burnt an Argentina flag he had stolen, then we charged into the Argies that had come out of the stadium. Duggie steamed in with us and we all got a couple of punches away, then the coppers steamed us and we were dispersed.

We walked down the dual carriageway; Argies were abusing us from cars. Stuart shouted at them to come back, but they just laughed at us.

We jumped on the back of a police tow van and managed to hang on. The coppers didn't mind. Me, Sprake, Shane and Stuart were all on it. They dropped us off in Tasquina square.

We got the tube back to the hotel, and I picked up my bag and got changed. Stuart Hill and Smoke decided they were coming with me, the rest were going to go for a Denny burger.

I had a carton of milk with them in Dennys, and as we talked about the match we were all wondering why Shilton was going mad when Maradona scored the first goal. At the time we thought it might have been because it was off side, but it turned out to be that Maradona had handled the ball.

I then said 'bye' to lads, as usual by this time of day it was now pissing down.

We tried to get a taxi but had no joy, so walked to the Reforma Road. We were soaked, but a taxi stopped and it took us past the church we went to on our trip, and out to the airport.

Stuart laughed when we told him that we refused to go in the church. At the airport Stuart and Smoke queued for tickets for the flight to Laredo.

It was a slow queue, but once they had bought their tickets we found a bar for the other match, which was Belgium versus Spain. We bought a beer and watched the penalty shoot-out, and then we were called through to departures. We cheered when Belgium won, which pissed off the Mexicans around us.

There was a few Argies and lots of Yanks about. The plane was delayed and we needed to get to the greyhound bus station in Laredo, to make the connections we needed home.

We took off two hours late. I sat next to Stuart, something I said I wouldn't do again, after our last dodgy flight back from Turkey. As we climbed we hit turbulence and he looked at me and laughed.

Coming into Laredo we bounced down the runway. The wheels bounced and banged before coming to rest. We took our bags with us into the cabin, so we were straight off the plane, and we walked to the customs. Stuart went straight through, but Smoke and me were told to wait over in corner.

Time was marching on, so we did a runner straight into a taxi, and that drove us straight to the US customs.

We got through those all right, and then managed to hitch a lift with a yank to the bus station down town. He said that he liked the English and that he was travelling in that direction, when we asked him for a lift as he was getting into his car!

That night in Mexico City there was trouble all over town, Eddie and some Chelsea lads were locked up, and there was lots of fighting around the 'Piccadilly bar'. Gerry was travelling around, in a police car, telling the coppers which Argies to lock up.

Meanwhile at the bus station, we asked when the next bus to Houston was, but we had missed the last one. We put our bags in the left luggage lockers and worked out our options. It was too late to get a flight, so we tried to get a hire car. It was now eleven on a Sunday night, as we lost an hour at the border. We were told the only car hire place was at the airport, and that was a long way away.

Things were looking bad, so we went for a walk and got some food and drink at a supermarket. The bars were closed, but there were still a few prostitutes about. We went to a park and tried to get some sleep on some benches, but some coppers moved us on, so we went back to the bus-station.

Monday

A bus to San Antonio was leaving at four so, as the station was packed, we decided to get that. I phoned up the airport in San Antonio and though it was difficult to use the automated phone, I found out there was a flight from San Antonio to Houston in the morning, at ten. The machine said this would connect with the Houston one o'clock flight to London. We decided to go for that.

Stuart told us how he was chatting to two girls about Austin, in Texas, on the flight out to America. Another woman overheard and said she was from there. He got talking to her, and ended up screwing her in the toilet. The woman was concerned her little boy, who was with her, would get scared if he noticed she had gone. Stuart told us that he gave her little boy his Man City scarf to play with, hoping this would occupy him! The lad thought his mum had got off the plane when he noticed she wasn't there, and the stewardesses had to knock on the toilet door to get her out.

I tried to get some sleep then at 3.30 started queuing for the bus, but it was packed so we had to wait a further half an hour for a relief bus.

The bus stunk, as it was full of Mexicans and general low-lifes. After about 5 miles some local cops stopped it at a roadblock, and boarded the bus. Two Mexicans were hiding under seats at back, but the police soon found them, and carted them off.

We all said 'good', but a Yank woman said 'they are only trying to better themselves'. We told her to piss off.

We arrived at San Antonio at about eight in the morning. We got off the bus and asked directions to the airport. Stuart was on about hiring a car so he went of in a different direction. The city appeared to be clean, but there were lots of tramps about. We walked past the remains of the 'Alamo' then got a bus to the airport.

We bought tickets for $37 from San Antonio to Houston, and the woman behind the counter checked our bags in, all the way to London. I went to the toilet and had a wash then waited for the flight. We watched as a woman drove to the terminal then couldn't undo her car boot; she ended up missing her flight. We then boarded the plane, children and the infirm first, as usual.

It was a short flight to Houston, then we just had a one-hour wait before we caught a plane to Washington. I tried to sleep on this. There were some massive busses at Washington Dulles Airport, which actually were the same height as the airport door. After disembarking we had a half hour wait. I bought some duty free and had a coffee, and then we got a Jumbo Jet back to London.

The pilot announced that we were passing New York on the left and as it was a clear day we got a good view of it. I had a couple of beers but didn't really feel like drinking. I ended up talking to an American woman next to me, as my armrest buttons were not working for the film. There seemed to be a lot of Indians on the plane. Smoke and me hardly said a word to each other on the flight home.

Tuesday

We arrived at Heathrow early the next morning and went through customs and waited for our bags, which didn't arrive. We were stood looking at the carousel after all the other passengers' bags had been collected.

I had to fill in a claim form; apparently the bags had gone via New York. I phoned Julie to let her know I was back, then we walked out into the concourse just as the England players were arriving.

There were lots of England fans at the airport, they had come down just to greet the players and they booed Smoke and me as we walked out!

We got on the tube and travelled into London. I said 'bye' to Smoke; we just shrugged our shoulders, as the trip was over. I got the first train home, and went straight into work for that afternoon.

Lightning Source UK Ltd.
Milton Keynes UK
UKOW06f1856260615

254209UK00007B/291/P

9 781782 223917